DYNAMICS OF TOURISM

DYNAMICS OF TOURISM

Ravindra Verma

CENTRUM PRESS
NEW DELHI-110002 (INDIA)

CENTRUM PRESS
H.O.: 4360/4, Ansari Road, Daryaganj,
New Delhi-110002 (India)
Tel: 23278000, 23261597, 23255577, 23286875
B.O.: No. 1015, Ist Main Road, BSK IIIrd Stage,
IIIrd Phase, IIIrd Block, Bangalore-560085 (INDIA)
Tel: 080-41723429
Email: centrumpress@gmail.com
Visit us at: www.centrumpress.com

Dynamics of Tourism

First Edition, 2010

ISBN 978-93-80540-80-1

PRINTED IN INDIA

Printed at Balaji Offset, Delhi.

Contents

Preface

The terms *tourism* and *travel* are sometimes used interchangeably. In this context, travel has a similar definition to tourism, but implies a more purposeful journey. The terms *tourism* and *tourist* are sometimes used pejoratively, to imply a shallow interest in the cultures or locations visited by tourists.

There has been an upmarket trend in the tourism over the last few decades, especially in Europe, where international travel for short breaks is common. Tourists have high levels of disposable income, considerable leisure time, are well educated, and have sophisticated tastes. There is now a demand for a better quality products, which has resulted in a fragmenting of the mass market for beach vacations; people want more specialised versions, quieter resorts, family-oriented holidays or niche market-targeted destination hotels.

The developments in technology and transport infrastructure, such as jumbo jets, low-cost airlines and more accessible airports have made many types of tourism more affordable. WHO estimates that up to 500,000 people are on planes at any time. There have also been changes in lifestyle, such as retiree-age people who sustain year round tourism. This is facilitated by internet sales of tourism products. Some sites have now started to offer dynamic packaging, in which an inclusive price is quoted for a tailor-made package requested by the customer upon impulse.

There have been a few setbacks in tourism, such as the September 11 attacks and terrorist threats to tourist destinations, such as in Bali and several European cities. Also, on December 26, 2004, a tsunami, caused by the 2004 Indian Ocean earthquake, hit the Asian countries on the Indian Ocean, including the Maldives. Thousands of lives were lost and many tourists died. This, together with the vast clean-up operation in place, has stopped or severely hampered tourism to the area.

This book portrays a real picture of the dynamics of tourism with all trends—vertical and horizontal. The publication focuses mainly on the major tourism issues. Basically, tourism is travel for recreational or leisure purposes.

—Ravindra Verma

1

Classification of Tourism

Tourism is travel for recreational, leisure or business purposes. The World Tourism Organization defines tourists as people who "travel to and stay in places outside their usual environment for more than twenty-four (24) hours and not more than one consecutive year for leisure, business and other purposes not related to the exercise of an activity remunerated from within the place visited". Tourism has become a popular global leisure activity. In 2008, there were over 922 million international tourist arrivals, with a growth of 1.9% as compared to 2007. International tourism receipts grew to US$944 billion (euro 642 billion) in 2008, corresponding to an increase in real terms of 1.8%.

As a result of the Late-2000s recession, international travel demand suffered a strong slowdown beginning in June 2008, with growth in international tourism arrivals worldwide falling to 2% during the boreal summer months, and this negative trend intensified as international tourist arrivals fell by 8% during the first four months of 2009. Thereafter this declining trend was exacerbated in some regions due to the outbreak of the influenza AH1N1 virus.

Tourism is vital for many countries, such as Egypt, Greece and Thailand, and many island nations, such as The Bahamas, Fiji, Maldives and the Seychelles, due to the large intake of money for businesses with their goods and services and the opportunity for employment in the service industries associated with tourism. These service industries include transportation services, such as airlines, cruise ships and taxis, hospitality services, such as accommodations, including hotels and resorts, and entertainment venues, such as amusement parks, casinos, shopping malls, various music venues and the theatre.

Definition

Theobald (1994) suggested that etymologically, the word "tour" is derived from the Latin 'tornare' and the Greek 'tornos,' meaning 'a lathe or circle; the movement around a central point or axis.' This meaning changed in modern English to represent 'one's turn.' The suffix -ism is defined as 'an action or process; typical behavior or quality' whereas the suffix -ist denotes one that performs a given action. When the word tour and the suffixes -ism and -ist are combined, they suggest the action of movement around a circle. One can argue that a circle represents a starting point, which ultimately returns back to its beginning. Therefore, like a circle, a tour represents a journey that is a round trip, i.e., the act of leaving and then returning to the original starting point, and therefore, one who takes such a journey can be called a tourist.

Hunziker and Krapf, in 1941, defined tourism as people who travel "the sum of the phenomena and relationships arising from the travel and stay of non-residents, insofar as they do not lead to permanent residence and are not connected with any earning activity." In 1976, the Tourism Society of England's definition was: "Tourism is the temporary, short-term movement of people to destination outside the places where they normally live and work and their activities during the stay at each destination. It includes movements for all purposes." In 1981, the International Association of Scientific Experts in Tourism defined tourism in terms of particular activities selected by choice and undertaken outside the home.

The United Nations classified three forms of tourism in 1994, in its "Recommendations on Tourism Statistics: Domestic tourism", which involves residents of the given country travelling only within this country; Inbound tourism, involving non-residents travelling in the given country; and Outbound tourism, involving residents travelling in another country. The UN also derived different categories of tourism by combining the three basic forms of tourism: Internal tourism, which comprises domestic tourism and inbound tourism; National tourism, which comprises domestic tourism and outbound tourism; and International tourism, which consists of inbound tourism and outbound tourism. *Intrabound tourism* is a term coined by the Korea Tourism Organization and widely accepted in Korea. Intrabound tourism differs from domestic tourism in that the former encompasses policymaking and implementation of national tourism policies. Recently, the tourism industry has shifted from the promotion of inbound tourism to the promotion of intrabound tourism, because many countries are experiencing tough competition for inbound tourists.

Terminology

Vacation, in English-speaking North America, describes recreational travel, such as a short pleasure trip, or a journey abroad. Most of the rest of the English-speaking whose of recent British or European descent, rarely say *going on holiday*. People in Commonwealth countries also use the phrase, *going on leave.*

Canadians often use *vacation* and *holiday* interchangeably referring to a trip away from home or time off work. In Australia, the term can refer to a vacation or a public holiday.

International Tourism Receipts

In 2008, there were over 922 million international tourist arrivals, with a growth of 1.9% as compared to 2007. International tourism receipts grew to US$944 billion (euro 642 billion) in 2008, corresponding to an increase in real terms of 1.8% on 2007. When the export value of international passenger transport receipts is accounted for, total receipts in 2008 reached a record of US$1. trillion, or over US$3 billion a day.

History

Wealthy people have always travelled to distant parts of the world, to see great buildings, works of art, learn new languages, experience new cultures and to taste different cuisines. Long ago, at the time of the Roman Republic, places such as Baiae were popular coastal resorts for the rich. The word *tourism* was used by 1811 and *tourist* by 1840. In 1936, the League of Nations defined *foreign tourist* as "someone travelling abroad for at least twenty-four hours". Its successor, the United Nations, amended this definition in 1945, by including a maximum stay of six months.

Leisure Travel

Leisure travel was associated with the Industrial Revolution in the United Kingdom – the first European country to promote leisure time to the increasing industrial population. Initially, this applied to the owners of the machinery of production, the economic oligarchy, the factory owners and the traders. These comprised the new middle class. Cox & Kings was the first official travel company to be formed in 1758.

The British origin of this new industry is reflected in many place names.

In Nice, France, one of the first and best-established holiday resorts on the French Riviera, the long esplanade along the seafront is known to this day as the *Promenade des Anglais*; in many other historic resorts in continental Europe, old, well-established palace hotels have names like the *Hotel Bristol*, the *Hotel Carlton* or the *Hotel Majestic* – reflecting the dominance of English customers.

Many leisure-oriented tourists travel to the tropics, both in the summer and winter. Places often visited are: Cuba, the Dominican Republic, Thailand, North Queensland in Australia and Florida in the United States.

Winter Tourism

Winter Sport

A winter sport is a sport commonly played during winter. As a formal term, it refers to a sport played on snow or ice; informally, it can refer to sports played in winter that are also played year-round, such as basketball. The main winter sports are ice hockey and figure skating, sledding events, such as luge, skeleton, and bobsleigh, skiing (Alpine and Nordic) and snowboarding. Other common winter sports include skiboarding, monoskiing, skwal, and snowmobiling.

List of Winter Sports

Note: an asterisk indicates that a particular sport is included in the Winter Olympic Games, as of the 2010 Vancouver Olympics.

Ice skating

- Figure skating
- Short-track speed skating
- Speed skating
- Synchronized skating

Skiing

- Alpine skiing
- Biathlon
- Cross country skiing
- Freestyle skiing
- Mogul skiing
- Newschool skiing
- Nordic combined
- Ski archery
- Skiboarding
- Skibob
- Skijoring
- Ski jumping
- Snowshoe
- Speed skiing
- Telemark skiing.

Sledding

Sports that use sleds going down ice tracks or pulled by something:

- Airboard
- Bobsled
- Dogsled racing
- Ice Blocking
- Luge
- Skeleton
- Work racing.

Snowboarding

- Alpine snowboarding
- Boardercross
- Freestyle snowboarding
- Slalom .

Snowmobiling

- free style
- snow-cross

- recreation
- cross country
- hill climbing.

Recreational Sports

Some 'sports' are competed (or simply enjoyed) on a more casual basis, often by children:

- Building snowmen
- Ice boating or sailing
- Ice fishing
- Ice swimming
- Shinny
- Snowball fight
- Tobogganing.

Team Sports

- Bandy
- Broomball
- Curling
- Ice hockey
- Ice stock sport
- Ringette
- Sledge hockey - (Winter Paralympic Sport)
- Snowball fight - (Last one standing)
- Snowman building - highest one.

Notable Winter Sport Resort Regions

- Alps
- Andes
- Appalachian Mountains
- Balkan Mountains
- Carpathian Mountains
- Karkonosze Mountains/Sudeten mountains
- Lapland
- Rocky Mountains
- Snowy Mountains
- Swiss Alps
- Whistler.

Notable Winter Sporting Events

- Winter Olympic Games
- Asian Winter Games
- Winter Paralympic Games
- Winter Universiade
- Winter Dew Tour.

Major ski resorts are located in the various European countries (e.g. Austria, Bulgaria, Czech Republic, France, Germany, Iceland, Italy, Norway, Poland, Sweden, Slovakia, Spain, Switzerland), Canada, the United States, Australia, New Zealand, Japan, South Korea, Chile and Argentina.

Mass Tourism

Mass tourism could only have developed with the improvements in technology, allowing the transport of large numbers of people in a short space of time to places of leisure interest, so that greater numbers of people could begin to enjoy the benefits of leisure time.

In the United States, the first seaside resorts in the European style were at Atlantic City, New Jersey and Long Island, New York.

In Continental Europe, early resorts included: Ostend, popularized by the people of Brussels; Boulogne-sur-Mer (Pas-de-Calais) and Deauville (Calvados) for the Parisians; and Heiligendamm, founded in 1797, as the first seaside resort on the Baltic Sea.

Adjectival Tourism

Adjectival tourism refers to the numerous niche or specialty travel forms of tourism that have emerged over the years, each with its own adjective. Many of these have come into common use by the tourism industry and academics. Others are emerging concepts that may or may not gain popular usage. Examples of the more common niche tourism markets include:

Introduction to Fish Tourism

Fish tourism is part of the wider context of marine ecotourism and involves special tourism services associated to fishing and aquaculture and related customs and traditions.

Fish tourism is part of the wider context of marine ecotourism and may involve the embarkation of persons (who are not members of the crew) on fishing vessels for recreational-tourism purposes, as well as the accommodation, catering and general provision of special tourism services associated to fishing and aquaculture and related customs and traditions.

The development of fish tourism may be perceived as an employment diversification opportunity aiming to help regenerate coastal communities, and fishermen in particular, that are experiencing economic hardship as a result of the decline of their income from traditional fishing activities. Moreover, fish tourism may propagate eco-awareness and the principles of sustainable development on both the parties involved, operators and customers, fishermen and tourists.

The need for such diversification in coastal regions -and the fishing communities in particular- has been long recognized by many national and international authorities, recommending that the inshore fisheries sector should be encouraged to pursue opportunities for diversification in addition to safeguarding traditional fishing activities.

Such diversification, which is considered a priority by the EU, has been successfully implemented in many costal regions of the EU. In all cases, apart from the economic, societal and demographic reasons that set the base for the development of fish tourism in a region, a supportive and comprehensive legal framework is required.

Fish tourism may be able to help regenerate fishing communities, and address low incomes, low levels of investment, high unemployment, out-migration, and so on.

Moreover, fish tourism is thought to offer a special opportunity to achieve environmentally sound, sustainable development – development that will help to meet the needs of the present generation without damaging the resource base for future generations.

It can also make a contribution to the objective of 'balanced spatial development' set out in the European Spatial Development Perspective (ESDP), by addressing regional disparities through sustainable use of the region's indigenous potential.

Case Studies

A Short Description of Fish Tourism in Italy and Ireland

What is the Case of Italy?

Italy is closely related to the sea as there are 7,600 km of coastline and many inland waters (lakes and rivers). There are more than 16,000 fishing vessels, the majority of which are costal and small scale fishing vessels, largely affected by diminishing fish stocks. The increasing rate of unemployment has led to the development of alternative forms of occupation (professional diversification) and fishtourism activities in particular.

Apart from sport fishing of large pelagic species like swordfish and tuna, pescaturismo has developed over the past few years, combining demonstration of fishing activities as well as participation. The Italians made one step further developing ittiturismo which is a form of agrotourism practiced in coastal areas with emphasis given on fishery related traditions and customs. This kind of tourism provides a chance to the local fishermen to improve their income and to the tourists to discover the local fishing culture and explore the coastal areas.

Fish tourism has developed not only close to the sea, but also in inland areas, in communities where inland water fishing is practiced, such as in lagoons, lakes and rivers. There are big national federations like FIPS (Federazione Italiana Pesca Sportivo) and KONI (Italian Olympic Commission) which organize occasionally sport fishing games across Italy. Carp, roach, trout, pike, eels are some of the species abundant to the lakes of Garda, Como, Iseo, Lago Maggiore, Trasimeno, Bracciano and Bolsena and of course salmon and trout to the rivers. Due to the tendency of the recreational fishermen to participate in such fishing activities, it is very likely that Pescaturismo will expand also to the inland waters.

What is the Case in Ireland?

The picturesque landscape of Ireland and the long fishing tradition of the country has aided the development of recreational fishing both in marine and inland waters.

The Bord Failte (Irish Tourism Organization) in cooperation with the Central Fisheries Board and the National Organization for the Fishery inform recreational fishermen on aspects concerning the legal framework covering the recreational fishing. There are many organizations chartering small vessels to recreational fishermen for inshore fishing, deep-sea fishing and wreck fishing. These types of fishing excursions are provided additionally to sightseeing ones. Recreational fishing is also allowed from the shore (shore angling) and to inland waters using fly-fishing or coarse angling. The high rate of environmental and nature conservation awareness of the Irish people has led to the development of many organisations whose mission is to educate fishermen and such issues.

In Ireland, there is a union of 21 specialized recreational fishing centres called "The Great Fishing Houses of Ireland", offering integrated thematic vacations, including subsistence and athletic activities like game fishing. Tourists pay a certain fee to fish or charter a fishing vessel and the rate depends on the season (high or low). The services are highly rated and provided by professionals of tourism management. Moreover, tourists are being informed on aspects concerning the local culture and tradition about fishing, also receiving maps and informative material.

Agritourism

Agritourism, as it is defined most broadly, involves any agriculturally-based operation or activity that brings visitors to a farm or ranch. Agritourism has different definitions in different parts of the world, and sometimes refers specifically to farm stays, as in Italy. Elsewhere, agritourism includes a wide variety of activities, including buying produce direct from a farm stand, navigating a corn maze, picking fruit, feeding animals, or staying at a B&B on a farm.

Agritourism is a form of niche tourism that is considered a growth industry in many parts of the world, including Australia, Canada, the United States, and the Philippines. Agritourism overlaps with geotourism, ecotourism, and culinary tourism. Other terms associated with agritourism are "agritainment", "value added products," "farm direct marketing", and "sustainable agriculture".

Agritourism in the United States

Agritourism is widespread in America. Agritourists can choose from a wide range of activities that include picking fruits and vegetables, riding horses, tasting honey, learning about wine and cheesemaking, or shopping in farm gift shops and farm stands for local and regional produce or hand-crafted gifts.

According the USDA, Cooperative State, Education and Extension Service, "Tourism is becoming increasingly important to the U.S. economy. A conservative estimate from the Federal Reserve Board in Kansas, based on 2000 data, shows that basic travel and tourism industries accounted for 3.6 percent of all U.S. employment. Even more telling, data from the Travel Industry Association of America indicate that 1 out of every 18 people in the U.S. has a job directly resulting from travel expenditures."

Through the Small Farm Centre at the University of California, "Agricultural tourism or agritourism, is one alternative for improving the incomes and potential economic viability of small farms and rural communities. Some forms of agritourism enterprises are well developed in California, including fairs and festivals. Other possibilities still offer potential for development." The UC Small Farm Centre has developed a California Agritourism Database that "provides visitors and potential entrepreneurs with information about existing agritourism locations throughout the state."

In Western North Carolina, the organization HandMade in America is using agritourism to develop their local economy and craft trades, and to educate visitors about agriculture practices. On the web site, *Hand Made in America,* they look at agritourism as a niche market [that] not only assists communities with solutions to help diversify their economic base, but it also helps our regional urban centres and increasingly suburban populations to understand the important role that farming and rural life plays in our history, by highlighting the need for it in our contemporary society. Agritourism projects reinforce the need to support local growers and sources and allow the visitor to experience what it is to be part of the land. The publication *Promoting Tourism in Rural America* explains the need for planning and marketing your rural community and weighing the pros and cons of tourism. According to the publication, local citizen participation is helpful and should be included in starting any kind of a tourism program. Citizen participation in planning tourism can contribute to buliding a successful program that enhances the community.

Additional websites that promote and publicize agritourism in the United States include Rural Bounty, founded by agritourism consultant Jane Eckert, Sleep in the Hay, a nationwide directory of farm stays, and Farm Stay USA, a blog that profiles farm stays and tracks agritourism news.

Reasons for Popularity

People have become more interested in how their food is produced. They want to meet farmers and processers and talk with them about what goes into food production. For many people who visit farms, especially children, the visit marks the first time they see the source of their food, be it a dairy cow, an ear of corn growing in the field, or an apple they can pick right off the tree.

Agritourism was featured in the satirical NBC television comedy series *The Office* in the episode entitled "Money" from season 4. The character Dwight Schrute lives on a beet farm, and in this episode reveals that he has opened a B&B in his farmhouse. The characters Jim and Pam proceed to visit the farm, where they choose the "irrigation" themed room. They choose to participate in various farm activities, including plowing the fields, making wine from beets, and watching a table making demonstration. In the episode, Dwight explains that Trip Advisor is the lifeblood of the agritourism industry. The episode portrayed agritourism in a somewhat unappealing light, as Dwight's beet farm and rural lifestyle are often objects of ridicule on the show. Still, the episode brought the concept of agritourism to the show's many viewers.

Dude Ranches

Dude (or guest) ranches offer tourists the chance to work on cattle ranches, and sometimes participate in cattle drives. The fact sheet, *Promoting the Farm and Ranch Recreation Business,* gives farmers and ranchers information on marketing and developing strategies to win tourism dollars. Dude ranches are common in the United States and Australian Outback.

Culinary Tourism

Judging by the surge since 2001 in the number of times "culinary tourism" has appeared as a subject matter or in a session title in tourism industry conferences and programs, we can see that Culinary Tourism is valued by tourism industry professionals as one of the most popular niches in the world's tourism industry.

This makes sense, given recent consumer focus on healthy and organic eating, culinary/food pedigrees, and the simple fact that all travellers must eat. Not every visitor goes shopping or visits museums, but all travellers eat. For anyone who doubts, look at the increase in cooking shows featured on The Travel Channel [Anthony Bourdain No Reservations] or travel shows featured on The Food Network [Rachel Ray's $40 a Day series], as examples.

Culinary Tourism is not just experiences of the highest caliber - that would be gourmet tourism. This is perhaps best illustrated by the notion that Culinary Tourism is about what is "unique and memorable, not what is necessarily pretentious and exclusive". Similarly, wine tourism, beer tourism and spa tourism are also regarded as subsets of culinary tourism.

Cultural Tourism

'Cultural tourism' (or culture tourism) is the subset of tourism concerned with a country or region's culture, specifically the lifestyle of the people in those geographical areas, the history of those peoples, their art, architecture, religion(s), and other elements that helped shape their way of life. Cultural tourism includes tourism in urban areas, particularly historic or large cities and their cultural facilities such as museums and theatres. It can also include tourism in rural areas showcasing the traditions of indigenous cultural communities (i.e. festivals, rituals), and their values and lifestyle. It is generally agreed that cultural tourists spend substantially more than standard tourists do. This form of tourism is also becoming generally more popular throughout the world, and a recent OECD report has highlighted the role that cultural tourism can play in regional development in different world regions. Cultural tourism has been defined as 'the movement of persons to cultural attractions away from their normal place of residence, with the intention to gather new information and experiences to satisfy their cultural needs'.

Destinations

One type of cultural tourism destination is living cultural areas. For an indigenous culture that has stayed largely separated from the surrounding majority, tourism can present both advantages and problems. On the positive side are the unique cultural practices and arts that attract the curiosity of tourists and provide opportunities for tourism and economic development.

On the negative side is the issue of how to control tourism so that those same cultural amenities are not destroyed and the people do not feel violated. Other destinations include historical sites, modern urban districts, theme parks and country clubs, coastal or island ecosystems, and inland natural areas.

Key Principles

Destination Planning

As the issue of globalization takes place to this modern time, the challenge of preserving the few remaining cultural community around the world is becoming hard. In a tribal based community, reaching economic advancement with minimal negative impacts is an essential objective to any destination planner. Since they are using the culture of the region as the main attraction, sustainable destination development of the area is vital for them to prevent the negative impacts (i.e. destroying the authentic identity of the tribal community) due to tourism.

Management Issues

Certainly, the principle of "one size fits all" doesn't apply to destination planning. The needs, expectations, and anticipated benefits from tourism vary greatly from one destination to another. This is clearly exemplified as local communities living in regions with tourism potential (destinations) develop a vision for what kind of tourism they want to facilitate, depending on issues and concerns they want to be settled or satisfied.

Destination Planning Resources

Planning Guides

Culture: the heart of development policy: It is important that the destination planner takes into account the diverse definition of culture as the term is subjective. Satisfying tourists' interests such as landscapes, seascapes, art, nature, traditions, ways of life and other products associated to them -which may be categorized cultural in the broadest sense of the word, is a prime consideration as it marks the initial phase of the development of a cultural destination. The quality of service and destination, which doesn't solely depend on the cultural heritage but more importantly to the cultural environment, can further be developed by setting controls and policies which shall govern the community and its stakeholders. It is therefore safe to say that the planner should be on the ball with the varying meaning of culture itself as this fuels the formulation of development policies that shall entail efficient planning and monitored growth. Local community, tourists, the destination and sustainable tourism: While satisfying tourists' interests and demands may be a top priority, it is also imperative to ruminate the subsystems of the destination's *(residents)*. Development pressures should be anticipated and set to their minimum level so as to conserve the area's resources and prevent a saturation of the destination as to not abuse the product and the residents correspondingly. The plan should incorporate the locals to its gain by training and employing them and in the process encourage them to participate to the travel business. Keep in mind that the plan should make travellers not only aware about the destination but also concern on how to help it sustain its character while broadening their travelling experience.

Planning Tools

Sources of Data

The core of a planner's job is to design an appropriate planning process and facilitate community decision. Ample information which is a crucial requirement is contributed through various technical researches and analyzes. Here are some of the helpful tools commonly used by planners to aid them:

1. Key Informant Interviews
2. Libraries, Internet, and Survey Research
3. Census and Statistical Analysis
4. Spatial Analysis with Geographical Information System (GIS) and Global Positioning System (GPS) technologies

Key Institutions

Participating structures are primarily led by the government's local authorities and the official tourism board or council, with the involvement of various NGOs, community and indigenous representatives, development organizations, and the academe.

Case Studies: Mountainous Regions of Central Asia and in the Himalayas

Tourism is coming to the previously isolated but spectacular mountainous regions of Central Asia, the Hindu Kush and the

Himalayas. Closed for so many years to visitors from abroad, it now attracts a growing number of foreign tourists by its unique culture and splendid natural beauty. However, while this influx of tourists is bringing economic opportunities and employment to local populations, helping to promote these little-known regions of the world, it has also brought challenges along with it: to ensure that it is well-managed and that its benefits are shared by all.

As a response to this concern, the Norwegian Government, as well as the UNESCO, organized an interdisciplinary project called the Development of Cultural and Ecotourism in the Mountainous Regions of Central Asia and the Himalayas project. It aims to establish links and promote cooperation between local communities, national and international NGOs, and tour agencies in order to heighten the role of the local community and involve them fully in the employment opportunities and income-generating activities that tourism can bring. Project activities include training local tour guides, producing high-quality craft items and promoting home-stays and bed-and-breakfast type accommodation.

As of now, the project is drawing on the expertise of international NGOs and tourism professionals in the seven participating countries, making a practical and positive contribution to alleviating poverty by helping local communities to draw the maximum benefit from their region's tourism potential, while protecting the environmental and cultural heritage of the region concerned.

The University of Travelhost, Dallas, Texas has an extensive travel library continually gathering travel related research and tourism economic impact studies nationwide.

Ecotourism

'Ecotourism' (also known as ecological tourism) is responsible travel to fragile, pristine, and usually protected areas that strives to be low impact and (often) small scale. It purports to educate the traveler; provide funds for conservation; directly benefit the economic development and political empowerment of local communities; and foster respect for different cultures and for human rights. Eco tourism is held as important by those who participate in it so that future generations may experience aspects of the environment relatively untouched by human intervention. Most serious studies of ecotourism including several university

programs now use this as the working definition. Ecotourism appeals to ecologically and socially conscious individuals. Generally speaking, it focuses on volunteering, personal growth and environmental responsibility. It typically involves travel to destinations where flora, fauna, and cultural heritage are the primary attractions. One of the goals of ecotourism is to offer tourists insight into the impact of human beings on the environment, and to foster a greater appreciation of our natural habitats.

Responsible ecotourism includes programs that minimize the negative aspects of conventional tourism on the environment and enhance the cultural integrity of local people. Therefore, in addition to evaluating environmental and cultural factors, an integral part of ecotourism is the promotion of recycling, energy efficiency, water conservation, and creation of economic opportunities for local communities.

Criteria

Ecotourism is a form of tourism that involves travelling to tranquil and unpolluted natural areas. According to the definition and principles of ecotourism established by The International Ecotourism Society (TIES) in 1990, ecotourism is "Responsible travel to natural areas that conserves the environment and improves the well-being of local people." (TIES, 1990). Martha Honey, expands on the TIES definition by describing the seven characteristics of ecotourism, which are:

- Involves travel to natural destinations.
- Minimizes impact.
- Builds environmental awareness.
- Provides direct financial benefits for conservation.
- Provides financial benefits and empowerment for local people.
- Respects local culture.
- Supports human rights and democratic movements.

Ideally, ecotourism should satisfy several criteria, such as:

- conservation of biological diversity and cultural diversity through ecosystem protection
- promotion of sustainable use of biodiversity, by providing jobs to local populations

- sharing of socioeconomic benefits with local communities and indigenous peoples by having their informed consent and participation in the management of ecotourism enterprises
- tourism to unspoiled natural resources, with minimal impact on the environment being a primary concern.
- minimization of tourism's own environmental impact
- affordability and lack of waste in the form of luxury
- local culture, flora and fauna being the main attractions

For many countries, ecotourism is not simply a marginal activity to finance protection of the environment, but is a major industry of the national economy. For example, in Costa Rica, Ecuador, Nepal, Kenya, Madagascar and Antarctica, ecotourism represents a significant portion of the gross domestic product and economic activity.

The concept of ecotourism is widely misunderstood and in practice is often used as a marketing tool to promote tourism that is related to nature. This is an especially frequent malpractice in the realm of Jungle tourism. Critics claim that these greenwashing practices, carried out in the name of ecotourism, often consist of placing a hotel in a splendid landscape, to the detriment of the ecosystem. According to them, ecotourism must above all sensitize people to the beauty and the fragility of nature. They condemn some operators as greenwashing their operations: using the labels of "green" and "eco-friendly", while behaving in environmentally irresponsible ways. Although academics disagree about who can be classified as an ecotourist and there is little statistical data, some estimate that more than five million ecotourists - the majority of the ecotourist population - come from the United States, with many others from Western Europe, Canada and Australia.

Currently, there are various moves to create national and international ecotourism accreditation programs, although the process is also controversial. National ecotourism certification programs have been put in place in countries such as Costa Rica, Australia, Kenya and Sweden.

History

Ecotourism, responsible tourism, jungle tourism, and sustainable development have become prevalent concepts since the late 1980s, and ecotourism has experienced arguably the fastest growth of all sub-sectors in the tourism industry. The popularity represents a change in tourist perceptions, increased environmental awareness, and a desire to explore natural environments. At times, such changes become as much a statement affirming one's social identity, educational sophistication, and disposable income as it has about preserving the Amazon rainforest or the Caribbean reef for posterity.

Criticisms

Definitional Problems and Greenwashing

To approach an understanding of the problem, a clear definition must delineate what is, and is not, ecotourism. Ideally, ecotourism satisfies several general criteria, including the conservation of biological diversity and cultural diversity through ecosystem protection, promotion of sustainable use of biodiversity, share of social-economic benefits with local communities through informed consent and participation, increase in environmental and cultural knowledge, affordability and reduced waste, and minimization of its own environmental impact. In such ways, it contributes to the long term benefits to both the environment and local communities.

However, in the continuum of tourism activities that stretch from conventional tourism to ecotourism proper, there has been a lot of contention to the limit at which biodiversity preservation, local social-economic benefits, and environmental impact can be considered "ecotourism". For this reason, environmentalists, special interest groups, and governments define ecotourism differently. Environmental organizations have generally insisted that ecotourism is nature-based, sustainably managed, conservation supporting, and environmentally educated. The tourist industry and governments, however, focus more on the product aspect, treating ecotourism as equivalent to any sort of tourism based in nature. As a further complication, many terms are used under the rubric of ecotourism. Nature tourism, low impact tourism, green tourism, bio-tourism, ecologically responsible tourism, and others have been used in literature and marketing, although they are not necessary synonymous with ecotourism.

The problems associated with defining ecotourism have led to confusion among tourists and academics alike. Definitional problems are also subject of considerable public controversy and concern because of green washing, a trend towards the commercialization of tourism schemes disguised as sustainable, nature based, and environmentally friendly ecotourism. According to McLaren, these schemes are environmentally destructive, economically exploitative, and culturally insensitive at its worst. They are also morally disconcerting because they mislead tourists and manipulate their concerns for the environment. Despite objections, green washing continues to grow unabated. The Nature's Sacred Paradise, a theme park in Quintana Roo, Mexico, is responsible for displacing local Mayan communities and illegally keeping endangered species in captivity to attract visitors. The development and success of such large scale, energy intensive, and ecologically unsustainable schemes are a testament to the tremendous profits associated with being labeled as ecotourism.

Negative Impact of Tourism

Ecotourism has become one of the fastest-growing sectors of the tourism industry, growing annually by 10-15% worldwide (Miller, 2007). One definition of ecotourism is "the practice of low-impact, educational, ecologically and culturally sensitive travel that benefits local communities and host countries" (Honey, 1999). Many of the ecotourism projects are not meeting these standards. Even if some of the guidelines are being executed, the local communities are still facing other negative impacts. South Africa is one of the countries that are reaping significant economic benefits from ecotourism, but negative effects - including forcing people to leave their homes, gross violations of fundamental rights, and environmental hazards - far outweigh the medium-term economic benefits (Miller, 2007). A tremendous amount of money is being spent and human resources continue to be used for ecotourism despite unsuccessful outcomes, and even more money is put into public relation campaigns to dilute the effects of criticism. Ecotourism channels resources away from other projects that could contribute more sustainable and realistic solutions to pressing social and environmental problems. "The money tourism can generate often ties parks and managements to eco-tourism" (Walpole et al. 2001). But there is a tension in this relationship because eco-tourism often causes conflict and changes in land-use rights, fails to deliver promises of community-level benefits, damages environments, and has plenty of other social impacts. Indeed many argue repeatedly that eco-tourism is neither ecologically nor socially beneficial, yet it persists as a strategy for conservation and development (West, 2006). While several studies are being done on ways to improve the ecotourism structure, some argue that these examples provide rationale for stopping it altogether.

The ecotourism system exercises tremendous financial and political influence. The evidence above shows that a strong case exists for restraining such activities in certain locations. Funding could be used for field studies aimed at finding alternative solutions to tourism and the diverse problems Africa faces in result of urbanization, industrialization, and the over exploitation of agriculture (Kamuaro, 2007). At the local level, ecotourism has become a source of conflict over control of land, resources, and tourism profits. In this case, ecotourism has harmed the environment and local people, and has led to conflicts over profit distribution. In a perfect world more efforts would be made towards educating tourists of the environmental and social effects of their travels. Very few regulations or laws stand in place as boundaries for the investors in ecotourism. These should be implemented to prohibit the promotion of unsustainable ecotourism projects and materials which project false images of destinations, demeaning local and indigenous cultures.

Direct Environmental Impacts

Ecotourism operations occasionally fail to live up to conservation ideals. It is sometimes overlooked that ecotourism is a highly consumer-centred activity, and that environmental conservation is a means to further economic growth.

Although ecotourism is intended for small groups, even a modest increase in population, however temporary, puts extra pressure on the local environment and necessitates the development of additional infrastructure and amenities. The construction of water treatment plants, sanitation facilities, and lodges come with the exploitation of non-renewable energy sources and the utilization of already limited local resources. The conversion of natural land to such tourist infrastructure is implicated in deforestation and habitat deterioration of butterflies in Mexico and squirrel monkeys in Costa Rica. In other cases, the environment suffers because local communities are unable to meet the infrastructure demands of ecotourism. The lack of adequate sanitation facilities in many East

African parks results in the disposal of campsite sewage in rivers, contaminating the wildlife, livestock, and people who draw drinking water from it.

Aside from environmental degradation with tourist infrastructure, population pressures from ecotourism also leaves behind garbage and pollution associated with the Western lifestyle. Although ecotourists claim to be educationally sophisticated and environmentally concerned, they rarely understand the ecological consequences of their visits and how their day-to-day activities append physical impacts on the environment. As one scientist observes, they "rarely acknowledge how the meals they eat, the toilets they flush, the water they drink, and so on, are all part of broader regional economic and ecological systems they are helping to reconfigure with their very activities." Nor do ecotourists recognize the great consumption of non-renewable energy required to arrive at their destination, which is typically more remote than conventional tourism destinations. For instance, an exotic journey to a place 10,000 kilometers away consumes about 700 litres of fuel per person.

Ecotourism activities are, in of itself, issues in environmental impact because they disturb fauna and flora. Ecotourists believe that because they are only taking pictures and leaving footprints, they keep ecotourism sites pristine, but even harmless sounding activities such as a nature hike can be ecologically destructive. In the Annapurna Circuit in Nepal, ecotourists have worn down the marked trails and created alternate routes, contributing to soil impaction, erosion, and plant damage. Where the ecotourism activity involves wildlife viewing, it can scare away animals, disrupt their feeding and nesting sites, or acclimate them to the presence of people. In Kenya, wildlife-observer disruption drives cheetahs off their reserves, increasing the risk of inbreeding and further endangering the species.

Environmental Hazards

Unfortunately, industrialization, urbanization, and unsustainable agriculture practices have all had serious effects on the environment. Ecotourism is now also playing a role in this depletion. While the term ecotourism may sound relatively benign, one of its most serious impacts is its consumption of virgin territories (Kamuaro, 2007). These invasions often include deforestation, disruption of ecological life systems and various forms of pollution, all of which contribute to environmental degradation. The number of motor vehicles crossing the park increases as tour drivers search for rare species. The number of roads has disrupted the grass cover which has serious effects on plant and animal species. These areas also have a higher rate of disturbances and invasive species because of all the traffic moving off the beaten path into new undiscovered areas (Kamuaro, 2007). Ecotourism also has an effect on species through the value placed on them. "Certain species have gone from being little known or valued by local people to being highly valued commodities. The commodification of plants may erase their social value and lead to overproduction within protected areas. Local people and their images can also be turned into commodities" (West, 2006). Kamuaro brings up a relatively obvious contradiction, any commercial venture into unspoiled, pristine land with or without the "eco" prefix as a contradiction in terms. To generate revenue you have to have a high number of traffic, tourists, which inevitably means a higher pressure on the environment.

Local People

Most forms of ecotourism are owned by foreign investors and corporations that provide few benefits to local communities. An overwhelming majority of profits are put into the pockets of investors instead of reinvestment into the local economy or environmental protection. The limited numbers of local people who are employed in the economy enter at its lowest level, and are unable to live in tourist areas because of meager wages and a two market system.

In some cases, the resentment by local people results in environmental degradation. As a highly publicized case, the Masai nomads in Kenya killed wildlife in national parks to show aversion to unfair compensation terms and displacement from traditional lands. The lack of economic opportunities for local people also constrains them to degrade the environment as a means of sustenance. The presence of affluent ecotourists encourage the development of destructive markets in wildlife souvenirs, such as the sale of coral trinkets on tropical islands and animal products in Asia, contributing to illegal harvesting and poaching from the environment. In Suriname, sea turtle reserves use a large portion of their budget to guard against these destructive activities.

Displacement of People

One of the most powerful examples of communities being moved in order to create a park is the story of the Masai. About 70% of national parks and game reserves in East Africa are on Masai land (Kamuaro, 2007). The first undesirable impact of tourism was that of the extent of land lost from the Masai culture. Local and national governments took advantage of the Masai's ignorance on the situation and robbed them of huge chunks of grazing land, putting to risk their only socioeconomic livelihood. In Kenya the Masai also have not gained any economic benefits. Despite the loss of their land, employment favours better educated workers. Furthermore the investors in this area are not local and have not put profits back into local economy. In some cases game reserves can be created without informing or consulting local people, who come to find out about the situation when an eviction notice is delivered (Kamuaro, 2007). Another source of resentment is the manipulation of the local people by their government. "Eco-tourism works to create simplistic images of local people and their uses and understandings of their surroundings. Through the lens of these simplified images, officials direct policies and projects towards the local people and the local people are blamed if the projects fail" (West, 2006). Clearly tourism as a trade is not empowering the local people who make it rich and satisfying. Instead ecotourism exploits and depletes, particularly in African Masai tribes. It has to be reoriented if it is to be useful to local communities and to become sustainable (Kamuaro, 2007).

Threats to Indigenous Cultures

Ecotourism often claims that it preserves and "enhances" local cultures. However, evidence shows that with the establishment of protected areas local people have illegally lost their homes, and most often with no compensation (Kamuaro, 2007). Pushing people onto marginal lands with harsh climates, poor soils, lack of water, and infested with livestock and disease does little to enhance livelihoods even when a proportion of ecotourism profits are directed back into the community. The establishment of parks can create harsh survival realities and deprive the people of their traditional use of land and natural resources. Ethnic groups are increasingly being seen as a "backdrop" to the scenery and wildlife. The local people struggle for cultural survival and freedom of cultural expression while being "observed" by tourists. Local indigenous people also have strong resentment towards the change, "Tourism has been allowed to develop with virtually no controls. Too many lodges have been built, too much firewood is being used and no limits are being placed on tourism vehicles. They regularly drive off-track and harass the wildlife. Their vehicle tracks crisscross the entire Masai Mara. Inevitably the bush is becoming eroded and degraded" (Kamuaro, 2007).

Mismanagement

While governments are typically entrusted with the administration and enforcement of environmental protection, they often lack the commitment or capability to manage ecotourism sites effectively. The regulations for environmental protection may be vaguely defined, costly to implement, hard to enforce, and uncertain in effectiveness. Government regulatory agencies, as political bodies, are susceptible to making decisions that spend budget on politically beneficial but environmentally unproductive projects. Because of prestige and conspicuousness, the construction of an attractive visitor's centre at an ecotourism site may take precedence over more pressing environmental concerns like acquiring habitat, protecting endemic species, and removing invasive ones. Finally, influential groups can pressure and sway the interests of the government to their favour. The government and its regulators can become vested in the benefits of the ecotourism industry which they are supposed to regulate, causing restrictive environmental regulations and enforcement to become more lenient.

Management of ecotourism sites by private ecotourism companies offers an alternative to the cost of regulation and deficiency of government agencies. It is believed that these companies have a self interest in limited environmental degradation, because tourists will pay more for pristine environments, which translates to higher profit. However, theory indicates that this practice is not economically feasible and will fail to manage the environment.

The model of monopolistic competition states that distinctiveness will entail profits, but profits will promote imitation. A company that protects its ecotourism sites is able to charge a premium for the novel experience and pristine environment. But when other companies view the success of this approach, they also enter the market with similar practices, increasing competition and reducing demand. Eventually, the demand will be reduced until the economic profit is zero. A cost-benefit analysis shows that the company bears the cost of environmental protection without receiving the gains. Without economic incentive, the whole premise of self interest through environmental protection is quashed; instead, ecotourism companies will minimize environment related expenses and maximize tourism demand.

The tragedy of the commons offers another model for economic unsustainability from environmental protection, in ecotourism sites utilized by many companies. Although there is a communal incentive to protect the environment, maximizing the benefits in the long run, a company will conclude that it is in their best interest to utilize the ecotourism site beyond its sustainable level. By increasing the number of ecotourists, for instance, a company gains all the economic benefit while paying only a part of the environmental cost. In the same way, a company recognizes that there is no incentive to actively protect the environment; they bear all the costs, while the benefits are shared by all other companies. The result, again, is mismanagement.

Taken together, the mobility of foreign investment and lack of economic incentive for environmental protection means that ecotourism companies are disposed to establishing themselves in new sites once their existing one is sufficiently degraded.

Improving Sustainability

Regulation and Accreditation

Because the regulation of ecotourism is poorly implemented or nonexistent, ecologically destructive greenwashed operations like underwater hotels, helicopter tours, and wildlife theme parks are categorized as ecotourism along with canoeing, camping, photography, and wildlife observation. The failure to acknowledge responsible, low impact ecotourism puts these companies at a competitive disadvantage.

Many environmentalists have argued for a global standard of accreditation, differentiating ecotourism companies based on their level of environmental commitment. A national or international regulatory board would enforce accreditation procedures, with representation from various groups including governments, hotels, tour operators, travel agents, guides, airlines, local authorities, conservation organizations, and non-governmental organizations. The decisions of the board would be sanctioned by governments, so that non-compliant companies would be legally required to disassociate themselves from the use of the ecotourism brand.

Crinion suggests a Green Stars System, based on criteria including a management plan, benefit for the local community, small group interaction, education value and staff training. Ecotourists who consider their choices would be confident of a genuine ecotourism experience when they see the higher star rating.

In addition, environmental impact assessments could be used as a form of accreditation. Feasibility is evaluated from a scientific basis, and recommendations could be made to optimally plan infrastructure, set tourist capacity, and manage the ecology. This form of accreditation is more sensitive to site specific conditions.

Guidelines and Education

An environmental protection strategy must address the issue of ecotourists removed from the cause-and-effect of their actions on the environment. More initiatives should be carried out to improve their awareness, sensitize them to environmental issues, and care about the places they visit.

Tour guides are an obvious and direct medium to communicate awareness. With the confidence of ecotourists and intimate knowledge of the environment, they can actively discuss conservation issues. A tour guide training program in Costa Rica's Tortuguero National Park has helped mitigate negative environmental impacts by providing information and regulating tourists on the parks' beaches used by nesting endangered sea turtles.

Small Scale, Slow Growth and Local Control

The underdevelopment theory of tourism describes a new form of imperialism by multinational corporations that control ecotourism resources. These corporations finance and profit from the development of large scale ecotourism that causes excessive environmental degradation, loss of traditional culture and way of life, and exploitation of local labour. In Zimbabwe and Nepal's

Annapurna region, where underdevelopment is taking place, more than 90 percent of ecotourism revenues are expatriated to the parent countries, and less than 5 percent go into local communities.

The lack of sustainability highlights the need for small scale, slow growth, and locally based ecotourism. Local peoples have a vested interest in the well being of their community, and are therefore more accountable to environmental protection than multinational corporations. The lack of control, westernization, adverse impacts to the environment, loss of culture and traditions outweigh the benefits of establishing large scale ecotourism.

The increased contributions of communities to locally managed ecotourism create viable economic opportunities, including high level management positions, and reduce environmental issues associated with poverty and unemployment. Because the ecotourism experience is marketed to a different lifestyle from large scale ecotourism, the development of facilities and infrastructure does not need to conform to corporate Western tourism standards, and can be much simpler and less expensive. There is a greater multiplier effect on the economy, because local products, materials, and labour are used. Profits accrue locally and import leakages are reduced. However, even this form of tourism may require foreign investment for promotion or start up. When such investments are required, it is crucial for communities for find a company or non-governmental organization that reflects the philosophy of ecotourism; sensitive to their concerns and willing to cooperate at the expense of profit. The basic assumption of the multiplier effect is that the economy starts off with unused resources, for example, that many workers are cyclically unemployed and much of industrial capacity is sitting idle or incompletely utilized. By increasing demand in the economy it is then possible to boost production. If the economy was already at full employment, with only structural, frictional, or other supply-side types of unemployment, any attempt to boost demand would only lead to inflation. For various laissez-faire schools of economics which embrace Say's Law and deny the possibility of Keynesian inefficiency and under-employment of resources, therefore, the multiplier concept is irrelevant or wrong-headed.

As an example, consider the government increasing its expenditure on roads by $one million, without a corresponding increase in taxation. This sum would go to the road builders, who would hire more workers and distribute the money as wages and profits. The households receiving these incomes will save part of the money and spend the rest on consumer goods. These expenditures in turn will generate more jobs, wages, and profits, and so on with the income and spending circulating around the economy.

The multiplier effect arises because of the induced increases in consumer spending which occur due to the increased incomes — and because of the feedback into increasing business revenues, jobs, and income again. This process does not lead to an economic explosion not only because of the supply-side barriers at potential output (full employment) but because at each "round", the increase in consumer spending is less than the increase in consumer incomes. That is, the marginal propensity to consume (mpc) is less than one, so that each round some extra income goes into saving, leaking out of the cumulative process. Each increase in spending is thus smaller than that of the previous round, preventing an explosion. Ecotourism has to be implemented with care.

Natural Resource Management

Natural resource management can be utilized as a specialized tool for the development of eco-tourism. There are several places throughout the world where the amount of natural resources are abundant. But, with human encroachment and habitats these resources are depleting. Without knowing the proper utilization of certain resources they are destroyed and floral and faunal species are becoming extinct. Ecotourism programmes can be introduced for the conservation of these resources. Several plans and proper management programmes can be introduced so that these resources remain untouched. Several organizations, NGO's, scientists are working on this field.

Natural resources of hill areas like Kurseong in West Bengal are plenty in number with various flora and fauna, but tourism for business purpose poised the situation. Researcher from Jadavpur University presently working in this area for the development of eco-tourism which can be utilized as a tool for natural resource management.

In South-East Asia government and Non-Government Organisations are working together with academics and industry operators to spread the economic benefits of tourism into the kampungs and villages of the region. A recently formed alliance, the South-East Asian Tourism Organisation - SEATO is bringing together these diverse players to allay resource management concerns.

Tour Operators, Travel Agencies & Retailers

Some companies specialise in ecotourism, designing their trips to be environmentally, culturally and socially friendly. Companies such as Intrepid Travel, Adventure Life, Frontier, and Marine Conservation Society, Family Nature Summit, Peregrine Adventures, World Expeditions, greentraveller, Explore Worldwide and Exodus offer trips catering for the thoughtful traveller. Some tour operators are keenly aware of the impacts that they may have on specific areas and rotate clients around to different sites for snorkeling, bird watching, and other activities. Others are just beginning to see the advantage of "green" travel destinations.

Extreme Tourism

Extreme tourism or shock tourism is a type of niche tourism involving travel to dangerous places (mountains, jungles, deserts, caves, etc.) or participation in dangerous events. Extreme tourism overlaps with extreme sport. The two share the main attraction, "adrenaline rush" caused by an element of risk, and differing mostly in the degree of engagement and professionalism.

Extreme tourism is a growing business in the countries of the former Soviet Union (Russia, Ukraine, Azerbaijan, etc.) and in South American countries like Peru, Chile and Argentina. The mountainous and rugged terrain of Northern Pakistan has also developed into a popular extreme tourism location.

While traditional tourism requires significant investments in hotels, roads, etc., extreme tourism requires much less to jump-start a business. In addition to traditional travel-based tourism destinations, various exotic attractions are suggested, such as flyovers in MiGs at Mach 2.5, ice diving in the White Sea, or travelling across the Chernobyl zone.

Geotourism

Geotourism is "best practice" tourism that sustains, or even enhances, the geographical character of a place, such as its culture, environment, heritage, and the well-being of its residents.

The concept was introduced publicly in a 2002 report by the Travel Industry Association of America (as of 2009 this organization adapted name to U.S. Travel Association) and National Geographic Traveler magazine. National Geographic senior editor Jonathan B. Tourtellot and his wife, Sally Bensusen, coined the term in 1997 in response to requests for a term and concept more encompassing than *ecotourism* and *sustainable tourism.*

Like ecotourism, geotourism promotes a virtuous circle whereby tourism revenues provide a local incentive to protect what tourists are coming to see, but extends the principle beyond nature and ecology to incorporate all characteristics that contribute to *sense of place,* such as historic structures, living and traditional culture, landscapes, cuisine, arts and artisanry, as well as local flora and fauna. Geotourism incorporates sustainability principles, but in addition to the do-no-harm ethic, geotourism focuses on the place as a whole. The idea of enhancement allows for development based on character of place, rather than standardized international branding, and generic architecture, food, and so on.

The Geotourism Charter

The National Geographic Society defines geoturism as tourism that sustains or enhances the geographical character of a place – its environment, culture, aesthetics, heritage, and the well-being of its residents.

National Geographic Society has also drawn up a "Geotourism Charter" based on 13 principles:

1. *Integrity of place:* Enhance geographical character by developing and improving it in ways distinctive to the local, reflective of its natural and cultural heritage, so as to encourage market differentiation and cultural pride.
2. *International codes:* Adhere to the principles embodied in the World Tourism Organization's Global Code of Ethics for Tourism and the Principles of the Cultural Tourism Charter established by the International Council on Monuments and Sites (ICOMOS).
3. *Market selectivity:* Encourage growth in tourism market segments most likely to appreciate, respect, and disseminate information about the distinctive assets of the locale.

4. *Market diversity:* Encourage a full range of appropriate food and lodging facilities, so as to appeal to the entire demographic spectrum of the geotourism market and so maximize economic resiliency over both the short and long term.
5. *Tourist satisfaction:* Ensure that satisfied, excited geotourists bring new vacation stories home and send friends off to experience the same thing, thus providing continuing demand for the destination.
6. *Community involvement:* Base tourism on community resources to the extent possible, encouraging local small businesses and civic groups to build partnerships to promote and provide a distinctive, honest visitor experience and market their locales effectively. Help businesses develop approaches to tourism that build on the area's nature, history and culture, including food and drink, artisanry, performance arts, etc.
7. *Community benefit:* Encourage micro- to medium-size enterprises and tourism business strategies that emphasize economic and social benefits to involved communities, especially poverty alleviation, with clear communication of the destination stewardship policies required to maintain those benefits.
8. *Protection and enhancement of destination appeal:* Encourage businesses to sustain natural habitats, heritage sites, aesthetic appeal, and local culture. Prevent degradation by keeping volumes of tourists within maximum acceptable limits. Seek business models that can operate profitably within those limits. Use persuasion, incentives, and legal enforcement as needed.
9. *Land use:* Anticipate development pressures and apply techniques to prevent undesired overdevelopment and degradation. Contain resort and vacation-home sprawl, especially on coasts and islands, so as to retain a diversity of natural and scenic environments and ensure continued resident access to waterfronts. Encourage major self-contained tourism attractions, such as large-scale theme parks and convention centres unrelated to character of place, to be sited in needier locations with no significant ecological, scenic, or cultural assets.

10. *Conservation of resources:* Encourage businesses to minimize water pollution, solid waste, energy consumption, water usage, landscaping chemicals, and overly bright nighttime lighting. Advertise these measures in a way that attracts the large, environmentally sympathetic tourist market.
11. *Planning:* Recognize and respect immediate economic needs without sacrificing long-term character and the geotourism potential of the destination. Where tourism attracts in-migration of workers, develop new communities that themselves constitute a destination enhancement. Strive to diversify the economy and limit population influx to sustainable levels. Adopt public strategies for mitigating practices that are incompatible with geotourism and damaging to the image of the destination.
12. *Interactive interpretation:* Engage both visitors and hosts in learning about the place. Encourage residents to show off the natural and cultural heritage of their communities, so that tourists gain a richer experience and residents develop pride in their locales.
13. *Evaluation:* Establish an evaluation process to be conducted on a regular basis by an independent panel representing all stakeholder interests, and publicize evaluation results.

Heritage Tourism

Cultural heritage tourism (or just heritage tourism) is a branch of tourism oriented towards the cultural heritage of the location where tourism is occurring.

Culture has always been a major object of travel, as the development of the Grand Tour from the 16th century onwards attests. In the 20th century, some people have claimed, culture ceased to be the objective of tourism: tourism is now culture. Cultural attractions play an important role in tourism at all levels, from the global highlights of world culture to attractions that underpin local identities. (Richards, 1996)

According to the Weiler and Hall, culture, heritage and the arts have long contributed to appeal of tourist destination. However, in recent years 'culture' has been rediscovered as an important marketing tool to attract those travellers with special interests in heritage and arts. According to the Hollinshead, cultural heritage tourism defines as cultural heritage tourism is the fastest growing segment of the tourism industry because there is a trend toward an increase specialization among tourists. This trend is evident in the rise in the volume of tourists who seek adventure, culture, history, archaeology and interaction with local people.

Cultural heritage tourism is important for various reasons; it has a positive economic and social impact, it establishes and reinforces identity, it helps preserve the cultural heritage, with culture as an instrument it facilitates harmony and understanding among people, it supports culture and helps renew tourism (Richards, 1996). Putangina Cultural heritage tourism has a number of objectives that must be met within the context of sustainable development such as; the conservation of cultural resources, accurate interpretation of resources, authentic visitors experience, and the stimulation of the earned revenues of cultural resources. We can see, therefore, that cultural heritage tourism is not only concerned with identification, management and protection of the heritage values but it must also be involved in understanding the impact of tourism on communities and regions, achieving economic and social benefits, providing financial resources for protection, as well as marketing and promotion. (J. M. Fladmark, 1994)

Heritage tourism involves visiting historical or industrial sites that may include old canals, railways, battlegrounds, etc. The overall purpose is to gain an appreciation of the past. It also refers to the marketing of a location to members of a diaspora who have distant family roots there.

Decolonization and immigration form the major background of much contemporary heritage tourism. Falling travel costs have also made heritage tourism possible for more people.

Another possible form involves religious travel or pilgrimages. Many Catholics from around the world come to the Vatican and other sites such as Lourdes or Fátima. Large numbers of Jews have both visited Israel and emigrated there. Many have also gone to Holocaust sites and memorials. Islam commands its followers to take the *hajj* to Mecca, thus differentiating it somewhat from tourism in the usual sense, though the trip can also be a culturally important event for the pilgrim.

Heritage Tourism can also be attributed to historical events that have been dramatised to make them more entertaining. For example a historical tour of a town or city using a theme such as ghosts or vikings.

LGBT Tourism

Gay tourism or LGBT tourism is a form of niche tourism marketed to gay, lesbian, bisexual and transgender (LGBT) people. They are usually open about their sexual orientation and gender identity but may be more or less open when travelling; for instance they may be closeted at home or if they have come out, may be more discreet in areas known for violence against LGBT people. The main components of LGBT tourism is for cities and countries wishing to attract LGBT tourists; people looking to travel to LGBT-friendly destinations; people wanting travel with other LGBT people when travelling regardless of the destination and LGBT travellers who are mainly concerned with cultural and safety issues. The slang term *gaycation* has come to imply a version of a vacation that includes a pronounced aspect of LGBT culture, either in the journey or destination. The LGBT tourism industry includes travel agents, tour companies, cruise lines and travel advertising and promotions companies who market these destinations to the gay community. Coinciding with the increased visibility of LGBT people raising children in the 1990s, an increase in family-friendly LGBT tourism has emerged in the 2000s, for instance R Family Vacations which includes activities and entertainment geared towards couples including same-sex weddings. R Family's first cruise was held aboard Norwegian Cruise Lines's *Norwegian Dawn* with 1600 passengers including 600 children.

Major companies in the travel industry have become aware of the substantial money (also known as the "pink dollar" or "pink pound") generated by this marketing niche, and have made it a point to align themselves with the gay community and gay tourism campaigns. According to a 2000 Tourism Intelligence International report 10% of international tourists were gay and lesbian accounting for more than 70 million arrivals worldwide. This market segment is expected to continue to grow as a result ongoing acceptance of LGBT people and changing attitudes towards sexual and gender minorities. The gay and lesbian segment is estimated at $55 billion annual market as of 2007. Outside larger companies, LGBT tourists are offered other traditional tourism tools, such as LGBT hospitality networks of LGBT individuals who offer each other hospitality during their travels and even home swaps where people live in each others homes. Also available are social groups for resident and visiting gay, lesbian, bisexual and transgender expatriates and friends exist worldwide.

Gay Travel Destinations

Gay travel destinations are popular among practitioners of gay tourism because they usually have permissive or liberal attitudes towards gays, feature a prominent gay infrastructure (bars, businesses, restaurants, hotels, nightlife, entertainment, media, organisations, etc.), the opportunity to socialize with other gays, and the feeling that one can relax safely among other gay people.

Gay travel destinations are often large cities, although not exclusively, and often coincide with the existence of gay neighborhoods. These municipalities and their tourism bureaus often work actively to develop their reputations as places for gays to travel to, commonly by aligning themselves to local gay organisations. Travel analysts state that the existence of a core gay friendly population is often the primary catalyst for the development of a gay-friendly tourist destination.

Gay tourism might also coincide with special gay events such as annual gay pride parades, gay neighborhood festivals and such gay community gatherings as gay chorus festivals and concerts, gay square dance conventions, gay sports meets such as Gay Games, World Outgames or Euro Games and conferences of national and international gay organisations. Gay tourism blossoms during these peak periods.

Gay tourism practitioners spend $64 billion a year on gay travel, according to Community Marketing Inc. The adult GLBT community has a total economic spending power of more than $600 billion per year, according to Wietck Combs. Philadelphia and Community Marketing found that for every one dollar invested in gay tourism marketing, $153 was returned in direct economic spending in shops, hotels, restaurants and attractions. Since 2002, there has been a historic rise in gay tourism marketing. Destinations such as Philadelphia, Dallas and Ft. Lauderdale have engaged in gay tourism campaigns. The gay cruise industry is experiencing a significant growth period. Community Marketing Inc. found in research studies that gay business travellers are 30% more likely to convert to a leisure visitor.

Philadelphia was the first destination in the world to create and air a television commercial specifically geared towards practitioners of gay tourism. Philadelphia was also the first destination to commission a research study aimed at a specific destination to learn about gay travel to a specific city.

Work is underway in conjunction with Israel's Ministry of Tourism to turn Tel Aviv into the international tourist destination for the gay-lesbian community in order to boost business in restaurants, hotels, city attraction sites and beaches. In an effort to boost gay tourism in Tel Aviv, the Gay and Lesbian Union has bid to host in Tel Aviv the 2009 Euro Pride, the largest annual gay parade in the world.

Gay Tourism Specialists

The International Gay and Lesbian Travel Association (IGLTA) holds an annual world convention and four symposia in different tourism destinations around the world. Each symposium attracts over 100 representatives of tour agencies and travel publications that specialise in the gay and lesbian market. The association was founded in 1983, and it currently represents over 900 members. Its headquarters are in Fort Lauderdale, Florida.

The "14th International Gay & Lesbian World Travel Expo" in 2006 will visit six U.S. cities. The annual Expo series is produced by Community Marketing, a gay tourism research and travel marketing firm.

Out Traveler, from the publishers of *Out* and *The Advocate,* is a glossy magazine aimed at gay and lesbian travellers. It is published six times yearly. Other LGBT-travel publications include Passport Magazine and Spartacus International. One of Europe's gay and lesbian travel marketing specialists is Out Now Consulting.

Medical Tourism

Medical tourism (also called medical travel, health tourism or global healthcare) is a term initially coined by travel agencies and the mass media to describe the rapidly-growing practice of travelling across international borders to obtain health care. It also refers pejoratively to the practice of healthcare providers travelling internationally to deliver healthcare.

Services typically sought by travellers include elective procedures as well as complex specialized surgeries such as joint replacement (knee/hip), cardiac surgery, dental surgery, and cosmetic surgeries. However, virtually every type of health care, including psychiatry, alternative treatments, convalescent care and even burial services are available. As a practical matter, providers and customers commonly use informal channels of communication-connection-contract, and in such cases this tends to mean less regulatory or legal oversight to assure quality and less formal recourse to reimbursement or redress, if needed.

Over 50 countries have identified medical tourism as a national industry. However, accreditation and other measures of quality vary widely across the globe, and there are risks and ethical issues that make this method of accessing medical care controversial. Also, some destinations may become hazardous or even dangerous for medical tourists to contemplate.

In the context of global health, "medical tourism" is a pejorative because during such trips health care providers often practice outside of their areas of expertise or hold different (i.e., lower) standards of care. Greater numbers than ever before of student volunteers, health professions trainees, and researchers from resource-rich countries are working temporarily and anticipating future work in resource-starved areas. This emphasizes the importance of understanding this other definition.

History

The concept of medical tourism is not a new one. The first recorded instance of medical tourism dates back thousands of years to when Greek pilgrims traveled from all over the Mediterranean to the small territory in the Saronic Gulf called Epidauria. This territory was the sanctuary of the healing god Asklepios. Epidauria became the original travel destination for medical tourism. Spa towns and sanitariums may be considered an early form of medical tourism. In eighteenth century England, for example, patients visited spas because they were places with supposedly health-giving mineral waters, treating diseases from gout to liver disorders and bronchitis.

Description

Factors that have led to the increasing popularity of medical travel include the high cost of health care, long wait times for certain procedures, the ease and affordability of international travel, and improvements in both technology and standards of care in many countries.

Medical tourists can come from anywhere in the First World, including Europe, the Middle East, Japan, the United States, and Canada. This is because of their large populations, comparatively high wealth, the high expense of health care or lack of health care options locally, and increasingly high expectations of their populations with respect to health care. An authority at the Harvard Business School recently stated that "medical tourism is promoted much more heavily in the United Kingdom than in the United States".

A forecast by Deloitte Consulting published in August 2008 projected that medical tourism originating in the US could jump by a factor of ten over the next decade. An estimated 750,000 Americans went abroad for health care in 2007, and the report estimated that a million and a half would seek health care outside the US in 2008. The growth in medical tourism has the potential to cost US health care providers billions of dollars in lost revenue.

A large draw to medical travel is convenience and speed. Countries that operate public health-care systems are often so taxed that it can take considerable time to get non-urgent medical care. Using Canada as an example, an estimated 782,936 Canadians spent time on medical waiting lists in 2005, waiting an average of 9.4 weeks. Canada has set waiting-time benchmarks, e.g. 26 weeks for a hip replacement and 16 weeks for cataract surgery, for non-urgent medical procedures.

Additionally, patients are finding that insurance either does not cover orthopedic surgery (such as knee/hip replacement) or imposes unreasonable restrictions on the choice of the facility, surgeon, or prosthetics to be used. Medical tourism for knee/hip replacements has emerged as one of the more widely accepted procedures because of the lower cost and minimal difficulties associated with the travelling to/from the surgery. Colombia provides a knee replacement for about $5,000 USD, including all associated fees, such as FDA-approved prosthetics and hospital stay-over expenses. However, many clinics quote prices that are not all inclusive and include only the surgeon fees associated with the procedure.

According to an article by the University of Delaware publication, Daily:

> *" The cost of surgery in India, Thailand or South Africa can be one-tenth of what it is in the United States or Western Europe, and sometimes even less. A heart-valve replacement that would cost $200,000 or more in the US, for example, goes for $10,000 in India—and that includes round-trip airfare and a brief vacation package. Similarly, a metal-free dental bridge worth $5,500 in the US costs $500 in India, a knee replacement in Thailand with six days of physical therapy costs about one-fifth of what it would in the States, and Lasik eye surgery worth $3,700 in the US is available in many other countries for only $730. Cosmetic surgery savings are even greater: A full facelift that would cost $20,000 in the US runs about $1,250 in South Africa."*

Popular medical travel worldwide destinations include: Argentina, Brunei, Cuba, Colombia, Costa Rica, Hong Kong, Hungary, India, Jordan, Lithuania, Malaysia, The Philippines, Singapore, South Africa, Thailand, and recently, Saudi Arabia, UAE, South Korea, Tunisia and New Zealand.

Popular cosmetic surgery travel destinations include: Argentina, Bolivia, Brazil, Colombia, Costa Rica, Cuba, Mexico and Turkey. In South America, countries such as Argentina, Bolivia, Brazil and Colombia lead on plastic surgery medical skills relying on their experienced plastic surgeons. In Bolivia and Colombia, plastic surgery has also become quite common. According to the Sociedad Boliviana de Cirugia Plasticay Reconstructiva", more than 70% of middle and upper class women in the country have had some form of plastic surgery. Colombia also provides advanced care in cardiovascular and transplant surgery.

In Europe Belgium, Poland and Slovakia are also breaking into the business. South Africa is taking the term "medical tourism" very literally by promoting their "medical safaris".

A specialized subset of medical tourism is reproductive tourism and reproductive outsourcing, which is the practice of travelling abroad to undergo in-vitro fertilization, surrogate pregnancy and other assisted reproductive technology treatments including freezing embryos for retro-production. However, perceptions of medical tourism are not always positive. In places like the US, which has high standards of quality, medical tourism is viewed as risky. In some parts of the world, wider political issues can influence where medical tourists will choose to seek out health care.

Health tourism providers have developed as intermediaries to unite potential medical tourists with provider hospitals and other organisations. Companies are beginning to offer global health care options that will enable North American and European patients to access world health care at a fraction of the cost of domestic care. Companies that focus on medical value travel typically provide nurse case managers to assist patients with pre- and post-travel medical issues. They also help provide resources for follow-up care upon the patient's return.

Process

The typical process is as follows: the person seeking medical treatment abroad contacts a medical tourism provider. The provider usually requires the patient to provide a medical report, including the nature of ailment, local doctor's opinion, medical history, and diagnosis, and may request additional information. Certified medical doctors or consultants then advise on the medical treatment. The approximate expenditure, choice of hospitals and tourist destinations, and duration of stay, etc., is discussed. After signing consent bonds and agreements, the patient is given recommendation letters for a medical visa, to be procured from the concerned embassy. The patient travels to the destination country, where the medical tourism provider assigns a case executive, who takes care of the patient's accommodation, treatment and any other form of care. Once the treatment is done, the patient can remain in the tourist destination or return home.

International Healthcare Accreditation

Because standards are important when it comes to health care, there are parallel issues around medical tourism, international healthcare accreditation, evidence-based medicine and quality assurance.

The oldest international accrediting body is Accreditation Canada, formerly known as the Canadian Council on Health Services Accreditation, which accredited the Bermuda Hospital Board as soon as 1968. Since then, it has accredited hospitals and health service organizations in ten other countries.

In the United States, the best known accreditation group is the Joint Commission International (JCI). They have been inspecting and accrediting health care facilities and hospitals outside of the United States since 1999. Many international hospitals today see obtaining international accreditation as a way to attract American patients.

Joint Commission International is a relative of the Joint Commission in the United States. Both are independent private sector not-for-profit organizations that develop nationally and internationally recognized procedures and standards to help improve patient care and safety. They work with hospitals to help them meet Joint Commission standards for patient care and then accredit those hospitals meeting the standards.

In the UK and Hong Kong, the Trent International Accreditation Scheme is a key player. The different international healthcare accreditation schemes vary in quality, size, cost, intent and the skill and intensity of their marketing. They also vary in terms of cost to hospitals and healthcare institutions making use of them. A forecast by Deloitte Consulting regarding medical tourism published in August 2008 noted the value of accreditation in ensuring quality of healthcare and specifically mentioned JCI, ISQUA and Trent.

Increasingly, some hospitals are looking towards dual international accreditation, perhaps having both JCI to cover potential US clientele, Trent for potential British and European clientele and Accreditation Canada. As a result of competition between clinics for American medical tourists, there have been initiatives to rank hospitals based on patient-reported metrics.

Other organizations providing contributions to quality practices include:

- The Society for International Healthcare Accreditation (SOFIHA), a free-to-join group providing a forum for discussion and for the sharing of ideas and good practice by providers of international healthcare accreditation and users of the same. The primary role of this organisation is to promote a safe hospital environment for patients.
- The United Kingdom Accreditation Forum (UKAF) is an established network of accreditation organisations with the intention of sharing experience good practice and new

ideas around the methodology for accreditation programmes, covering issues such as developing healthcare quality standards, implementation of standards within healthcare organisations, assessment by peer review and exploration of the peer review techniques to include the recruitment, training, monitoring and evaluation of peer reviewers and the mechanisms for awards of accredited status to organisations.

Organizations and Associations

International hospitals, insurance companies and medical travel facilitators have in recent years sought affiliations through various organizations such as the International Medical Travel Association, based in Singapore.

Medical Tourism Association (MTA), the second non-profit trade association for medical tourism (after the International Medical Travel Association), is made up of international hospitals, healthcare providers, medical travel facilitators, insurance companies, and other affiliated companies and members with the common goal of promoting medical tourism in a global environment. The Association promotes the interests of its healthcare provider and medical travel facilitator members. The MTA claims three tenets: Transparency, Communication and Education. These tenets were recently called into question in a Reuters article during the time of one if its conferences. Further questions about the legitimacy of the organization were discussed in an International Medical Travel Journal piece on a legal dispute involving the MTA. Some in the medical tourism industry have complained of unethical or illegal practices such as redirecting non-MTA member web sites to the MTA web site or the MTA claiming to be the sole voice of the entire medical tourism industry.

The goal of these types of associations is often to raise awareness of medical tourism in the hopes of expanding the industry.

Risks

Medical tourism carries some risks that locally-provided medical care does not. Some countries, such as India, Malaysia, or Thailand have very different infectious disease-related epidemiology to Europe and North America. Exposure to diseases without having built up natural immunity can be a hazard for weakened individuals, specifically with respect to gastrointestinal diseases (e.g. Hepatitis A, amoebic dysentery, paratyphoid) which could weaken progress, mosquito-transmitted diseases, influenza, and tuberculosis. However, because in poor tropical nations diseases run the gamut, doctors seem to be more open to the possibility of considering any infectious disease, including HIV, TB, and typhoid, while there are cases in the West where patients were consistently misdiagnosed for years because such diseases are perceived to be "rare" in the West.

The quality of post-operative care can also vary dramatically, depending on the hospital and country, and may be different from US or European standards. However, JCI and Trent fulfill the role of accreditation by assessing the standards in the healthcare in the countries like India, China and Thailand. Also, travelling long distances soon after surgery can increase the risk of complications. Long flights and decreased mobility in a cramped airline cabin are a known risk factor for developing blood clots in the legs such as venous thrombosis or pulmonary embolus economy class syndrome. Other vacation activities can be problematic as well — for example, scars may become darker and more noticeable if they sunburn while healing. To minimise these problems, medical tourism patients often combine their medical trips with vacation time set aside for rest and recovery in the destination country.

Also, health facilities treating medical tourists may lack an adequate complaints policy to deal appropriately and fairly with complaints made by dissatisfied patients.

Differences in healthcare provider standards around the world have been recognised by the World Health Organization, and in 2004 it launched the World Alliance for Patient Safety. This body assists hospitals and government around the world in setting patient safety policy and practices that can become particularly relevant when providing medical tourism services.

Legal Issues

Receiving medical care abroad may subject medical tourists to unfamiliar legal issues. The limited nature of litigation in various countries is one reason for the lower cost of care overseas. While some countries currently presenting themselves as attractive medical tourism destinations provide some form of legal remedies for medical malpractice, these legal avenues may be unappealing to the medical tourist. Should problems arise, patients might not be covered by adequate personal insurance or might be unable to seek compensation via malpractice lawsuits. Hospitals and/or doctors in some countries may be unable to pay the financial damages awarded by a court to a patient who has sued them, owing to the hospital and/or the doctor not possessing appropriate insurance cover and/or medical indemnity.

Ethical Issues

There can be major ethical issues around medical tourism. For example, the illegal purchase of organs and tissues for transplantation has been alleged in countries such as India and China prior to 2007. Medical tourism may raise broader ethical issues for the countries in which it is promoted. For example in India, some argue that a "policy of 'medical tourism for the classes and health missions for the masses' will lead to a deepening of the inequities" already embedded in the health care system. In Thailand, in 2008 it was stated that, "Doctors in Thailand have become so busy with foreigners that Thai patients are having trouble getting care". Medical tourism centred on new technologies, such as stem cell treatments, is often criticized on grounds of fraud, blatant lack of scientific rationale and patient safety. However, when pioneering advanced technologies, such as providing 'unproven' therapies to patients outside of regular clinical trials, it is often challenging to differentiate between acceptable medical innovation and unacceptable patient exploitation.

Employer-sponsored Health Care in the US

Some US employers have begun exploring medical travel programs as a way to cut employee health care costs. Such proposals have raised stormy debates between employers and trade unions representing workers, with one union stating that it deplored the "shocking new approach" of offering employees overseas treatment in return for a share of the company's savings. The unions also raise the issues of legal liability should something go wrong, and potential job losses in the US health care industry if treatment is outsourced.

Employers may offer incentives such as paying for air travel and waiving out-of-pocket expenses for care outside of the US. For example, in January 2008, Hannaford Bros., a supermarket chain based in Maine, began paying the entire medical bill for employees to travel to Singapore for hip and knee replacements, including travel for the patient and companion. Medical travel packages can integrate with all types of health insurance, including limited benefit plans, preferred provider organizations and high deductible health plans. In 2000 Blue Shield of California began the United States' first cross border health plan. Patients in California could travel to one of the three certified hospitals in Mexico for treatment under California Blue Shield. In 2007, a subsidiary of BlueCross BlueShield of South Carolina, Companion Global Healthcare, teamed up with hospitals in Thailand, Singapore, Turkey, Ireland, Costa Rica and India. A 2008 article in *Fast Company* discusses the globalization of healthcare and describes how various players in the US healthcare market have begun to explore it.

Subfields

Dental: Dental tourism involves individuals seeking dental care outside of their local healthcare systems.

Fertility: Fertility tourism is the practice of travelling to another country for fertility treatments. The main reasons for fertility tourism are legal regulation of the sought procedure in the home country, or lower price. In-vitro fertilization, donor insemination and surrogacy are major procedures involved.

Destinations

Africa and Middle East

Countries in this region involved in medical tourism include Saudi Arabia, South Africa, and Tunisia.

Israel

Israel is emerging as a popular destination for medical tourists. In 2006, 15,000 foreigners travelled to the country for medical procedures, bringing in $40 million of revenue.

Medical tourists choose Israel for several reasons. Some come from European nations such as Romania where certain procedures are not available. Others come to Israel, perhaps most commonly from the US, because they can receive quality health care at a fraction of the cost it would be at home, for both surgeries and in-vitro fertilization treatments. Other medical tourists come to Israel to visit the Dead Sea, a world-famous therapeutic resort. The Israel Ministry of Tourism and several professional medical services providers have set out to generate awareness of Israel's medical capabilities.

Jordan

Jordan is an emerging medical tourism destination, with related revenues exceeding one billion dollars in 2007. More than 250,000 patients from other countries sought treatment in Jordan that year. This included an estimated 45,000 Iraqis and approximately 25,000 patients each from Palestine and Sudan. An estimated 1,800 US citizens, 1,200 UK citizens, and 400 Canadians also sought treatment in Jordan that year. Treatment costs can be as low as 25 percent of costs in the US. The kingdom was rated as number one in the region and fifth in the world as a medical tourism hub in a study by the World Bank.

UAE

Hospitals in Dubai and other emirates have expressed an intent to develop in medical tourism. Some have American-sourced international healthcare accreditation, while others are looking towards the UK, Australia and Canada for accreditation services.

The Americas

Countries in the Americas that are treating foreign patients include Argentina, Bolivia, Brazil, Colombia, Costa Rica, Cuba, Dominican Republic, Guatemala, Mexico, Panama, Peru and Uruguay.

Brazil

Brazil has long been known as a destination for cosmetic surgery. For non-cosmetic procedures, Brazil is only now entering the global market. However, Albert Einstein Jewish Hospital in Sao Paulo was the first JCI-accredited facility outside of the US, and more than a dozen Brazilian medical facilities have since been similarly accredited. Brazil requires visas for US citizens based on a reciprocal arrangement since Brazilians are required to obtain a visa to visit the US.

Canada

Canada has entered the medical tourism field. In comparison to US health costs, medical tourism patients can save 30 to 60 percent on health costs in Canada.

Cuba

Cuba has been a popular medical tourism destination for more than 40 years. Thousands of patients travel to Cuba, particularly from Latin America and Europe, attracted by the "fine reputation of Cuban doctors, the low prices and nearby beaches on which to recuperate." In 2006, Cuba attracted nearly 20,000 health tourists. Medical treatments included joint replacement, cancer treatment, eye surgery, cosmetic surgery and addictions rehabilitation. Costs are about 60 to 80 percent less than US costs.

Cuba has hospitals for Cuban residents and others that focus on serving foreigners and diplomats. In the 2007 American documentary film, *Sicko,* which criticizes the US healthcare system, producer Michael Moore leads a group of uninsured American patients to Cuba to obtain more affordable medical treatment. *Sicko* has greatly increased foreigners' interest in Cuban healthcare. A recent Miami Herald story focused on the high quality of health care that Canadian and American medical tourism patients receive in Cuba. The Cuban government has developed Cuban medical tourism to generate income for the country. Residents of Canada, the UK and most other countries can travel to Cuba without any difficulty a tourist visa is generally required. For Americans, however, because of the US trade policy towards Cuba, travellers must either obtain US government approval, or, more frequently, travel to Cuba from Canada, Mexico, the Bahamas, Jamaica or the Dominican Republic. Cuban immigration authorities do not stamp the passports of US visitors so that Americans can keep their travels a private matter. To date no Cuban facility has achieved JCI Accreditation.

Mexico

Americans, particularly those living near the Mexican border, now routinely cross to Mexico for medical care. Popular specialties include dentistry and plastic surgery. Mexican dentists often charge one-fifth to one-fourth of US prices, while other procedures typically cost a third what they would in the US.

This trend has alarmed American healthcare providers who, fearing a loss of business, warn patients away from Mexico. "The phenomenon has unsettled US-based dentists who tell horror stories of rampant infections, undetected cases of oral cancer and shoddy work south of the border", claims hotly disputed by Mexican dentists. "In Texas, legislators explored the possibility of allowing health maintenance organizations to operate on both sides of the border. However, physicians in south Texas lobbied against the changes, arguing that local doctors could not compete with the lower costs in Mexico". US doctors point out that the

Mexican legal system makes it almost impossible to sue Mexican doctors for malpractice. However, many who travel to Mexico for care report that they are satisfied. According to a report commissioned by Families U.S.A., a Washington advocacy group for health-care issues, "About 90 percent [feel] the care they had received in Mexico had been good or excellent. About 80 percent rated the care they had received in the United States as good or excellent". Indeed "some U.S. dentists ... have conceded to the competition and begun a 'reverse migration' opening offices in Mexico to take advantage of lower costs". More American insurers are providing coverage for travellers, as the out-of-pocket costs to them are much lower. "With healthcare costs in the United States continuing to rise, many employers in Southern California are turning to insurance plans that send their workers to Mexico for routine care, plans that are growing by nearly 3,000 people a year."

In addition to dental and plastic surgery, Mexican hospitals are popular for bariatric surgery for weight loss, considered an elective procedure that is not covered by some US insurers. A popular bariatric procedure, lap band surgery, which was approved by the FDA in the US in 2001, has been performed for longer by Mexican surgeons.

Panama

In Panama, health and medical tourism is growing rapidly. Factors drawing medical tourists include Panama's tourist appeal, position as a hub for international travel, and use of the American dollar as the official currency. Many of Panama's doctors are bilingual, board certified, and accustomed to working with the same medical equipment and technology used in the United States and Europe. On most procedures, Panama offers savings of more than 50% compared to the US and Europe. No Panamanian hospitals currently have international healthcare accreditation, whether through US, British, Australian or Canadian sources.

United States

Although much attention has been given to the growing trend of uninsured Americans travelling to foreign countries, a report from 2008 found that a plurality of an estimated 60,000 to 85,000 medical tourists were travelling to the United States for the purpose of receiving inpatient medical care. The availability of advanced medical technology and sophisticated training of physicians are cited as driving motivators for growth in foreigners travelling to the U.S. for medical care. Also, it has been noted that the decline in value of the U.S. dollar is offering additional incentive for foreign travel to the U.S. However, costs differences between the US and many locations in Asia far outweigh any currency fluctuations. Several major medical centres and teaching hospitals offer international patient centres that cater to patients from foreign countries who seek medical treatment in the U.S. Many of these organizations offer service coordinators to assist international patients with arrangements for medical care, accommodations, finances and transportation including air ambulance services.

It should be noted that many locations in the US that offer medical care comparable in price to foreign medical facilities are not Joint Commission Accredited.

Uruguay

Uruguay recently entered the medical tourism market. A private medical tourism initiative, Uruhealth, has been created with support from the Ministries of Tourism and Public Health. The initiative involves the infrastructuıe, human resources and experience of two healthcare companies: MP Personalized Medicine (Montevideo) and SEMM-Mautone Hospital (Punta del Este).

Asia/Pacific

Many Asian Pacific countries are medical tourism destinations.

China

China is fast emerging as a desirable destination for individuals seeking medical care in a wide range of medical specialties, including cardiology, neurology, orthopedics and others. A number of private and government hospitals in major cities have established international departments. Many leading hospitals provide treatments integrating Traditional Chinese Medicine with Western medical technology and techniques. China is home to leading stem cell research and treatment hospitals that offer Westerners who want to take advantage of stem cell treatments that are still considered experimental or have yet to be approved in their home country.

Hong Kong

As of 2006, Hong Kong had 12 private hospitals and 39 public hospitals, providing 3,124 and 27,755 beds respectively. A wide range of health care services are offered. All 12 of Hong Kong's private hospitals have been surveyed and accredited by the UK's Trent Accreditation Scheme since early 2001. This has been a major factor in the ascent of standards in Hong Kong's private hospitals. The Trent scheme works closely with the hospitals it assesses to generate standards appropriate to the locality (with respect to culture, geography, public health, primary care interfaces etc.), and always uses combinations of UK-sourced and Hong Kong-sourced surveyors. Some of Hong Kong's private hospitals have now gone on to obtain dual international accreditation, with both Trent and JCI (and have therefore attained a standard surpassing some of the best hospitals in Thailand and Singapore). Others are looking towards dual international accreditation with Trent and the Australian group. Hong Kong public hospitals have yet to commit to external accreditation.

India

India's medical tourism sector is expected to experience an annual growth rate of 30%, making it a Rs. 9,500-crore industry by 2015. Estimates of the value of medical tourism to India go as high as $2 billion a year by 2012. Advantages for medical tourists include reduced costs, the availability of latest medical technologies and a growing compliance on international quality standards, as well as the fact that foreigners are not likely to face a language barrier in India. The Indian government is taking steps to address infrastructure issues that hinder the country's growth in medical tourism. Most estimates claim treatment costs in India start at around a tenth of the price of comparable treatment in America or Britain. The most popular treatments sought in India by medical tourists are alternative medicine, bone-marrow transplant, cardiac bypass surgery, eye surgery and orthopedic surgery. India is known in particular for heart surgery, hip resurfacing and other areas of advanced medicine. Ministry of Tourism India (MoT) is planning to extend its Market Development Assistance (MDA) scheme to cover Joint Commission International (JCI) and National Accreditation Board of Hospitals (NABH) certified hospitals. A policy announcement of this effect is likely soon. The south Indian city of Chennai is regarded as the healthcare capital of India.

Korea, Republic of

Listed on CNN.com as one of the "hot destinations" for medical tourism, Korea is quickly establishing itself in the field of medical tourism.

However, *The Korea Times* reported in a series of articles that Korean hospitals have adopted a discriminatory pricing policy, charging foreigners two to three times more than the full-fee for locals.

The paper revealed that the price disparity in medical fees for foreign patients is extremely high, considering that the difference between the lowest and highest fees for the most-sought-after procedures exceeds more than 10 times on average.

It claims the government is overlooking soaring medical fees on foreign patients, who are unprotected from malpractice, discriminatory charging, overpricing and patient privacy rights under the Korean Medical Law.

In 2008, Korea had 27,480 foreign-based patients and the Korean health ministry expects that number to increase to 140,000 by 2015. Due to legislation passed in May 2009, state-licensed clinics and hospitals are now allowed to directly seek out foreign patients through various promotional activities.

Korean hospitals and clinics provide a variety of medical services for medical tourists including comprehensive health screening, cancer treatment, organ transplantation, joint/ rheumatism care, spinal treatment, ophthalmology, dental care, infertility treatment, otorhinolaryngology, and Korean traditional medicine. Currently, the most popular treatments for medical tourists are cosmetic procedures such as eyelid surgery, nose jobs, facelifts, and skin lightening.

Over 30 Korean hospitals and clinics are member providers under the Council for Korea Medicine Overseas Promotion (CKMOP). Among these facilities are the "Big Four" – Seoul National University Hospital, Samsung Medical Centre, Asan Medical Centre, and Yonsei Severance Hospital.

Malaysia

Malaysia is well on its way to develop itself as a medical tourism hub. The country has excellent hospitals, English is widely spoken, and many staff have been trained to a high level in the UK or in the US. There is a highly active Association for Private Hospitals of Malaysia working to develop medical tourism. However, while Malaysia has a national accreditation healthcare scheme (MSQH) and many Malaysia's hospitals are currently firmly on the way to achieve international healthcare accreditation.

Malaysian hospitals International Specialist Eye Centre, Penang Adventist Hospital and many others such as Gleneagles Hospital Kuala Lumpur have or are going to be JCI accredited. The Ministry of Health has launched a medical tourism page with medical tourism portals such as Wellness Visit.

New Zealand

New Zealand is a relatively new destination to medical travel. It has all the hallmarks of a very successful destination especially for North American based patients. This includes being a first world, developed economy with a sophisticated and comprehensive medical system. It is first and foremost English speaking with a rich heritage of producing world class doctors and medical research.

Many of its private hospitals are internationally accredited, state of the art and offer an integrated package of care. The surgeons in New Zealand are trained both in New Zealand and abroad, usually spending years of their training in either North America or Western Europe.

While New Zealand is aligned medically and culturally to North America, the cost of the surgical care is significantly cheaper. On average it is considered that New Zealand's surgical costs are around 15 to 20% the cost of the same surgical procedure in the USA. One patient who had his prosthetic hip replaced in New Zealand said the total cost including travel, lodging and the surgery at a private hospital was $20,000, as opposed to the $80,000 - $140,000 he was told the operation would have cost at home.

Added to this the personalized level of medical care, the world renown natural beauty and tranquility, the fact that New Zealand is one of the safest places in the world and only 12 hours direct flight from the west coast of North America, then New Zealand as a medical travel destination looks set to develop.

Philippines

The Philippines has been growing as a destination for medical tourism. The US Medical Tourism Association magazine reported that this services sub-sector grew 8.0% in 2007. The number can be expected to grow as American health-care costs rise, or if pending legislation results in an increase in patient wait times for surgical procedures (as has been seen in other countries where care has been nationalized), due to the traditional political, economic and cultural connections between the United States and the Philippines. The Philippines is one of a few countries that sends qualified nurses, physicians and dentists to the US, the thousands serving in American medical facilities being a testament to its quality of medical education. According to year 2000 WHO rankings of the world's health systems, the Philippines takes its position on no.60.

Singapore

Singapore has a dozen hospitals and health centres with JCI accreditation. In 1997 (published 2000), the World Health Organization ranked Singapore's health care system sixth best in the world and the highest ranked system in Asia. "Singapore Medicine" is a multi-agency government-industry partnership committed to strengthening Singapore's position as a medical hub and promoting Singapore as a destination for advanced patient care. Patients come from neighboring countries, such as Indonesia and Malaysia, and patient numbers from Indochina, South Asia, the Middle East and Greater China are growing. Patients from developed countries such as the United States and the UK are also beginning to choose Singapore as their medical travel destination for relatively affordable health care services in a clean cosmopolitan city.

Taiwan

The Taiwanese government has declared its determination for the country to become a medical tourism centre. In 2007, the Department of Health launched a campaign to promote inbound medical tourism, focusing on integrating the resources of the government and academia to build Taiwan's brand as a medical tourism destination. Costs for procedures remain comparatively low. Taiwan is known for liver transplants, joint replacement surgery, bone marrow transplants, and reconstructive and plastic surgery.

Thailand

Medical tourism has been a growing segment of Thailand's tourism and health-care sectors. In 2005, one Bangkok hospital took in 150,000 treatment seekers from abroad. In 2006, medical tourism was projected to earn the country 36.4 billion baht.

Treatments for medical tourists in Thailand range from cosmetic, organ transplants, cardiac, and orthopaedic treatments to dental and cardiac surgeries. Treatments also include spa, physical and mental therapies. One patient who had coronary artery bypass surgery at Bumrungrad International hospital in Bangkok said the operation cost him US$12,000 (8,200 euros), as opposed to the $100,000 (68,000 euros) he estimated the operation would have cost him at home. Bumrungrad treated approximately 55,000 American patients in 2005 alone, a 30% increase from the previous year. Hospitals in Thailand are a popular destination for other Asians. Bangkok Hospital, which caters to medical tourists, has a Japanese wing, and Phyathai Hospitals Group has interpreters for over 22 languages, besides the English-speaking medical staff. When Nepal Prime Minister Girija Prasad Koirala needed medical care in 2006, he went to Bangkok.

Many Thai physicians hold US or UK professional certification. Bumrungrad International hospital states that many of its doctors and staff are trained in the UK, Europe and the US. Bumrungrad International was accredited most recently in 2005 by the Joint Commission. Some of the country's major hospitals have also achieved certification by the International Organization for Standardization's ISO 9001:2000. However, ISO 2000 is not an accreditation scheme.

The World Health Organization's 2000 ranking put the Thai healthcare system at number 47, below the USA's ranking at 37 and the United Kingdom's ranking at 18.

Serious political problems during late 2008, including mass demonstrations and the complete closure of major airports, have made travel to Thailand less appealing than in the past, and the US State Department has issued a travel alert for the country.

Europe

Countries in Europe that have active medical tourism sectors include Turkey, Cyprus, Germany, Hungary, Lithuania, Malta, Poland, Portugal, Czech Republic, Slovakia, Spain, and Ukraine.

Czech Republic

Czech Republic has built its medical tourism on spas and medical care equalling the world standards.

Germany

Germany is a destination for patients seeking advanced medical technology, high standards, safety, and quick treatment. All German citizens have health coverage, resulting in a high hospital density, with twice as many hospitals per capita as the United States. The high hospital density results in shorter waitlists for treatment. Costs for medical treatment compete well with other developed European countries and are commonly 50% of those in in the USA.

Germany is an attractive destination for patients from the Middle East since travelling to the USA has become more difficult for them since the September 11 attacks. US citizens sometimes travel to Germany to seek treatments such as artificial cervical disc replacement that are not US Food and Drug Administration (FDA) approved.

Poland

Since 2004, when Poland joined the European Union, it has become another locale for people seeking cheaper medical treatments. The quality of care in Poland must comply with EU standards.

Turkey

Turkey has since many years attracted medical tourists from Europe and the Balkans, the United States, Eurasia and the Middle East.

The Turkish private healthcare system is striving to become a strategic global health service provider manufacturing centre. The site contains information on prices and hospital statistics, information about the healthcare, pharmaceutical and insurance environments as well as an international patient guide.

Turkey has the highest number of JCI accredited healthcare institutions in the world except for the US. The German Hospital in Istanbul operates the country's first ISO-certified IVF centre, while Memorial Hospital was the first private hospital to receive American JCI accreditation. Since then, over 34 hospitals and medical institutions have achieved Joint Commission International accreditation.

2

Kinds of Modern Tourism

Nautical Tourism

Nautical tourism is an increasingly popular way to combine love of sailing and boating with vacation and holiday activities. First defined as an industry segment in Europe and South America, it has since caught on in the United States and the Pacific Rim.

Not only is nautical tourism an enjoyable way to see unique parts of the world, it is also a very profitable industry. Many tourists who enjoy sailing combine water travel with other activities. Supplying the equipment and accessories for those activities has spawned businesses for those purposes. With many nautical enthusiasts living on board their vessels even in port, nautical tourists bring demand for a variety of goods and services. Marinas developed especially for nautical tourists have been built in Europe, South America and Australia.

Tourist services available at marinas catering to nautical tourists include:

- Leasing of berths for sailing vessels and nautical tourists who live on board.
- Leasing of sailing vessels for holiday and recreational use,
- Reception, safe-guarding and maintenance of sailing vessels.
- Provision of stock (water, fuel, supplies, spare parts, equipment and similar).
- Preparation and keeping sailing vessels in order.
- Providing information to nautical enthusiasts (weather forecasts, nautical guides etc.)

- Leasing of water scooters, jet skis, and other water equipment.

Nautical Tourism in Europe and Along the Mediterranean Coast

Among the more interesting locations frequented by nautical tourists, the Croatian coast offers services at 15 ports, touting it as "Mediterranean as it once was." Croatia's efforts have been so successful they have been offered to the tourism industry as a model for sustainable nautical tourism. Italy has gone to great lengths to attract boating tourists to its ports as well.

Nautical Tourism in the Pacific

Australia has invested $1.5 billion in facilities designed to attract nautical tourists and promote development of nautical tourism as a segment of the tourist trade.

Nautical Tourism in South America

A growing worldwide industry segment, nautical tourism has become popular in South America. The Brazilian Ministry of Tourism has a website devoted to the subject. Puerto Rico has seen its share of growth in nautical tourism as well. Not to be outdone, the Chilean Economic Development Agency has launched the Chilean Patagonia Nautical Tourism Program to develop and attract nautical tourists to the Chilean coast.

Nautical Tourism in the United States

Nautical tourism is big business, even in the United States. In the Southeast, the Tennessee-Tombigbee Waterway, a meandering river and canal system that traverses Alabama and Mississippi linking the Tennessee River with the Gulf of Mexico, has become a favourite boating trail for nautical tourists who want a diverse route with a scenic view. Originally conceived as an alternate shipping route for barges destined for the Midwest, the route proved too awkward for large tows. However, boating enthusiasts discovered it as a great way to see Middle-America. Stops along the way include Mobile, Alabama, Demopolis, Alabama, and Amory and Columbus in Mississippi. Travelling north from the Gulf, boaters can follow the Tennessee River its intersection with the Ohio and travel a circuitous route back to the Gulf by way of New Orleans.

Likewise, the Intracoastal Waterway system, which stretches from Texas to New Jersey, has long provided nautical tourists with a well-marked channel and an inside passage that allows boaters to travel from southern Texas up the eastern seaboard without having to venture onto the high seas. Using this route, boaters can stop at Galveston, Texas, any number of towns in southern Louisiana, including New Orleans. Farther west, Apalachicola, Florida provides a glimpse of Florida the way it used to be.

Pop-culture Tourism

Pop-culture tourism is the act of travelling to locations featured in literature, film, music, or any other form of popular entertainment.

Popular destinations have included:

- Los Angeles, California film studios.
- The Dyersville, Iowa cornfields featured in *Field of Dreams*
- New Zealand after *The Lord of the Rings* was filmed there
- Tom's Restaurant which is known to many as Monk's from *Seinfeld*
- Prince Edward Island, in which the Canadian novel *Anne of Green Gables* takes place, is a popular attraction for tourists, notably from Japan.
- South Korea because of the recent Hallyu phenomenon in East Asia.
- Japan for japanophiles or lovers of Japanese pop-culture.
- North Bend, Washington and in particular Twede's Cafe where much of the television show Twin Peaks was shot.
- Roslyn, Washington, which stood in for Cicely, Alaska in the television show Northern Exposure.
- Tunisia, location of the filming of the Star Wars movies.
- Pin Oak Court, Vermont South, Victoria, a suburban Melbourne shooting location for internationally popular soap opera *Neighbours*
- Santa Ynez Valley in Central California where much of Sideways took place.
- Burkittsville, Maryland, where tourists re-create the most gruesome scenes from The Blair Witch Project.
- Salzburg, Austria, where many scenes from the musical The Sound of Music were filmed.

Pop-culture tourism is in some respects akin to pilgrimage, with its modern equivalents of places of pilgrimage, such as Elvis Presley's Graceland and the grave of Jim Morrison in Pere Lachaise Cemetery.

Another pop-culture tourism destination is Vulcan, Alberta Canada. In the early 1990s this small rural community began to explore ways it could capitalize on the coincidence of the Town's name being the same as popular Star Trek Character, Mr. Spock's home planet: Vulcan, to develop its local tourism industry.

Poverty Tourism

Poverty tourism or poorism, also known as township tourism or slumming is a type of tourism, in which tourists travel to less developed places to observe people living in poverty. Poorism travel tours are popular in places like India, Ethiopia, and even places that have had natural disasters such as hurricanes and tsunamis. After Hurricane Katrina, Louisiana became a big poorism site.

Critics say poorism is likened to a kind of voyeurism, exploiting people less fortunate, snapping pictures and leaving nothing in return. Some poorism tours do use portions of the profits to help out however.

Slumming

Slumming (derived from *slum*) originally referred to a practice, fashionable among certain segments of the middle class in many Western countries, whereby one deliberately patronizes areas or establishments which are populated by, or intended for, people well below one's own socioeconomic level, motivated by curiosity or a desire for adventure. Most often these establishments take the form of bars or restaurants in low-income areas.

Recreational slumming was popular in Victorian London, where omnibus rides through Whitechapel were in vogue. Similarly, slumming tours were documented through the Five Points slums in Manhattan during the 1840s.

It's also associated with the middle 1980s, as an outgrowth of the yuppie subculture. The sense that upper-class establishments were phony, overpriced, and affected (ironically, the very criticisms levelled at yuppies themselves) made it fashionable among middle-class professionals to frequent "dives", due to their supposed authenticity and local colour. "Slumming" (also known as "class tourism") has come to refer to many activities that involve interaction with the less fortunate, especially when motivated by curiosity, adventure, laziness, boredom, and even outright greed and miserliness. The term, and to some extent, the practice, have consequently acquired an unpleasant connotation, having become associated with condescension, exploitation, affectation, and bourgeois insensitivity. Unlike bohemianism or voluntary simplicity, slumming rarely involves more than a temporary or superficial commitment on the part of its participants; it is by nature a touristic or voyeuristic activity.

In *Good Will Hunting*, for example, the main character uses "slumming" to describe sexual relationships between rich, well-educated girls and poorer boys, whom they might encounter around their universities.

South Africa

Township tourism is a term used to describe a form of tourism that emerged in post-apartheid South Africa and Namibia. South African settements are still visibly divided into wealthy, historically white suburbs and poor, historically black townships, because of the effects of apartheid and racial segregation. Before 1994 it was rare for tourists to visit townships. Increasingly the established South African tourism industry sees the townships as a resource for attracting tourism revenue. Smaller operations, including many emerging black tourism operators, see township tourism as a means of empowerment and of bolstering the self-esteem of people in these historically marginalised communities. Although township tours vary in form, they often differ from other tourism experiences in being interactive, socially minded, and potentially empowering for the communities involved. However they have also courted controversy, because of disputes about their safety, their voyeurism, and fears that they misrepresent South African culture(s).

Religious Tourism

Religious tourism, also commonly referred to as faith tourism, is a form of tourism, whereby people of faith travel individually or in groups for pilgrimage, missionary, or leisure (fellowship) purposes. North American religious tourists comprise an estimated $10 billion of this industry.

Tourism segments

Religious tourism comprises many facets of the travel industry including:

- Pilgrimages
- Missionary travel
- Leisure (fellowship) vacations
- Faith-based cruising
- Crusades, conventions and rallies
- Retreats
- Monastery visits and guest-stays
- Faith-based camps
- Religious tourist attractions.

Videos on Religious Tourism;

- Discover the World of Religious Tourism Video.

Hindu Religious Tourism Centres in India

The major Hindu religious tourism centres in India are:-

- Thirupathi temple, Andhra Pradesh.
- Akshar Dham, Gandhi Nagar, Gujarat.
- Amarnath Temple, Pahalgam, Jammu & Kashmir.
- Somnath Temple, Gujarat.
- Vaishnodevi Temple, Jammu, Jammu & Kashmir.
- Kailash Temple, Aurangabad, Maharashtra.
- Sun Temple, Konark, Orissa.
- Chidambaram Temple, Chidambaram, Tamil Nadu.
- Mahabalipuram Temple, Tamil Nadu.
- Rameswaram Temple, Tamil Nadu.
- Meenakshi Temple, Madurai, Tamil Nadu.
- Badarinath Temple, Uthranchal.
- Naina Devi Temple, Bilaspur, Himachalpradesh.
- Sabarimala Temple, Pathanamthitta, Kerala.
- Guruvayoor Temple, Guruvayoor, Trichur, Kerala
- Kodungallor Temple, Trichur, Kerala
- Chettikulangara Temple, Mavelikkara, Kerala.
- Padmanabhaswamy Temple, Trivandrum, Kerala.

Statistics

Although no definitive study has been completed on worldwide religious tourism, some segments of the industry have been measured:

- According to the World Tourism Organization, an estimated 300 to 330 million pilgrims visit the world's key religious sites every year.
- According to the U.S. Office of Travel and Tourism Industries, Americans travelling overseas for "religious or pilgrimage" purposes has increased from 491,000 travellers in 2002 to 633,000 travellers in 2005 (30% increase).
- According to the Religious Conference Management Association, in 2006 more than 14.7 million people attended religious meetings (RCMA members), an increase of more than 10 million from 1994 with 4.4 million attendees.
- The United Methodist Church experienced an increase of 455% in mission volunteers from 1992 with almost 20,000 volunteers compared to 110,000 volunteers in 2006.
- The Christian Camp and Conference Association states that more than eight million people are involved in CCCA member camps and conferences, including more than 120,000 churches.
- Religious attractions including Sight & Sound Theatre attracts 800,000 visitors a year while the Holy Land Experience and Focus on the Family Welcome Centre each receives about 250,000 guests annually. Religious tourism, also commonly referred to as *faith tourism,* is a form of tourism whereby people of faith travel individually or in groups for pilgrimage, missionary, or leisure (fellowship) purposes.
- 50,000 churches in the United States with religious travel programs
- One-quarter (25%) of travellers said they were currently interested in taking a spiritual vacation.

Space Tourism

Space tourism is the phenomenon of tourists paying for flights into space. As of 2009, orbital space tourism opportunities are limited and expensive, with only the Russian Space Agency providing transport. The price for a flight brokered by Space Adventures to the International Space Station aboard a Soyuz spacecraft is US$20–35 million. The space tourists usually sign contracts with third parties to conduct certain research while in orbit. This helps to minimize their own expenses.

Infrastructure for a suborbital space tourism industry is being developed through the construction of spaceports in numerous locations, including California, Oklahoma, New Mexico, Florida, Virginia, Alaska, Wisconsin, Esrange in Sweden as well as the United Arab Emirates. Some use the term "personal spaceflight" as in the case of the Personal Spaceflight Federation.

A number of startup companies have sprung up in recent years, hoping to create a space tourism industry. For a list of such companies, and the spacecraft they are currently building.

Russia announced on 3 March 2010 that they would be ending their space tourism program, at least for the next several years.

Early Dreams

After early successes in space, much of the public saw intensive space exploration as inevitable. Those aspirations are remembered in science fiction such as Arthur C. Clarke's *A Fall of Moondust* and also *2001: A Space Odyssey*, Roald Dahl's *Charlie and the Great Glass Elevator*, Joanna Russ's 1968 novel *Picnic on Paradise*, and Larry Niven's Known Space stories. Lucian in the second century AD in his book *True History* examines the idea of a crew of men whose ship travels to the Moon during a storm. Jules Verne also took up the theme of lunar visits in his books, *From the Earth to the Moon* and *Around the Moon*.

Robert A. Heinlein's short story *The Menace from Earth*, published in 1957, was one of the first to incorporate elements of a developed space tourism industry within its framework. During the 1960s and 1970s, it was common belief that space hotels would be launched by 2000. Many futurologists around the middle of the 20th century speculated that the average family of the early 21st century would be able to enjoy a holiday on the Moon. In the 1960s, Pan Am established a waiting list for future flights to the moon, issuing free "First Moon Flights Club" membership cards to those who requested them.

The end of the Space Race, however, signified by the Moon landing, decreased the emphasis placed on space exploration by national governments and therefore led to decreased demands for public funding of manned space flights.

Precursors

The Soviet space program was aggressive in broadening the pool of cosmonauts. The Soviet Intercosmos program also included cosmonauts selected from Warsaw Pact members (from Czechoslovakia, Poland, East Germany, Bulgaria, Hungary, Romania) and later from allies of the USSR (Cuba, Mongolia, Vietnam) and non-aligned countries (India, Syria, Afghanistan). Most of these cosmonauts received full training for their missions and were treated as equals, but especially after the Mir program began, were generally given shorter flights than Soviet cosmonauts. The European Space Agency took advantage of the program as well.

The U.S. space shuttle program included payload specialist positions which were usually filled by representatives of companies or institutions managing a specific payload on that mission. These payload specialists did not receive the same training as professional NASA astronauts and were not employed by NASA. In 1983, Ulf Merbold from ESA and Byron Lichtenberg from MIT (engineer and Air Force fighter pilot) were the first Payload Specialists to fly on the shuttle, becoming the first non-NASA astronauts. In 1984, Charlie Walker became the first non-government astronaut to fly, with his flight paid for by his employer, McDonnell Douglas. NASA was also eager to prove its capability to Congressional sponsors. Senator Jake Garn was flown on the shuttle in 1985, followed by Representative Bill Nelson (now Senator) in 1986. As the shuttle program expanded, the Teacher in Space program was developed as a way to expand publicity and educational opportunities for NASA. Christa McAuliffe would have been the first Teacher in Space, but was killed in the Challenger disaster and the program was canceled. During the same period a Journalist in Space program was frequently discussed, with individuals such as Walter Cronkite and Miles O'Brien considered front-runners, but no formal program was ever developed. McAuliffe's backup in the Teacher in Space Program, Barbara Morgan, eventually got hired in 1998 as a professional astronaut and flew on STS-118 as a mission specialist where she spoke to many students as an educator during the trip.

With the realities of the post-Perestroika economy in Russia, its space industry was especially starved for cash. The Tokyo Broadcasting System (TBS) offered to pay for one of its reporters to fly on a mission. For $28 million, Toyohiro Akiyama was flown in 1990 to Mir with the eighth crew and returned a week later with the seventh crew. Akiyama gave a daily TV broadcast from orbit and also performed scientific experiments for Russian and Japanese companies. However, since the cost of the flight was paid by his employer, Akiyama could be considered a business traveler rather than a tourist.

In 1991, British chemist Helen Sharman was selected from a pool of 13,000 applicants to be the first Briton in space. The program was known as Project Juno and was a cooperative arrangement between the Soviet Union and a group of British companies. The Project Juno consortium failed to raise the funds required, and the program was almost cancelled. Reportedly Mikhail Gorbachev ordered it to proceed under Soviet expense in the interests of international relations, but in the absence of Western underwriting, less expensive experiments were substituted for those in the original plans. Sharman flew aboard Soyuz TM-12 to Mir and returned aboard Soyuz TM-11.

Orbital Space Tourism

At the end of the 1990s, MirCorp, a private venture by then in charge of the space station, began seeking potential space tourists to visit Mir in order to offset some of its maintenance costs. Dennis Tito, an American businessman and former JPL scientist, became their first candidate.

In conjunction with the Federal Space Agency of the Russian Federation and Rocket and Space Corporation (Energia), Space Adventures facilitated the flights for all of the world's first private space explorers. The first three participants paid in excess of $20 million (USD) each for their 10-day visit to the ISS.

On April 28, 2001, Dennis Tito became the first "fee-paying" space tourist when he visited the International Space Station (ISS) for seven days. He was followed in 2002 by South African computer millionaire Mark Shuttleworth. The third was Gregory Olsen in 2005, who was trained as a scientist and whose company produced specialist high-sensitivity cameras. Olsen planned to use his time on the ISS to conduct a number of experiments, in part to test his company's products. Olsen had planned an earlier flight, but had to cancel for health reasons.

After the Columbia disaster, space tourism on the Russian Soyuz program was temporarily put on hold, because Soyuz vehicles became the only available transport to the ISS. However, in 2006, space tourism was resumed. On September 18, 2006, Anousheh Ansari, an Iranian American, became the fourth space tourist (she prefers "private space explorer"). On April 7, 2007, Charles Simonyi, an American businessman of Hungarian descent, joined their ranks.

In 2003, NASA and the Russian Space Agency agreed to use the term 'Spaceflight Participant' to distinguish those space travellers from astronauts on missions coordinated by those two agencies. Tito, Shuttleworth, Olsen, Ansari, and Simonyi were designated as such during their respective space flights. NASA also lists Christa McAuliffe as a "Space Flight Participant" (although she did not pay a fee), apparently due to her non-technical duties aboard the STS 51-L flight.

Suborbital Flights

More affordable suborbital space tourism is viewed as a money-making proposition by several other companies, including Space Adventures, Virgin Galactic, Starchaser, Blue Origin, Armadillo Aerospace, XCOR Aerospace, Rocketplane Limited, the European "Project Enterprise", and others. Most are proposing vehicles that make suborbital flights peaking at an altitude of 100-160 kilometres. Passengers would experience three to six minutes of weightlessness, a view of a twinkle-free starfield, and a vista of the curved Earth below. Projected costs are expected to be about $200,000 per passenger.

As of November 2007 Virgin Galactic had pre-sold nearly 200 seats for their suborbital space tourism flights, according to the company's president.

The X Prize

On October 4, 2004, the SpaceShipOne, designed by Burt Rutan of Scaled Composites, won the $10,000,000 X Prize, which was designed to be won by the first private company who could reach and surpass an altitude of 62 miles (100 km) twice within two weeks. The altitude is beyond the Karman Line, the arbitrarily defined boundary of space. The first flight was flown by Michael Melvill on June 21, 2004 to a height of 62 miles, making him the first commercial astronaut. The prize-winning flight was flown by Brian Binnie, which reached a height of 69.6 miles, breaking the X-15 record.

Virgin Galactic

Virgin Galactic, one of the leading potential space tourism groups, is planning to begin passenger service aboard the VSS Enterprise, a Scaled Composites Space Ship Two type spacecraft. The initial seat price will be $200,000, but that price is expected to eventually fall to $20,000. To date, over two hundred people have made down payments on bookings. Headed by Sir Richard Branson's Virgin Group, Virgin Galactic hopes to be the first private space tourism company to regularly send civilians into space. A citizen astronaut will only require three days of training before spaceflight. Space Ship Two is a scaled up version of SpaceShipOne, the spacecraft which claimed the Ansari X Prize. Both spacecraft were designed by Burt Rutan's Scaled Composites. Launches will initially occur at the Mojave Spaceport in California, and will then be moved to Spaceport America in Upham, New Mexico. Tourists will also be flown from Kiruna, Sweden. The spacecraft will travel 360,000 feet (109.73 km/68.18 miles) high. This goes beyond the internationally defined boundary between Earth and space of 100 km. Spaceflights will last 2.5 hours, carry 6 passengers, and reach a speed of Mach 3. Space Ship Two will not require a space shuttle-like heat shield for atmospheric reentry as it will not experience the extreme aerodynamic heating experienced during reentry at orbital velocities (approximately Mach 22.5 at a typical shuttle altitude of 300 km, or 185 miles). The glider will employ a "feathering" technique to manage drag during the unpowered descent and landing. Space Ship Two will use a single hybrid rocket motor to launch from mid-air after detaching from a mother ship at 50,000 feet, instead of NASA's space shuttle's ground-based launch.

Project Enterprise

Project Enterprise was launched by the German TALIS Institute in 2004 and is the first project of its kind in Europe. The goal is to develop a rocket-propelled spaceplane by 2011 that will carry one pilot and up to five passengers into suborbital space. The plane will launch from the ground using rockets, and will return in an unpowered flight like Virgin Galactic's Space Ship Two. The prototypes and finished spaceplane will be launched from an airport near Cochstedt (Germany; Saxony-Anhalt).

Since 2004, the TALIS Institute has gained many industrial partners, including XtremeAir, who will manufacture the airframe, and Swiss Propulsion Laboratory SPL, who will deliver the propulsion components. XtremeAir is known for their acrobatic airplanes, and SPL has designed and tested liquid propellant rocket engines since 1998.

Current work is focusing on the first prototype, the "Black Sky": An existing acrobatic airplane that would be fitted with a single rocket engine and a new wing. The rocket engine is expected to deliver a thrust of 10 kN. The test program for this engine started in 2007 at SPL and is expected to fly by 2010.

Legality

United States: In December 2005, the U.S. Government released a set of proposed rules for space tourism. These included screening procedures and training for emergency situations, but not health requirements.

Under current US law, any company proposing to launch paying passengers from American soil on a suborbital rocket must receive a license from the Federal Aviation Administration's Office of Commercial Space Transportation (FAA/AST). The licensing process focuses on public safety and safety of property, and the details can be found in the Code of Federal Regulations. This is in accordance with the Commercial Space Launch Amendments Act passed by Congress in 2004.

Orbital Flights, Space Stations and Space Hotels

- EADS Astrium, a subsidiary of European aerospace giant EADS, announced its space tourism project on June 13, 2007.
- SpaceX is a private space company which is developing their own rocket family called *Falcon* and a capsule named Dragon, capable of sending up to 7 people to any space station, either ISS or a possible station by Bigelow Aerospace. Falcon 1 has already undertaken testflights and successfully completed its first commercial flight on

July 14, 2009, deploying the Malaysian Razak SAT into orbit. Falcon 9 (which will be the rocket for the Dragon capsule) is currently in vertical position at Space Launch Complex 40 in Cape Canaveral, and will make its first testflight in late 2009. An initial prototype of the Dragon capsule is expected to be used on this test flight; SpaceX anticipates that Dragon could be qualified for human spaceflight within 3 years of the receipt of NASA CCDV funding.

- Space Adventures Ltd. have also announced that they are working on circumlunar missions to the moon, with the price per passenger being $100,000,000. They are currently developing spaceports at the United Arab Emirates (Ras al-Khaimah) and in Singapore.
- Orbital space tourist flights are also being planned by Excalibur Almaz, using modernized *TKS* space capsules.

Several plans have been proposed for using a space station as a hotel. American motel tycoon Robert Bigelow has acquired the designs for inflatable space habitats from the Transhab program abandoned by NASA. His company, Bigelow Aerospace, has already launched two first inflatable habitat modules. The first, named Genesis I, was launched 12 July 2006. The second test module, Genesis II, was launched 28 June 2007. Both Genesis habitats remain in orbit as of mid-2009. As of 2006, Bigelow planned to officially launch the first commercial space station by 2012 (tagged *Nautilus*) which will have 330 cubic meters (almost as big as the ISS's 425 cubic meters of usable volume).

Bigelow Aerospace is currently offering the America's Space Prize, a $50 million prize to the first US company to create a reusable spacecraft capable of carrying passengers to a Nautilus space station.

Other companies have also expressed interest in constructing "space hotels". For example, Excalibur Almaz plans to modernize and launch its Soviet-era Almaz space stations, which will feature the largest windows ever on spacecraft. Virgin's Richard Branson has expressed his hope for the construction of a space hotel within his lifetime. He expects that beginning a space tourism program will cost $100 million. Hilton International announced the Space Islands Project, a plan to connect together used space shuttle fuel tanks, each the diameter of a Boeing 747 aircraft. A separate organization, Space Island Group announced their distinct Space Island Project (note the singular "Island"), and plans on having 20,000 people on their "space island" by 2020, with the number of people doubling for each decade. British Airways has expressed interest in the venture. If and when Space Hotels develop, it would initially cost a passenger $60,000, with prices lowering over time.

Fashion designer Eri Matsui has designed clothing, including a wedding gown, intended to look best in weightless environments.

Advocacy, Education, and Industry Organizations

Several organizations have been formed to promote the space tourism industry, including the Space Tourism Society, and others. More information about the future of Space Tourism can be found at Space Tourism Lecture, which is a free online Space Tourism Lecture handout collection. Since 2003 Dr. Robert A. Goehlich and Pierluigi Polignano teaches the world's first and only Space Tourism class at Keio University, Yokohama, Japan. UniGalactic Space Travel Magazine is a bi-monthly educational publication covering space tourism and space exploration developments in companies like SpaceX, Orbital Sciences, Virgin Galactic and organizations like NASA. The content of UniGalactic Space Travel Magazine can be found on UniGalactic web site.

Opinions of Commercial Space Tourism

A web-based survey suggested that over 70% of those surveyed wanted less than or equal to 2 weeks in space; in addition, 88% wanted to spacewalk (only 74% of these would do it for a 50% premium), and 21% wanted a hotel or space station.

The concept has met with some criticism from bureaucrats, notably Gunter Verheugen, vice-president of the European Commission, who said of the EADS Astrium Space Tourism Project "It's only for the super rich, which is against my social convictions".

Objections to "Space Tourist" Terminology

Dennis Tito, Mark Shuttleworth, Gregory Olsen, Anousheh Ansari and Richard Garriott have all expressed a preference to be called something other than "space tourist". In each case, they explained their preferences by pointing out that they carried out scientific experiments as part of their journey; Garriott additionally emphasized their training is identical to requirements of non-

Russian Soyuz crew members, and that teachers and other non-professional astronauts chosen to fly with NASA are called astronauts. Garriott prefers "cosmonaut" or "astronaut", but will accept "private" in front of either. Tito has asked to be known as an "independent researcher". Shuttleworth proposed "pioneer of commercial space travel". Olsen preferred "private researcher." Ansari prefers the term "private space explorer". Alone among those who have paid to go to orbit so far, Charles Simonyi seems to have no concerns about calling it "space tourism", even in reference to his own experience. Asked in an interview "Do you foresee a day when space tourism is not just the province of billionaires - when it will be as affordable as plane travel?", he did not object to the implicit categorization of his own trip, but rather answered "Yes, the only question is when ...."

NASA and the Russian Federal Space Agency agreed to use the term "spaceflight participant" to distinguish those space travellers from astronauts on missions coordinated by those two agencies.

Although many space enthusiasts subscribe to the notion of space tourism as a potential burgeoning industry that could further the development and settlement of space, some of these same enthusiasts object to the use of the term "space tourist". Rick Tumlinson of the Space Frontier Foundation, for example, has said;

> *"I hate the word tourist, and I always will .... 'Tourist' is somebody in a flowered shirt with three cameras around his neck."*
>
> *Others with perhaps less enthusiasm for space development seem to agree. Alex Tabarrok has categorized it as a kind of "adventure travel". The mere fact of people paying for a travel experience does not, in his view, make that activity "tourism". "At best and for the foreseeable future space travel will remain akin to climbing Everest, dangerous and uncommon. Yes, we might see 100 flights a year but that's not space tourism - tourism is fat guys with cameras."*

War Tourism

War tourism is a term the media uses to describe the idea of recreational travel to war zones for purposes of sightseeing and superficial voyeurism. War tourist is also a pejorative term to describe thrill seeking in dangerous and forbidden places. There has been no proof of the concept in real life but the idea has gained currency in a number of media reports, none of which have actually interviewed or found a tourist who have visited active combat areas as a tourist.

There have been a number of tourists caught up in war torn regions, many who visit active war zones like Israel, Lebanon, Myanmar, Algeria, Colombia and other regions at war. There are many freelance journalists who describe themselves humorously as "war tourists" (P.J. O'Rourke is the most famous) and mercenaries who have pretended to be tourists to avoid discovery as in Michael Hoare's attempt to take over the Seychelles disguised as "The Royal Order of Frothblowers".

During the 2006 Israel-Lebanon crisis, for example, Beirut was full of tourists who were forced to leave when fighting with Israel broke out. Tourists have also been targeted in Kenya, the Philippines and other regions due to their media value and damage to the country's tourist industry. It could be argued that continued tourism to these regions is war tourism, even though active combat is free from tourist access.

The initial myth of war tourism was actually started by a collection of stories by P.J. O'Rourke. His mocking and cynical view of journalism in conflict areas entitled 'Holidays in Hell: In Which Our Intrepid Reporter Travels to the World's Worst Places and Asks, "What's Funny About This" planted the idea that maybe journalists are after all tourists on an expense account.

The PBS TV show, Frontline, used the phrase war tourism to describe a practice in Iraq of US troops going on daylight patrols and returning in the evening to heavily defended large bases.

A book on this topic is Dark Tourism (Tourism, Leisure & Recreation) by Malcolm Foley and John Lennon. The authors explore the idea that people are attracted to regions and sites where "inhuman acts" have occurred. They claim that motivation is driven by media coverage and a desire to see for themselves, and that there is a symbiotic relationship between the attraction and the visitor, whether it be a death camp or site of a celebrity's death. Much of their focus in on ancient sites where "acts of inhumanity are celebrated as heritage sites in Britain (for example, the Tower of London, Edinburgh Castle), and the Berlin Wall" War tourism is also confused with "Battlefield tourism": going to places of historic importance or famous battle sites such as the German WW2 fortification, Ground Zero in New York, the Atlantic Wall or the Maginot Line in France.

Wildlife Tourism

Wildlife tourism can be an eco and animal friendly tourism, usually showing animals in their natural habitat. Wildlife tourism, in its simplest sense, is watching wild animals in their natural habitat. Wildlife tourism is an important part of the tourism industries in many countries including many African and South American countries, Australia, India, Canada, Indonesia, Malaysia and Maldives among many. It has experienced a dramatic and rapid growth in recent years world wide and is closely aligned to eco-tourism and sustainable-tourism.

Wildlife tourism is also a multi-million dollar industry offering customized tour packages and safaris.

Recent Developments

There has been an upmarket trend in the tourism over the last few decades, especially in Europe, where international travel for short breaks is common. Tourists have high levels of disposable income, considerable leisure time, are well educated, and have sophisticated tastes. There is now a demand for a better quality products, which has resulted in a fragmenting of the mass market for beach vacations; people want more specialised versions, quieter resorts, family-oriented holidays or niche market-targeted destination hotels.

The developments in technology and transport infrastructure, such as jumbo jets, low-cost airlines and more accessible airports have made many types of tourism more affordable. WHO estimates that up to 500,000 people are on planes at any time. There have also been changes in lifestyle, such as retiree-age people who sustain year round tourism. This is facilitated by internet sales of tourism products. Some sites have now started to offer dynamic packaging, in which an inclusive price is quoted for a tailor-made package requested by the customer upon impulse.

There have been a few setbacks in tourism, such as the September 11 attacks and terrorist threats to tourist destinations, such as in Bali and several European cities. Also, on December 26, 2004, a tsunami, caused by the 2004 Indian Ocean earthquake, hit the Asian countries on the Indian Ocean, including the Maldives. Thousands of lives were lost and many tourists died. This, together with the vast clean-up operation in place, has stopped or severely hampered tourism to the area. The terms *tourism* and *travel* are sometimes used interchangeably. In this context, travel has a similar definition to tourism, but implies a more purposeful journey. The terms *tourism* and *tourist* are sometimes used pejoratively, to imply a shallow interest in the cultures or locations visited by tourists.

Sustainable Tourism

"Sustainable tourism is envisaged as leading to management of all resources in such a way that economic, social and aesthetic needs can be fulfilled while maintaining cultural integrity, essential ecological processes, biological diversity and life support systems."

Sustainable development implies "meeting the needs of the present without compromising the ability of future generations to meet their own needs" (World Commission on Environment and Development, 1987).

Recession Tourism

Recession tourism is a travel trend, which evolved by way of the world economic crisis. Identified by American entrepreneur Matt Landau (2007), recession tourism is defined by low-cost, high-value experiences taking place of once-popular generic retreats. Various recession tourism hotspots have seen business boom during the recession thanks to comparatively low costs of living and a slow world job market suggesting travellers are elongating trips where the dollar travels further.

Educational Tourism

Educational tourism developed, because of the growing popularity of teaching and learning of knowledge and the enhancing of technical competency outside of the classroom environment. In educational tourism, the main focus of the tour or leisure activity includes visiting another country to learn about the culture, such as in Student Exchange Programs and Study Tours, or to work and apply skills learned inside the classroom in a different environment, such as in the International Practicum Training Program.

Creative Tourism

Creative tourism has existed as a form of cultural tourism, since the early beginnings of tourism itself. Its European roots date back to the time of the Grand Tour, which saw the sons of aristocratic families travelling for the purpose of mostly interactive, educational experiences.

More recently, creative tourism has been given its own name by Crispin Raymond and Greg Richards, who as members of the Association for Tourism and Leisure Education (ATLAS), have directed a number of projects for the European Commission, including cultural and crafts tourism, known as sustainable tourism. They have defined "creative tourism" as tourism related to the active participation of travellers in the culture of the host community, through interactive workshops and informal learning experiences.

Meanwhile, the concept of creative tourism has been picked up by high-profile organizations such as UNESCO, who through the Creative Cities Network, have endorsed creative tourism as an engaged, authentic experience that promotes an active understanding of the specific cultural features of a place.

More recently, creative tourism has gained popularity as a form of cultural tourism, drawing on active participation by travellers in the culture of the host communities they visit. Several countries offer examples of this type of tourism development, including the United Kingdom, the Bahamas, Jamaica, Spain, Italy and New Zealand.

Dark Tourism

One emerging area of special interest tourism has been identified by Lennon and Foley (2000) as "dark" tourism. This type of tourism involves visits to "dark" sites, such as battlegrounds, scenes of horrific crimes or acts of genocide, for example: concentration camps. Dark tourism poses severe ethical and moral dilemmas: should these sites be available for visitation and, if so, what should the nature of the publicity involved be. Dark tourism remains a small niche market, driven by varied motivations, such as mourning, remembrance, macabre curiosity or even entertainment. Its early origins are rooted in fairgrounds and medieval fairs.

Growth

The World Tourism Organization (UNWTO) forecasts that international tourism will continue growing at the average annual rate of 4 %. With the advent of e-commerce, tourism products have become one of the most traded items on the internet. Tourism products and services have been made available through intermediaries, although tourism providers (hotels, airlines, etc.) can sell their services directly. This has put pressure on intermediaries from both on-line and traditional shops.

It has been suggested there is a strong correlation between tourism expenditure per capita and the degree to which countries play in the global context. Not only as a result of the important economic contribution of the tourism industry, but also as an indicator of the degree of confidence with which global citizens leverage the resources of the globe for the benefit of their local economies. This is why any projections of growth in tourism may serve as an indication of the relative influence that each country will exercise in the future.

Space tourism is expected to "take off" in the first quarter of the 21st century, although compared with traditional destinations the number of tourists in orbit will remain low until technologies such as a space elevator make space travel cheap.

Technological improvement is likely to make possible air-ship hotels, based either on solar-powered airplanes or large dirigibles. Underwater hotels, such as Hydropolis, expected to open in Dubai in 2009, will be built. On the ocean, tourists will be welcomed by ever larger cruise ships and perhaps floating cities.

Latest Trends

As a result of the Late-2000s recession, international arrivals suffered a strong slowdown beginning in June 2008. Growth from 2007 to 2008 was only 3.7% during the first eight months of 2008. The Asian and Pacific markets were affected and Europe stagnated during the boreal summer months, while the Americas performed better, reducing their expansion rate but keeping a 6% growth from January to August 2008. Only the Middle East continued its rapid growth during the same period, reaching a 17% growth as compared to the same period in 2007. This slowdown on international tourism demand was also reflected in the air transport industry, with a negative growth in September 2008 and a 3.3%

growth in passenger traffic through September. The hotel industry also reports a slowdown, as room occupancy continues to decline. As the global economic situation deteriorated dramatically during September and October as a result of the global financial crisis, growth of international tourism is expected to slow even further for the remaining of 2008, and this slowdown in demand growth is forecasted to continue into 2009 as recession has already hit most of the top spender countries, with long-haul travel expected to be the most affected by the economic crisis. This negative trend intensified as international tourist arrivals fell by 8% during the first four months of 2009, and the decline was exacerbated in some regions due to the outbreak of the influenza AH1N1 virus.

Types of Tourism in India

All types of tourism in India have registered phenomenal growth in the last decade ever since the Indian government decided to boost revenues from the tourism sector by projecting India as the ultimate tourist spot.

The reason why India has been doing well in all types of tourism in India is that India has always been known for its hospitality, uniqueness, and charm – attributes that have been attracting foreign travellers to India in hordes. The Indian government, in order to boost tourism of various kinds in India, has set up the Ministry of Tourism and Culture. This ministry recently launched a campaign called 'Incredible India!' in order to encourage different types of tourism in India.

The result was that in 2004, foreign tourists spent around US$ 15.4 billion during their trips to India. Being a country with tremendous diversity, India has a lot to offer in terms of tourism and related activities. The diversity that India is famous for, ensures that there is something to do for all tourists in India, no matter what their interests.

The different types of tourism in India are as follows:

Heritage Tourism

India has always been famous for its rich heritage and ancient culture. So the onset of heritage tourism in India was long anticipated. India's glorious past and cultural diversity make a potent blend which attracts millions of tourists each year to its heritage tourist attractions. The government of India and the

Ministry of Tourism and Culture encourage heritage tourism in India by offering several benefits to the Indian states that are particularly famous for attracting tourists.

India's rich heritage is amply reflected in the various temples, palaces, monuments, and forts that can be found everywhere in the country. This has led to the increase in India's heritage tourism. The most popular heritage tourism destinations in India are:

- Taj Mahal in Agra
- Mandawa castle in Rajasthan
- Mahabalipuram in Tamil Nadu
- Madurai in Tamil Nadu
- Lucknow in Uttar Pradesh
- Delhi, the Indian capital.

Taj Mahal was built by a grief stricken Emperor Shahjahan as a memorial to his beloved wife Mumtaj Mahal. A world-renowned wonder, Taj Mahal Sits pretty on the northern side of this green paradise. It looks the same from all the four sides! The Quranic inscriptions on its four entrances are carved in such subtle increase in size that may appear to be of the same size from top to bottom! Shahjahan invited master craftsmen from as far as Italy and Persia to help design his ambitious tribute to love. The Taj Mahal is phenomenal not in the beauty alone that shines forth, but in the deep planning and design that went into its making, and the ethereal idea of immortalizing love. Delicate carvings in marble vie with gorgeous pietra dura for attention. Lapiz, Lazuli, Carnation, Mother of pearl, Agate and Emerald are inlayed in floral and geometrical patterns in the marble itself. This enchanting mausoleum, on the bank of river Yamuna started in 1631 it took 22 years to complete with the help of an estimated 20000 workers. The Mandawa castle in Rajasthan, built in 1775 reflects India's rich heritage and attracts thousands of tourists each year to Rajasthan which seems especially popular for its antique paintings, jade jewelry, palaces, and costumes. Mahabalipuram has sculptural and architectural sites which are considered the greatest in India. Mahabalipuram has cave temples that have been carved from granite blocks and belong to the 7th century. This is the primary reason why many heritage tourists in India visit this place.

The tourism of heritage in India has also increased due to the interest of many foreigners in the temples of India. Madurai is known as the 'temple city' due to the presence of a large number of temples in the city. And for this reason, many tourists go and visit the place each year. The most important temple in Madurai is the Meenakshi temple. Heritage tourism India has also been popularized because a lot of tourists go to Delhi which is not only the capital of India but also has many heritage sites. The most famous heritage sites in Delhi are the Red fort, Jama Masjid, Humayun's tomb, and Tughlaqabad fort. Heritage tourism India has grown in recent years but there is scope for further development which can be attained only through combined efforts of the government of India and the tourism boards.

Ecotourism

Ecotourism India has developed recently, for the concept itself is a relatively new one. Ecotourism entails travelling to places that are renowned for their natural beauty and social culture, while making sure not to damage the ecological balance.

Ecotourism pertains to a conscious and responsible effort to preserve the diversity of a naturally endowed region and sustaining its beauty and local culture. Indians have been known since ages to worship and conserve nature. So the growth of ecotourism in India is but natural. Also the government of India has set up the Ministry of Tourism and Culture to promote ecotourism in India alongside other types of tourism.

Ecotourism in India has grown significantly in recent years in India since the country has a diverse geography which led to the development of many tourists destinations. These various destinations not only de-stress the tourists but also rejuvenate them. There are various ways in which tourists can enjoy nature in India. And this has given ecotourism in India a major boost.

Places such as Kerala, Lakshdweep Islands, the Himalayan region, north-east India, and Andaman and Nicobar Islands are some destinations in

India where tourists can participate in ecotourism-related activities. In Kerala, Thenmala is a planned ecotourism spot and is the first of its kind in India. Great care has gone into the care and preservation of Thenmala so that it caters to nature lovers and eco- tourists. Eco-tourists have been thronging India in large numbers for it has a rich source of flora and fauna. A great number of endangered and rare species are also to be found in the various national parks in India. The major national parks in India for ecotourism are:

- Corbett National Park in Uttar Pradesh
- Bandhavgarh National Park in Madhya Pradesh
- Kanha National Park in Madhya Pradesh
- Gir National Park and Sanctuary in Gujarat
- Ranthambore National Park in Rajasthan .

Ecotourism India has increased in the last few years. The government of India and Ministry of Tourism need to make concerted efforts to ensure that ecotourism in India is able to keep pace with ecotourism destinations across the world and making sustainable tourism a priority.

Adventure Tourism

Adventure tourism has recently grown in India. This involves exploration of remote areas and exotic locales and engaging in various activities. For adventure tourism in India, tourists prefer to go for trekking to places like Ladakh, Sikkim and Himalaya. Himachal Pradesh and Jammu and Kashmir are popular for the skiing facilities they offer. Whitewater rafting is also catching on in India and tourists flock to places such as Uttranchal, Assam, and Arunachal Pradesh for this adrenalin-packed activity.

Wildlife Tourism

India has a rich forest cover which has some beautiful and exotic species of wildlife – some of which that are even endangered and very rare. This has boosted wildlife tourism in India. The places where a foreign tourist can go for wildlife tourism in India are the Sariska Wildlife Sanctuary, Keoladeo Ghana National Park, and Corbett National Park.

Pilgrimage Tourism

India is probably the ultimate destination of all kinds of pilgrims following any faith around the world. The great religions like Hinduism, Buddhism, Jainism, Islam, Christianity and Sikhism are the integral part of Indian culture and heritage whose values and faiths are mingled with the air, soil and the sky of India. You can feel the blissful serenity of the Indian atmosphere where Lord Buddha, Mahabir Jain, Shri Sathya Sai Baba and Guru Nanak once walked turning the Indian soil pious and blessed at the different circle of time wheel. There are numerous destinations in India which are considered sacred by people following different faith because of their religious importance. A visit to the Kedarnath or Badrinath will take you to the Himalayas which is believed to be the abode of 330 million gods and goddesses and you can feel the immense divinity in the air itself. It is widely believed that after breathing in the holy atmosphere of Varanasi or Haridwar or taking a dip into the sacred Pushkar Lake or river Ganges washes away the sins and helps one to attain nirvana (salvation). The divine Buddha pilgrimages, Bodhgaya and Sarnath are the destinations of thousands of Buddhist pilgrims every year coming from each and every corner of the earth.

Famous Pilgrimage

- Ajmer
- Pushkar
- Haridwar
- Amarnath
- Badrinath
- Gangotri
- Kedarnath
- Yamunotri
- Chardham Yatra
- Rishikesh
- Manikaran
- Paonta Sahib
- Rewalsar
- Omkareshwar
- Ajmer Sharief
- Rameswaram
- Mathura Vrindavan
- Puri
- Guruvayur
- Shirdi Saibaba
- Amarnath Cave
- Vaishno Devi
- Jagannath Temple

- Konark Sun Temple
- Tirupati Temple.

Pilgrimage Places

- Himachal Pradesh
- Rajasthan
- Uttranchal
- Kerala
- Maharashtra
- Tamil Nadu
- Jammu And Kashmir
- Madhya Pradesh
- Madhya Pradesh
- Karnataka
- Andhra Pradesh
- Temples
- Mosques
- Gurudwaras
- Churches.

Famous Tourist Destinations

The World Tourism rankings are compiled by the World Tourism Organization (UNWTO) as part of their World Tourism Barometer publication.

International Tourist Arrivals by Country of Destination 2008

The top international destinations in 2008 are:

Rank	*Country*	*International tourist arrivals*
1	France	79.3 million
2	United States	58.0 million
3	Spain	57.3 million
4	China	53.0 million
5	Italy	42.7 million
6	United Kingdom	30.1 million
7	Ukraine	25.4 million
8	Turkey	25.0 million
9	Germany	24.9 million
10	Mexico	22.6 million

10 Unique Tourist Destinations in the World

Let's tour the world and see these unique places.

Let's begin our travel in the third largest continent – North America.

Dinosaur Provincial Park: Canada

The first destination in our list is Dinosaur Provincial Park. This unique tourist destination which is a UNESCO World Heritage Site is located in Alberta, Canada.

The park is famous for being one of the greatest dinosaur fossil beds in the world, attracting more than 350,000 tourists annually. Thirty-nine dinosaur species have been discovered at the park and more than 500 specimens have been removed and exhibited in museums across the globe.

From North America, let's slide down to South America – the land of the Incas, who were regarded as "Romans of Americas" because of their ability to conquer.

Salar De Uyuni, Salt Flat: Bolivia

Second on the list is the Salar de Uyuni. This is the world's largest salt flat at 10,582 km^2 or 4,085 square miles. It is located in the southwest of Bolivia, near the crest of the Andes, 3,650 meters high. The major minerals found in the salar are halite and gypsum.

Due to its large size, smooth surface, high surface reflectivity when covered with shallow water, and minimal elevation deviation, Salar de Uyuni makes an ideal target for the testing and calibration of remote sensing instruments on orbiting satellites used to study the Earth.

Salar de Uyuni is estimated to contain 10 billion tons of salt, of which less than 25,000 tons is extracted annually. Every November, Salar de Uyuni is also the breeding grounds for three species of South American flamingoes: the Chilean, James's and Andean flamingoes.

From South America let's proceed to Asia, the continent with the largest population.

Chocolate Hills: Bohol, Philippines

Chocolate Hills is the most famous tourist attraction in Bohol. This popular tourist spot is currently ranked number 6 in the list of New Seven Wonders of the world. Chocolate Hills consist of around 1,268 perfectly cone-shaped haycock hills with heights ranging from 40 to 120 meters. The Chocolate Hills is a wonder of nature The Hills are considered as a Philippine National Geological Monument. During the summer, the dome-shaped, grass-covered limestone hills dry up and turn brown transforming the areas into rows and rows of chocolate "kisses," hence the name. There is no natural formation like these in the world. From a distance, they look like half a ball grown out of the ground. The molehill-shaped and almost uniformly sized hills dot the landscape with green and brown.

Fansipan Mountain: Vietnam

For mountain climbers, Fansipan Mountain is one of the best mountains to climb. This tourist spot is currently ranked number 12 in the list of the New Seven Wonders of the world. Fansipan Mountain is located 9 km south-west of Sapa Townlet in the Hoang Lien Mountain Range. Fansipan is branded "the Roof of Indochina" with a towering height of 3,143 m. Fansipan had been proposed to be one of the very few eco-tourist spots of Vietnam, with about 2,024 floral varieties and 327 faunal species.

The peak of Fansipan is accessible all year round. The best time to make the ascent is from mid-October to mid-November, and again in March, when the flowers all flourish and the climbers may behold the carpets of brilliant blossoms, violets and orchids, rhododendrons and aglaias. Fansipan Mountain also contains rice terraces like the famous Banawe Rice Terraces in the Philippines.

Mount Mayon: Albay, Philippines

The majestic Mount Mayon, which is considered as the world's near perfect cone-shaped volcano, is one of the candidates of the New 7 Wonders of Nature and is currently ranked number 9 in the list. This scenic volcano is located south of Manila, in the province of Albay, Philippines. Mayon Volcano is the Philippines' most active volcano (47 eruptions since 1616) and is considered to be the world's most perfectly formed volcano for its symmetrical cone.

Pamukkale Springs: Turkey

Do you want to experience a new kind of bathing? Well, then try taking a bath in a hot springs at Pamukkale. Pamukkale which means "cotton castle" in Turkish, are located in south-western Turkey. It is a natural site and a famous tourist attraction. This unique hot spring is 2,700 meters long and 160 meters high and can be seen from a great distance. About 250 litres of hot water that contains large amount of hydrogen carbonate and calcium rises from the spring every second. This natural phenomenon leaves thick white layers of limestone and travertine cascading down the mountain slope, which resemble a frozen waterfall.

The Burren: Ireland

This place is truly a unique place to see. It is a place where there are no trees to hang a man. A place where there is not enough water to drown him. And if you finally succeeded in killing him, it's too rocky to bury him. This place occupies an area of approximately 300 sq. kilometers.

Burren's landscape is special. The limestone is split and weathered. Everywhere are traces of Megalithic Tombs (like this famous Poulnabrone), ring forts, souterrains, cairns, holy wells and stone rows. There are relics of human habitation dating back almost 6000 years. In this area alone there are more than 60 wedge tombs and the densest concentration in Ireland.

The Burren is situated south of Galway in County Clare, Ireland. Burren means "stony places." The vast amount of stone works on the imagination of people. Not only 3000 years BC, but even today stones are piled up into nice shapes, maybe even with some (unknown) purpose.

There are also different rock formations in this place. This area is also rich in historical ecclesiastical sites.

Camargue Marsh: France

The Camargue is home to more than 400 species of birds, the brine ponds providing one of the few European habitats for the greater flamingo.

The marshes are also a prime habitat for many species of insects, notably (and notoriously) some of the most ferocious mosquitoes to be found anywhere in France. It is also famous for bulls and the Camargue horse.

From Europe, let's go down to the hottest continent in the world – Africa.

Djoudj Sanctuary: Senegal

The Djoudj National Bird Sanctuary is a UNESCO World Heritage Site. It lies on the southeast bank of the River Senegal in Senegal, north east of St-Louis. It provides a range of wetland habitats which prove very popular with migrating birds. Situated in the Senegal River delta, the Djoudj Sanctuary is a wetland of 16,000 ha, comprising a large lake surrounded by streams, ponds and backwaters.

It forms a living but fragile sanctuary for some 1.5 million birds, such as the white pelican, the purple heron, the African spoonbill, the great egret and the cormorant. There are about 400 species of birds and a wide range of wildlife that inhabit the park.

Mariana Trench: Pacific Ocean

This is the right place for those who are fond of underwater or deep-sea adventure – the Mariana Trench. It is good place to see some of the most unique deep-sea creatures too, like the amphipod above.

Marianas Trench is the deepest part of the world's oceans, and the deepest location on the surface of the Earth's crust. It has a maximum depth of about 11 km (6.8 mi), and is located in the western North Pacific Ocean, to the east and south of the Mariana Islands, near Guam.

Tourism in Indian Sub-continent

The vast and varied region that we call Southeast Asia offers something for everyone. Hot sun and warm water, dense jungle, frigid mountaintops, crowded cities, steamy markets and a wealth of outdoor pursuits, from scuba diving to bungee jumping to off-road dirt biking. Existing under a diverse cultural, historical and linguistic framework that remains as varied and complex as ever, along with plenty of tourist-friendly infrastructure, you'll remember your trip from the moment you first step into the humid air to your last bowl of spicy street-noodles.

Thailand is without a doubt the transport hub of the region, as well as the most popular country in terms of tourist numbers. Extensive and cheap road, rail and air travel networks ensure easy access to Vietnam, Malaysia and Singapore, which follow closely in terms of popularity; all three offer pristine natural beauty of all forms - from bamboo forests to endless rice paddies - and huge, bustling cities to shop, sleep, eat and play in (indeed, Singapore is one huge city in and of itself). Indonesia and the Philippines cover vast areas of ocean with thousands of islands, some as big as a small country, some as small as a city block. Both offer rugged and nearly untouched marine and forest parks - dive with endangered green sea turtles near the Philippine island of Palawan or climb into the clouds on Indonesia's volcanic Dieng Plateau. The less-populated but still culturally rich Laos and Myanmar offer stunning ruins, ancient but active customs, and a glimpse into what their richer and more populous neighbours were like before the endless incursion of Coca-Cola, 7-Eleven and the internet.

Some Highlights

Asian Metropolises

Large, sprawling and endlessly fascinating, the streets of Bangkok, Jakarta, Hanoi, Phnom Penh, Manila and Kuala Lumpur each offer enough variety and spectacle to satiate any thirst - as long as you don't mind the hustle and bustle

Beaches

From the pristine water around Malaysia's east-coast islands to the party beaches of Krabi in Thailand, every country in the region can offer several beach-bum paradise locales where you can tan during the day and dance into the night.

Ruins

Some of the most fantastic archaeological ruins on the globe lay here; from the majestic Angkor Wat in Cambodia, to the sprawling Bagan plain in Myanmar, to the ancient and mysterious Hindu temples in My Son, Vietnam. Countless others masterpieces of history are dotted around the region.

Ho Chi Minh Trail

During the Vietnam War, this nature-trail from hell helped the Viet Cong move supplies, troops and weapons around while fighting the war that could not be won. Most of it snakes through Vietnam, but it also runs through parts of Laos and Cambodia.

Cameron Highlands

A lush, elevated plain of rolling hills and tea plantations, Malaysia's answer to a Canadian prairie is a popular way to escape the coastal heat.

Mt. Kinabalu

See nearly the entire Malaysian province of Sabah from as high as you can go, at the top of this massive but surprisingly easy to climb mountain that dominates the north-eastern tip of Borneo.

Ha Long Bay

A postcard photographer's dream, this bay on Vietnam's north-eastern tip is possibly the most visited natural attraction the country has, with craggy limestone spires jutting out of the blue waters of the South China Sea.

The Killing Fields

A sobering reminder of one of Asia's darkest moments, this sorrowful but historically important site is one of the locations used by Cambodia's Khmer Rouge to detain, torture and ultimately kill over 1 million Cambodians in the late 1970's.

Sri Lanka

Sri Lanka is one of the most visited tourists destinations in the world. Surrounded by water all around, Sri Lanka is situated in the midst of Arabian Sea. The most remarkable features of Sri Lanka is the beauty of its exotic beaches. The island country's rich cultural heritage and majestic landscape makes it an amazing tourists destinations. The world famous Maria band of Sri Lanka will surely get your booty pooping to its beats.

Bangladesh

Bangladesh is blessed with unique beauty from nature. Explore the various archaeological, historical and cultural sites of Bangladesh which will contribute towards an unparalleled travel experience to this part of the world. The main attractions of for tourists includes the famous Bangladeshi cuisine, beautifully hand crafted items, many serpentine rivers and green hills of Bangladesh. Get face to face with the famous Royal Bengal Tiger in this part of the world.

Bhutan

Bhutan can be termed as a cultural destination. Endowed with rich cultural heritage of Buddhism, Bhutan has different shades of this religion in many different aspects. Besides this, numerous places of spiritual atraction are admired by tourists across the world. The neatly carved wooden houses and superior quality crafts of Bhutan makes it a preferred location for tourists around the globe.

Maldives

Tourism forms the backbone of Maldives. The island country enjoys tropical climate with plenty of sunshine throughout the year. The palm fringed islands, pretty beaches, clear waters and beautiful flora and fauna of Maldives will provide you the most admired hospitality and accommodation for a memorable travelling experience. With the latest threat of its submergence in water, Maldives is a must tour destination.

Pakistan

Pakistan has numerous places of tourists interests. The Karakoram highway, Hunza valley, Khyber pass and the ancient civilization ruins - Mohen Jo Daro and Harappa are on the top chart and comes under the most visited attractions in Pakistan. Pakistan is blessed with a variety of natures work in the form of excellent mix of dry mountains, sea, deserts, waterfalls, forests and ice covered mountains.

Nepal

Nepal is the land of adventure. Home to 8 out of the 10 highest peaks in the world, Nepal is an ideal place for adventurous sports such as trekking, climbing etc. The world highest peak Mt. Everest stands tall in the crown of Nepal and attracts a lot of tourists from across the world. Shopping in Nepal will drive you crazy. Pokhara, Chitwan National Park, Nepal Ganj, Nagarkot and Annapurna are some of the most visited destinations in Nepal.

3

Development of Rural Tourism

Rural Tourism Development: Constraints and Possibilities with a Special Reference to Agri Tourism

The Indian Agriculture and Tourism Industry Scenario

India is known as "Land of villages". More than 77 crore farmers live in 5.5 lakhs of village (2001).

Agriculture contributed about 18.5% of the national income (2006-07) as compared to a high 50% in 1950.

85% of population of India still depends on Agriculture hence Agriculture is not mere business, but is still the "True Culture of India".

Indian Agriculture Scenario

Today the Indian Agriculture has to face tremendous competition because of the driven global trends. To add to this the agriculture crop growth is also weakened due to the uncertain climatic conditions. There is no minimum support price guarantee also. These changes have altered the form and practices of farming operation. Farmers are looking beyond traditional farming to generate income via various forms of direct on farm marketing and farm based non-agriculture business.

Indian Tourism Industry

The Indian Tourism sector contributes 5.3 percent of India's GDP 2006-07. The tourism industry shows that India had 367 million domestic tourists and 3.92 million international tourists. The Forex earnings from the tourism industry were 25,000 crores. The tourism industry created 38.8 million direct and indirect jobs.

The tourism trend shows as per the 10th five year plan Indian government is willing to spend over

Rs.2900 crores in the next five years to boost the growth in this sector. It is also seen that domestic tourism has displayed greater buoyancy and resilience. The centre has committed to contribute 765 crores for the state tourism development.

Domestic Tourism Growth

India has achieved great prosperity in tourism as a product. India being the home to many leading religions of the world has many important pilgrim sites of different religions scattered throughout the country.

Besides the average Indian is also an avid sightseer. As per the study report of FICCI A.F. Ferguson and Co. 2004, every additional Rs.10 lakhs invested can create 47.5 direct jobs and each direct job can create 11 indirect jobs. It also stated that every 30 million additional tourist translate into Rs.4300 crores in revenue. It also stated that farm tourism if developed along unique indigenous lines could have a multiplier effect and high revenue capital ratio.

Within last 15 years, domestic tourism has grown by more than 304 million from 63 million in 1990 to 367 million in 2005 registering a growth of 20% p.a.

The World Travel and Tourism Council has Rated India as one of the Five Fastest Growing Tourism Economies in the World

Tourism Potential in Maharashtra

Maharashtra is the third largest state of India, both in area and population. It is located on the West Coast of India with a 720 km long coastline along the lush green Konkan region of Maharashtra, with its dense forests is home to several wild life sanctuaries and nature parks.

Maharashtra abounds in numerous tourist attractions ranging from ancient cave, temples, unspoiled beaches, ancient forts and monuments, forest and wild life unique hill stations, pilgrimage centres, a rich tradition of festivals, art and culture. The tourism market in Maharashtra is estimated to be around 250 million domestic tourists in 2005.

Objectives of the Study

With the growing importance of Agri-tourism and the thrust given by the government to promote tourism:

1) examines the key issues involved in the development of Agri-tourism in India
2) the challenges faced by Agri-tourism industry
3) suggest recommendations for the success of this industry.

The Agri-tourism industry being a very vast subject and also considering the several diversities of the Indian sub-continent, it was physically not possible to study the Agri-tourism market for the whole country.

Consequently, a study was conducted in Malegaon, Baramati district of Maharashtra.

Status of Agri-Tourism Internationally with Specific Focus on Europe

Most of the European countries pay lots of attention to rural tourism. The growth of rural tourism is difficult to quantify because few countries collect statistics in a way, which separates purely rural from other forms of tourism. The concept of Agri-Tourism developed in 80's in Europe, the participating farms have doubled in countries like Italy, the United Kingdom, and France. The number of agri-tourism accommodation units exceeds 600.00.

In the middle of the 90s, 12 European countries (Belgium, Denmark, Greece, Netherlands, Portugal, Spain, Ireland, Great Britain, Italy, Austria, France and Germany had more than 100.00 farm enterprises involve with different tourism activities. It is obvious that most of the European countries have positive attitude towards rural tourism development because of the advantages this strategy has on rural areas and their overall development. Agritourism in India: Innovative Income generating activity for Enterprising Farmers

Agriculture is backbone of Indian economy. This sector's contribution towards GDP is decreasing and farmers are finding it difficult to carry the agricultural activities without an additional income. Whereas

tourism is termed as an instrument for employment generation, poverty alleviation and development, Agri-Tourism brings in together the declining and booming sector.

Advantages of Agri-Tourism:

1. It brings major primary sector Agriculture closer to major service sector tourism expected to create win-win situation for both the sectors.
2. Tourism sector has the potential to enlarge.
3. Agriculture sector has the capacity to absorb expansion in Tourism sector.

Scope of Agri-Tourism

1. An inexpensive gateway: The cost of food, accommodation, recreation and travel and tourism is low, widening the scope of tourism.
2. Curiosity for the urban about farming industry and life style: Agri-tourism, which involves villages and agriculture, has the capacity to satisfy the curiosity of the urban segment by providing scope for re-discovering the rural life, which is rich in diversity.
3. Strong family oriented recreational activities: through rural games, festivals, food, dress.
4. Finding solace with nature friendly life style: Peace and tranquility are in-built in Agri-tourism.
5. Nostalgia for their roots on the farm: For tourists it is like returning back to their roots.
6. Educational value of Agri-Tourism spreading knowledge about Agriculture science where urban students are moving with the pace of technology.

Basic Principles of Agri-Tourism

1. Have something for visitors to see: Animals, birds, farms, culture of the village, dress and festivals.
2. Have something for visitors to do: Participating in agricultural operations, riding camel, buffalo, cooking and participating in the rural games i.e. gillidanda, gotti (marble etc.).
3. Have something for visitors to buy: Rural crafts, dress materials, farm gate fresh processed food are few items.

Detailed discussions with various knowledgeable persons indicated the following three factors:

1. Farmer: Majority cases farmer is less educated, less exposed and innocent for him outsider as guest is (like god) is treated wholeheartedly without any commercial motive. He entertains the guest while entertaining himself in the process he fills all the service gaps . This makes him a natural businessman.
2. Village: Village being located far from the city lacks urban facilities but is rich in natural resources. The investment is the natural resources itself.
3. Agriculture field: Each field is unique which adds to the attraction of the urban population. This is the incentive wealth of the rural people.

Facts 40 years back

- Only 22 villages in the tehsil received water from Neera river left bank canal, and few more villages were fed water from Karha River which presents a picture of prosperity and happiness.
- In glaring contrast to this, there were 43 villages which were at the mercy of fate and famine with neither any hope of river nor any water resource around.

Year 1967

- Group of farmers came together to do some concrete rural development work in the Baramati tehsil.
- Their development work was construction of percolation tanks, providing loans for digging wells, blasting units, supply of seeds and fertilizers of improved variety and also agricultural equipments.
- Baramati receives on an average, just 16 – 18" of rainfall for the whole year. Further the entire water is lost due to poor storage/ reservoir facilities.
- Farmers were restless, they started exploring the ways and solutions and thus the idea of "percolation tanks" came up.
- Drought sufferers came forward to share the dream of self-sufficiency.

Year 1968

Tandulwadi village: 1st percolation tanks were constructed providing irrigation to thousand areas of agricultural land. 250 percolation tanks were executive and computed. To give an impetus to the work accomplish by these group of former, the trust was formed on June 22.

1971 (Agriculture Development Trust)

The objective of the Agriculture Development Trust was :-

- To popularize and spread the actual demonstration and cultivation of new varieties of crops.
- To test and spread the use of improved seed varieties.
- To improve methods of crop cultivation.
- To develop vocations supplementary to Agriculture.
- To undertake various projects of water supply.
- To train the farmers for the vocational projects.
- To undertake afforestation in barren and fallow land.
- To spread the use of cross bred cows.
- To educate and provide facilities to poor, promising and deserving women for earning their livelihood.
- Agricultural research laboratory to guide farmers to built library providing books to update farmers knowledge.
- To organize seminars, workshop related to agricultural activities.

Year 1970: The year 1970 was a landmark for Malegaon, Baramati it came with the Model Demonstration Farm.

The trust did not rest on its laurels, to prove that an uncultivable rocky land of 110 across was converted into a fertile track of cultivable land on which grows various crops, fruits, fodder for cattle. This was initiated by Dr. Appasaheb Pawar and is now followed by Mr. Rajendra Pawar who is the present President of the trust.

Today the Model Demonstration farm encloses:

- Horticulture Unit.
- Dairy Division.
- Sericulture unit.

- Bee Hive Unit.
- Alternative Energy Unit.
- Krishi Vigyan Kendra.
- Analytical Laboratory – Provides farmers about weather, forecast, velocity of wind, and maximum and minimum temperature and undertakes analysis of soil, water, fertilizers animal.

As years passed by Agriculture as a business was becoming more and more expensive that many farmers were not able to afford it. To add to this there was gradual loss of fertility of land giving the farmers to brainstorm to meet the expense by retaining the farm and opening a supplementary business unit.

Formation of Agri-Tourism Development Corporation

ATDC's mission is "To promote agriculture tourism to achieve income, employment and economic stability in rural communities in India. To help boosting a range of activities, services and amenities provided by farmers and rural people to attract urban tourists to their area. Thus providing opportunity to urban people to get back to the rural roots".

ATDC's Role in Agri-Tourism

- Prepare Agri Tourism project report and business plan for ·each applicant agriculture farm.
- Help to facilitate the financial support from Nationalize banks, institutes and government agencies to built agri and rural tourism facilities and infrastructure like accommodation, sanitation, approach road etc.
- Conduct Agri Tourism Business Training Program.
- Conduct Seminars and conferences on agri-tourism business.
- Provide sales and marketing support.
- Co-ordinate tours from urban areas to the farms.

The trust decided to experiment Agri-Tourism concept on a pilot scale on its own 110 acres model farm, Malegaon, Baramati.

Prior to setting up the successful Pilot Agri and Rural Tourism Project in Maharashtra, Malegaon, Baramati

Taluka, Dist. Pune in October, 2005 a market survey was conducted by ATDC with sample size of 2,440.

The analysis of the survey was:

- 35% do not have relatives in village.
- 43% never stayed or visited village.
- 57% never visited dairy farm.

This survey promoted to experiment Agri-Tourism in the 110 acre model farm of the agriculture development trust.

The Agri Tourism Destination Malegaon village, Taluka Baramati, Dist. Pune, Maharashtra, India (Pilot Project)

This Agri Tourism destination belongs to "Agricultural Development Trust Malegaon". The detailed study has helped in bringing to light the following facts about the model project at Malegaon, Baramati.

Attractions

Agri Tourism activities include farm tours; tractor and bullock cart rides; grapes, mangoes, and other horticulture farms and by-product farms; birds and animal farms; There are lot of things the visitors or guests can enjoy in this agri tourism unit/farm.

Total area under cultivation here is of 110 acres, primarily use for agricultural purposes, out of which 65 acres is used for Horticultural plantations and cultivation, consisting of various seasonal fruits farms.

The added attractions here are the poultry farm; dairy farm; goat farm; and most visited point silk processing unit.

The visitors here can also visit the gram panchayat village office and school; village fairs and markets, near by Jaggery making unit; Emu bird Farm; Sugar factory; Taluka Milk Collection Centres and some of the oldest religious temples and also Museum.

Accomodation

The over night stay arrangement is at the farm itself, there are 12 rooms and 1 big hall. The occupancy is quadruple sharing every room having 4 single beds. One Room is allotted to each Family. The accommodation facilities are basic but very hygienic neat and clean. Two toilets (one western style) (and one bathroom attached to block of every three rooms, this arrangement is purposely kept to experience the joint family atmosphere. The Solar Water heaters at the rooftop are fitted to provide the running hot water for bathing in the morning. There is also the facility of dormitory hall, wherein more than 250 people can easily accommodate.

Outdoor Recreational Activities

The outdoor recreational activities for children and adults during daytime are farm tours and agricultural education programs, how to grow sugarcane, grapes, pomegranate, guava, watermelon, other fruits and what are the food values of each fruits, how to take care of the cattle, nature education programs, domestic animals and emu bird farms visits and education of the different trees, demonstrations such as goat and cow milking, honey making, silk making, jaggery making, rural games that they can play as gotya; bovhra; surparanbhya; vittidandu; Buffalo ride; bullock cart ride; tractor rides; watching domestic animals; clay molding; painting the nature scenery; tree climbing or simply run with the cycle tree.

Entertainment Programs

The Evenings are generally fun filled, star gazing activity and the rural Maharashtra folk dances and folk song programs is organized. Bonfire/campfire during winter seasons, family games, children games, and lots of fun filled programs.

Meals for Tourists

The food served is pure vegetarian Maharashtrian style, for breakfast Poha, Upma, or Shira, for the lunch usually jawar or bajra bhakri, chapattis, rice, varan, pickle, papad, kurdaya, bhaji, thecha, wangeche bharit, jhunka/pitla, any fresh green vegetable sabji, matki/ chawli usual shabji, etc.

Safety & Security Aspects

The Agri Tourism unit at Malegaon is very safe and secure for all the guests and visitors, there is only one main entrance gate, during daytime almost 400 people work in the farm, plus the entire area of 110 acres is barbed wire fenced and over and above there is adequate 24 hours security persons at the main entrance gate and for the entire area.

Medical Facilities

This Agri Tourism unit is just 1 km from the Malegaon village. Apart from the onsite medical doctor there are specialist doctors available 24 hours on call.

Risk And Liability in Case of Accidents

ATDC has examined the risks associated with some of the activities of agri-tourism. For example: one may decide to ride the bullock cart ride or tractor tailor ride which is not risk free, since there is always a possibility that a guest will fall off the bullock cart or the tractor tailor, however ATDC has established rules and regulations that protects the guests from potential risks.

Sometimes accidents cannot be avoided during agri tourism visits at the farms, However, ATDC makes sure that the operations and the farm activity and the sight seeing tours at the farm and outside the farms to sugar factory, jaggery making unit is safe as possible and they have taken appropriate safety precautions.

4

Health and Medical Tourism

Medical tourism (also called medical travel, health tourism or global healthcare) is a term initially coined by travel agencies and the mass media to describe the rapidly-growing practice of travelling across international borders to obtain health care. It also refers pejoratively to the practice of healthcare providers travelling internationally to deliver healthcare.

Services typically sought by travellers include elective procedures as well as complex specialized surgeries such as joint replacement, cardiac surgery, dental surgery, and cosmetic surgeries. However, virtually every type of health care, including psychiatry, alternative treatments, convalescent care and even burial services are available. As a practical matter, providers and customers commonly use informal channels of communication-connection-contract, and in such cases this tends to mean less regulatory or legal oversight to assure quality and less formal recourse to reimbursement or redress, if needed.

Over 50 countries have identified medical tourism as a national industry. However, accreditation and other measures of quality vary widely across the globe, and there are risks and ethical issues that make this method of accessing medical care controversial. Also, some destinations may become hazardous or even dangerous for medical tourists to contemplate.

In the context of global health, "medical tourism" is a pejorative because during such trips health care providers often practice outside of their areas of expertise or hold different (i.e., lower) standards of care. Greater numbers than ever before of student volunteers, health professions trainees, and researchers from resource-rich countries are working temporarily and anticipating future work in resource-starved areas. This emphasizes the importance of understanding this other definition.

History

The concept of medical tourism is not a new one. The first recorded instance of medical tourism dates back thousands of years to when Greek pilgrims traveled from all over the Mediterranean to the small territory in the Saronic Gulf called Epidauria. This territory was the sanctuary of the healing god Asklepios. Epidauria became the original travel destination for medical tourism.

Spa towns and sanitariums may be considered an early form of medical tourism. In eighteenth century England, for example, patients visited spas because they were places with supposedly health-giving mineral waters, treating diseases from gout to liver disorders and bronchitis.

Description

Factors that have led to the increasing popularity of medical travel include the high cost of health care, long wait times for certain procedures, the ease and affordability of international travel, and improvements in both technology and standards of care in many countries.

Medical tourists can come from anywhere in the First World, including Europe, the Middle East, Japan, the United States, and Canada. This is because of their large populations, comparatively high wealth, the high expense of health care or lack of health care options locally, and increasingly high expectations of their populations with respect to health care. An authority at the Harvard Business School recently stated that "medical tourism is promoted much more heavily in the United Kingdom than in the United States".

A forecast by Deloitte Consulting published in August 2008 projected that medical tourism originating in the US could jump by a factor of ten over the next decade. An estimated 750,000 Americans went abroad for health care in 2007, and the report estimated that a million and a half would seek health care outside the US in 2008. The growth in medical tourism has the potential to cost US health care providers billions of dollars in lost revenue.

A large draw to medical travel is convenience and speed. Countries that operate public health-care systems are often so taxed that it can take considerable time to get non-urgent medical care. Using Canada as an example, an estimated 782,936 Canadians spent time on medical waiting lists in 2005, waiting an average of 9.4 weeks. Canada has set waiting-time benchmarks, e.g. 26 weeks for a hip replacement and 16 weeks for cataract surgery, for non-urgent medical procedures.

Additionally, patients are finding that insurance either does not cover orthopedic surgery (such as knee/hip replacement) or imposes unreasonable restrictions on the choice of the facility, surgeon, or prosthetics to be used. Medical tourism for knee/hip replacements has emerged as one of the more widely accepted procedures because of the lower cost and minimal difficulties associated with the travelling to/from the surgery. Colombia provides a knee replacement for about $5,000 USD, including all associated fees, such as FDA-approved prosthetics and hospital stay-over expenses. However, many clinics quote prices that are not all inclusive and include only the surgeon fees associated with the procedure.

According to an article by the University of Delaware publication, Daily:

> *"The cost of surgery in India, Thailand or South Africa can be one-tenth of what it is in the United States or Western Europe, and sometimes even less. A heart-valve replacement that would cost $200,000 or more in the US, for example, goes for $10,000 in India—and that includes round-trip airfare and a brief vacation package. Similarly, a metal-free dental bridge worth $5,500 in the US costs $500 in India, a knee replacement in Thailand with six days of physical therapy costs about one-fifth of what it would in the States, and Lasik eye surgery worth $3,700 in the US is available in many other countries for only $730. Cosmetic surgery savings are even greater: A full facelift that would cost $20,000 in the US runs about $1,250 in South Africa."*

Popular medical travel worldwide destinations include: Argentina, Brunei, Cuba, Colombia, Costa Rica, Hong Kong, Hungary, India, Jordan, Lithuania, Malaysia, The Philippines, Singapore, South Africa, Thailand, and recently, Saudi Arabia,

UAE, South Korea, Tunisia and New Zealand. Popular cosmetic surgery travel destinations include: Argentina, Bolivia, Brazil, Colombia, Costa Rica, Cuba, Mexico and Turkey. In South America, countries such as Argentina, Bolivia, Brazil and Colombia lead on plastic surgery medical skills relying on their experienced plastic surgeons. In Bolivia and Colombia, plastic surgery has also become quite common. According to the "Sociedad Boliviana de Cirugia Plastica y Reconstructiva", more than 70% of middle and upper class women in the country have had some form of plastic surgery. Colombia also provides advanced care in cardiovascular and transplant surgery.

In Europe Belgium, Poland and Slovakia are also breaking into the business. South Africa is taking the term "medical tourism" very literally by promoting their "medical safaris".

A specialized subset of medical tourism is reproductive tourism and reproductive outsourcing, which is the practice of travelling abroad to undergo in-vitro fertilization, surrogate pregnancy and other assisted reproductive technology treatments including freezing embryos for retro-production.

However, perceptions of medical tourism are not always positive. In places like the US, which has high standards of quality, medical tourism is viewed as risky. In some parts of the world, wider political issues can influence where medical tourists will choose to seek out health care.

Health tourism providers have developed as intermediaries to unite potential medical tourists with provider hospitals and other organisations. Companies are beginning to offer global health care options that will enable North American and European patients to access world health care at a fraction of the cost of domestic care. Companies that focus on medical value travel typically provide nurse case managers to assist patients with pre- and post-travel medical issues. They also help provide resources for follow-up care upon the patient's return.

Process

The typical process is as follows: the person seeking medical treatment abroad contacts a medical tourism provider. The provider usually requires the patient to provide a medical report, including the nature of ailment, local doctor's opinion, medical history, and diagnosis, and may request additional information. Certified medical doctors or consultants then advise on the medical treatment. The approximate expenditure, choice of hospitals and tourist destinations, and duration of stay, etc., is discussed. After signing consent bonds and agreements, the patient is given recommendation letters for a medical visa, to be procured from the concerned embassy. The patient travels to the destination country, where the medical tourism provider assigns a case executive, who takes care of the patient's accommodation, treatment and any other form of care. Once the treatment is done, the patient can remain in the tourist destination or return home.

International Healthcare Accreditation

Because standards are important when it comes to health care, there are parallel issues around medical tourism, international healthcare accreditation, evidence-based medicine and quality assurance.

The oldest international accrediting body is Accreditation Canada, formerly known as the Canadian Council on Health Services Accreditation, which accredited the Bermuda Hospital Board as soon as 1968. Since then,.it has accredited hospitals and health service organizations in ten other countries.

In the United States, the best known accreditation group is the Joint Commission International (JCI). They have been inspecting and accrediting health care facilities and hospitals outside of the United States since 1999. Many international hospitals today see obtaining international accreditation as a way to attract American patients.

Joint Commission International is a relative of the Joint Commission in the United States. Both are independent private sector not-for-profit organizations that develop nationally and internationally recognized procedures and standards to help improve patient care and safety. They work with hospitals to help them meet Joint Commission standards for patient care and then accredit those hospitals meeting the standards.

In the UK and Hong Kong, the Trent International Accreditation Scheme is a key player. The different international healthcare accreditation schemes vary in quality, size, cost, intent and the skill and intensity of their marketing. They also vary in terms of cost to hospitals and healthcare institutions making use of them. A forecast by Deloitte Consulting regarding medical tourism published in August 2008 noted the value of accreditation in ensuring quality of healthcare and specifically mentioned JCI, ISQUA and Trent.

Increasingly, some hospitals are looking towards dual international accreditation, perhaps having both JCI to cover potential US clientele, Trent for potential British and European clientele and Accreditation Canada. As a result of competition between clinics for American medical tourists, there have been initiatives to rank hospitals based on patient-reported metrics.

Other organizations providing contributions to quality practices include:

- The Society for International Healthcare Accreditation, a free-to-join group providing a forum for discussion and for the sharing of ideas and good practice by providers of international healthcare accreditation and users of the same. The primary role of this organisation is to promote a safe hospital environment for patients.
- Medical Tourism Association (MTA), the second non-profit trade association for medical tourism (after the International Medical Travel Association), is made up of the top international hospitals, healthcare providers, medical travel facilitators, insurance companies, and other affiliated companies and members with the common goal of promoting the highest level of quality of healthcare to patients in a global environment. The Association promotes the interests of its healthcare provider and medical travel facilitator members. The MTA claims three tenets: Transparency, Communication and Education. These tenets were recently called into question in a Reuters article during the time of one if its conferences. Further questions about the legitimacy of the organization were discussed in an International Medical Travel Journal piece on a legal dispute involving the MTA.
- The United Kingdom Accreditation Forum (UKAF) is an established network of accreditation organisations with the intention of sharing experience good practice and new ideas around the methodology for accreditation programmes, covering issues such as developing

healthcare quality standards, implementation of standards within healthcare organisations, assessment by peer review and exploration of the peer review techniques to include the recruitment, training, monitoring and evaluation of peer reviewers and the mechanisms for awards of accredited status to organisations.

Risks

Medical tourism carries some risks that locally-provided medical care does not. Some countries, such as India, Malaysia, or Thailand have very different infectious disease-related epidemiology to Europe and North America. Exposure to diseases without having built up natural immunity can be a hazard for weakened individuals, specifically with respect to gastrointestinal diseases (e.g. Hepatitis A, amoebic dysentery, paratyphoid) which could weaken progress, mosquito-transmitted diseases, influenza, and tuberculosis. However, because in poor tropical nations diseases run the gamut, doctors seem to be more open to the possibility of considering any infectious disease, including HIV, TB, and typhoid, while there are cases in the West where patients were consistently misdiagnosed for years because such diseases are perceived to be "rare" in the West.

The quality of post-operative care can also vary dramatically, depending on the hospital and country, and may be different from US or European standards. However, JCI and Trent fulfill the role of accreditation by assessing the standards in the healthcare in the countries like India, China and Thailand.

Also, travelling long distances soon after surgery can increase the risk of complications. Long flights and decreased mobility in a cramped airline cabin are a known risk factor for developing blood clots in the legs such as venous thrombosis or pulmonary embolus economy class syndrome. Other vacation activities can be problematic as well — for example, scars may become darker and more noticeable if they sunburn while healing. To minimise these problems, medical tourism patients often combine their medical trips with vacation time set aside for rest and recovery in the destination country.

Also, health facilities treating medical tourists may lack an adequate complaints policy to deal appropriately and fairly with complaints made by dissatisfied patients.

Differences in healthcare provider standards around the world have been recognised by the World Health Organization, and in 2004 it launched the World Alliance for Patient Safety. This body assists hospitals and government around the world in setting patient safety policy and practices that can become particularly relevant when providing medical tourism services.

Legal Issues

Receiving medical care abroad may subject medical tourists to unfamiliar legal issues. The limited nature of litigation in various countries is one reason for the lower cost of care overseas. While some countries currently presenting themselves as attractive medical tourism destinations provide some form of legal remedies for medical malpractice, these legal avenues may be unappealing to the medical tourist. Should problems arise, patients might not be covered by adequate personal insurance or might be unable to seek compensation via malpractice lawsuits. Hospitals and/or doctors in some countries may be unable to pay the financial damages awarded by a court to a patient who has sued them, owing to the hospital and/or the doctor not possessing appropriate insurance cover and/or medical indemnity.

Ethical Issues

There can be major ethical issues around medical tourism. For example, the illegal purchase of organs and tissues for transplantation has been alleged in countries such as India and China prior to 2007.

Medical tourism may raise broader ethical issues for the countries in which it is promoted. For example in India, some argue that a "policy of 'medical tourism for the classes and health missions for the masses' will lead to a deepening of the inequities" already embedded in the health care system. In Thailand, in 2008 it was stated that, "Doctors in Thailand have become so busy with foreigners that Thai patients are having trouble getting care". Medical tourism centred on new technologies, such as stem cell treatments, is often criticized on grounds of fraud, blatant lack of scientific rationale and patient safety. However, when pioneering advanced technologies, such as providing 'unproven' therapies to patients outside of regular clinical trials, it is often challenging to differentiate between acceptable medical innovation and unacceptable patient exploitation.

Employer-sponsored Health Care in the US

Some US employers have begun exploring medical travel programs as a way to cut employee health care costs.

Such proposals have raised stormy debates between employers and trade unions representing workers, with one union stating that it deplored the "shocking new approach" of offering employees overseas treatment in return for a share of the company's savings. The unions also raise the issues of legal liability should something go wrong, and potential job losses in the US health care industry if treatment is outsourced.

Employers may offer incentives such as paying for air travel and waiving out-of-pocket expenses for care outside of the US. For example, in January 2008, Hannaford Bros., a supermarket chain based in Maine, began paying the entire medical bill for employees to travel to Singapore for hip and knee replacements, including travel for the patient and companion. Medical travel packages can integrate with all types of health insurance, including limited benefit plans, preferred provider organizations and high deductible health plans.

In 2000 Blue Shield of California began the United States' first cross border health plan. Patients in California could travel to one of the three certified hospitals in Mexico for treatment under California Blue Shield. In 2007, a subsidiary of BlueCross BlueShield of South Carolina, Companion Global Healthcare, teamed up with hospitals in Thailand, Singapore, Turkey, Ireland, Costa Rica and India. A 2008 article in *Fast Company* discusses the globalization of healthcare and describes how various players in the US healthcare market have begun to explore it.

Dental

Dental tourism involves individuals seeking dental care outside of their local healthcare systems.

Fertility

Fertility tourism is the practice of travelling to another country for fertility treatments. The main reasons for fertility tourism are legal regulation of the sought procedure in the home country, or lower price. In-vitro fertilization, donor insemination and surrogacy are major procedures involved.

Destinations

Africa and Middle East

Countries in this region involved in medical tourism include Saudi Arabia, South Africa, and Tunisia.

Israel

Israel is emerging as a popular destination for medical tourists. In 2006, 15,000 foreigners travelled to the country for medical procedures, bringing in $40 million of revenue.

Medical tourists choose Israel for several reasons. Some come from European nations such as Romania where certain procedures are not available. Others come to Israel, perhaps most commonly from the US, because they can receive quality health care at a fraction of the cost it would be at home, for both surgeries and in-vitro fertilization treatments.

Other medical tourists come to Israel to visit the Dead Sea, a world-famous therapeutic resort. The Israel Ministry of Tourism and several professional medical services providers have set out to generate awareness of Israel's medical capabilities.

Jordan

Jordan is an emerging medical tourism destination, with related revenues exceeding one billion dollars in 2007. More than 250,000 patients from other countries sought treatment in Jordan that year. This included an estimated 45,000 Iraqis and approximately 25,000 patients each from Palestine and Sudan. An estimated 1,800 US citizens, 1,200 UK citizens, and 400 Canadians also sought treatment in Jordan that year. Treatment costs can be as low as 25 percent of costs in the US. The kingdom was rated as number one in the region and fifth in the world as a medical tourism hub in a study by the World Bank.

UAE

Hospitals in Dubai and other emirates have expressed an intent to develop in medical tourism. Some have American-sourced international healthcare accreditation, while others are looking towards the UK, Australia and Canada for accreditation services.

The Americas

Countries in the Americas that are treating foreign patients include Argentina, Bolivia, Brazil, Colombia, Costa Rica, Cuba,

Dominican Republic, Guatemala, Mexico, Panama, Peru and Uruguay.

Brazil

Brazil has long been known as a destination for cosmetic surgery. For non-cosmetic procedures, Brazil is only now entering the global market. However, Albert Einstein Jewish Hospital in Sao Paulo was the first JCI-accredited facility outside of the US, and more than a dozen Brazilian medical facilities have since been similarly accredited. Brazil requires visas for US citizens based on a reciprocal arrangement since Brazilians are required to obtain a visa to visit the US.

Canada

Canada has entered the medical tourism field. In comparison to US health costs, medical tourism patients can save 30 to 60 percent on health costs in Canada.

Cuba

Cuba has been a popular medical tourism destination for more than 40 years. Thousands of patients travel to Cuba, particularly from Latin America and Europe, attracted by the "fine reputation of Cuban doctors, the low prices and nearby beaches on which to recuperate." In 2006, Cuba attracted nearly 20,000 health tourists.

Medical treatments included joint replacement, cancer treatment, eye surgery, cosmetic surgery and addictions rehabilitation. Costs are about 60 to 80 percent less than US costs.

Cuba has hospitals for Cuban residents and others that focus on serving foreigners and diplomats. In the 2007 American documentary film, *Sicko,* which criticizes the US healthcare system, producer Michael Moore leads a group of uninsured American patients to Cuba to obtain more affordable medical treatment. *Sicko* has greatly increased foreigners' interest in Cuban healthcare. A recent Miami Herald story focused on the high quality of health care that Canadian and American medical tourism patients receive in Cuba.

The Cuban government has developed Cuban medical tourism to generate income for the country. Residents of Canada, the UK and most other countries can travel to Cuba without any difficulty a tourist visa is generally required. For Americans, however, because of the US trade policy towards Cuba, travellers must either obtain US government approval, or, more frequently, travel to Cuba from Canada, Mexico, the Bahamas, Jamaica or the Dominican Republic. Cuban immigration authorities do not stamp the passports of US visitors so that Americans can keep their travels a private matter.

Mexico

Americans, particularly those living near the Mexican border, now routinely cross to Mexico for medical care. Popular specialties include dentistry and plastic surgery. Mexican dentists often charge one-fifth to one-fourth of US prices, while other procedures typically cost a third what they would in the US.

This trend has alarmed American healthcare providers who, fearing a loss of business, warn patients away from Mexico. "The phenomenon has unsettled US-based dentists who tell horror stories of rampant infections, undetected cases of oral cancer and shoddy work south of the border", claims hotly disputed by Mexican dentists.

"In Texas, legislators explored the possibility of allowing health maintenance organizations to operate on both sides of the border. However, physicians in south Texas lobbied against the changes, arguing that local doctors could not compete with the lower costs in Mexico". US doctors point out that the Mexican legal system makes it almost impossible to sue Mexican doctors for malpractice.

However, many who travel to Mexico for care report that they are satisfied. According to a report commissioned by Families U.S.A., a Washington advocacy group for health-care issues, "About 90 percent [feel] the care they had received in Mexico had been good or excellent. About 80 percent rated the care they had received in the United States as good or excellent".

Indeed "some U.S. dentists ... have conceded to the competition and begun a 'reverse migration' opening offices in Mexico to take advantage of lower costs". More American insurers are providing coverage for travellers, as the out-of-pocket costs to them are much lower. "With healthcare costs in the United States continuing to rise, many employers in Southern California are turning to insurance plans that send their workers to Mexico for routine care, plans that are growing by nearly 3,000 people a year."

In addition to dental and plastic surgery, Mexican hospitals are popular for bariatric surgery for weight loss, considered an elective procedure that is not covered by some US insurers. A popular bariatric procedure, lap band surgery, which was approved by the FDA in the US in 2001, has been performed for longer by Mexican surgeons.

Panama

In Panama, health and medical tourism is growing rapidly. Factors drawing medical tourists include Panama's tourist appeal, position as a hub for international travel, and use of the American dollar as the official currency. Many of Panama's doctors are bilingual, board certified, and accustomed to working with the same medical equipment and technology used in the United States and Europe. On most procedures, Panama offers savings of more than 50% compared to the US and Europe. No Panamanian hospitals currently have international healthcare accreditation, whether through US, British, Australian or Canadian sources.

United States

Although much attention has been given to the growing trend of uninsured Americans travelling to foreign countries, a report from 2008 found that a plurality of an estimated 60,000 to 85,000 medical tourists were travelling to the United States for the purpose of receiving inpatient medical care. The availability of advanced medical technology and sophisticated training of physicians are cited as driving motivators for growth in foreigners travelling to the U.S. for medical care. Also, it has been noted that the decline in value of the U.S. dollar is offering additional incentive for foreign travel to the U.S. However, costs differences between the US and many locations in Asia far outweigh any currency fluctuations.

Several major medical centres and teaching hospitals offer international patient centres that cater to patients from foreign countries who seek medical treatment in the U.S. Many of these organizations offer service coordinators to assist international patients with arrangements for medical care, accommodations, finances and transportation including air ambulance services.

It should be noted that many locations in the US that offer medical care comparable in price to foreign medical facilities are not Joint Commission Accredited.

Uruguay

Uruguay recently entered the medical tourism market. A private medical tourism initiative, Uruhealth, has been created with support from the Ministries of Tourism and Public Health. The initiative involves the infrastructure, human resources and experience of two healthcare companies: MP Personalized Medicine (Montevideo) and SEMM-Mautone Hospital (Punta del Este).

Asia/Pacific

Many Asian Pacific countries are medical tourism destinations.

China

China is fast emerging as a desirable destination for individuals seeking medical care in a wide range of medical specialties, including cardiology, neurology, orthopedics and others. A number of private and government hospitals in major cities have established international departments. Many leading hospitals provide treatments integrating Traditional Chinese Medicine with Western medical technology and techniques. China is home to leading stem cell research and treatment hospitals that offer Westerners who want to take advantage of stem cell treatments that are still considered experimental or have yet to be approved in their home country.

Hong Kong

As of 2006, Hong Kong had 12 private hospitals and 39 public hospitals, providing 3,124 and 27,755 beds respectively. A wide range of health care services are offered. All 12 of Hong Kong's private hospitals have been surveyed and accredited by the UK's Trent Accreditation Scheme since early 2001. This has been a major factor in the ascent of standards in Hong Kong's private hospitals.

The Trent scheme works closely with the hospitals it assesses to generate standards appropriate to the locality (with respect to culture, geography, public health, primary care interfaces etc.), and always uses combinations of UK-sourced and Hong Kong-sourced surveyors.

Some of Hong Kong's private hospitals have now gone on to obtain dual international accreditation, with both Trent and JCI (and have therefore attained a standard surpassing some of the best hospitals in Thailand and Singapore). Others are looking towards dual international accreditation with Trent and the Australian group. Hong Kong public hospitals have yet to commit to external accreditation.

India

India's medical tourism sector is expected to experience an annual growth rate of 30%, making it a Rs. 9,500-crore industry by 2015. Estimates of the value of medical tourism to India go as high as $2 billion a year by 2012. Advantages for medical tourists include reduced costs, the availability of latest medical technologies and a growing compliance on international quality standards, as well as the fact that foreigners are not likely to face a language barrier in India. The Indian government is taking steps to address infrastructure issues that hinder the country's growth in medical tourism.

Most estimates claim treatment costs in India start at around a tenth of the price of comparable treatment in America or Britain. The most popular treatments sought in India by medical tourists are alternative medicine, bone-marrow transplant, cardiac bypass surgery, eye surgery and orthopedic surgery. India is known in particular for heart surgery, hip resurfacing and other areas of advanced medicine.

Ministry of Tourism India (MoT) is planning to extend its Market Development Assistance (MDA) scheme to cover Joint Commission International (JCI) and National Accreditation Board of Hospitals (NABH) certified hospitals. A policy announcement of this effect is likely soon.

The south Indian city of Chennai is regarded as the healthcare capital of India.

Korea, Republic of

Listed on CNN.com as one of the "hot destinations" for medical tourism, Korea is quickly establishing itself in the field of medical tourism.

However, *The Korea Times* reported in a series of articles that Korean hospitals have adopted a discriminatory pricing policy, charging foreigners two to three times more than the full-fee for locals.

The paper revealed that the price disparity in medical fees for foreign patients is extremely high, considering that the difference between the lowest and highest fees for the most-sought-after procedures exceeds more than 10 times on average.

It claims the government is overlooking soaring medical fees on foreign patients, who are unprotected from malpractice, discriminatory charging, overpricing and patient privacy rights under the Korean Medical Law.

In 2008, Korea had 27,480 foreign-based patients and the Korean health ministry expects that number to increase to 140,000 by 2015. Due to legislation passed in May 2009, state-licensed clinics and hospitals are now allowed to directly seek out foreign patients through various promotional activities.

Korean hospitals and clinics provide a variety of medical services for medical tourists including comprehensive health screening, cancer treatment, organ transplantation, joint/rheumatism care, spinal treatment, ophthalmology, dental care, infertility treatment, otorhinolaryngology, and Korean traditional medicine. Currently, the most popular treatments for medical tourists are cosmetic procedures such as eyelid surgery, nose jobs, facelifts, and skin lightening.

Over 30 Korean hospitals and clinics are member providers under the Council for Korea Medicine Overseas Promotion (CKMOP). Among these facilities are the "Big Four" – Seoul National University Hospital, Samsung Medical Centre, Asan Medical Centre, and Yonsei Severance Hospital.

Malaysia

Malaysia is well on its way to develop itself as a medical tourism hub. The country has excellent hospitals, English is widely spoken, and many staff have been trained to a high level in the UK or in the US. There is a highly active Association for Private Hospitals of Malaysia working to develop medical tourism. However, while Malaysia has a national accreditation healthcare scheme (MSQH) and many Malaysia's hospitals are currently firmly on the way to achieve international healthcare accreditation.

Malaysian hospitals International Specialist Eye Centre, Penang Adventist Hospital and many others such as Gleneagles Hospital Kuala Lumpur have or are going to be JCI accredited. The Ministry of Health has launched a medical tourism page with medical tourism portals such as Wellness Visit.

New Zealand

New Zealand is a relatively new destination to medical travel. It has all the hallmarks of a very successful destination especially for North American based patients. This includes being a first world, developed economy with a sophisticated and comprehensive medical system. It is first and foremost English speaking with a rich heritage of producing world class doctors and medical research.

Many of its private hospitals are internationally accredited, state of the art and offer an integrated package of care. The surgeons in New Zealand are trained both in New Zealand and abroad, usually spending years of their training in either North America or Western Europe.

While New Zealand is aligned medically and culturally to North America, the cost of the surgical care is significantly cheaper. On average it is considered that New Zealand's surgical costs are around 15 to 20% the cost of the same surgical procedure in the USA. One patient who had his prosthetic hip replaced in New Zealand said the total cost including travel, lodging and the surgery at a private hospital was $20,000, as opposed to the $80,000 - $140,000 he was told the operation would have cost at home.

Added to this the personalized level of medical care, the world renown natural beauty and tranquility, the fact that New Zealand is one of the safest places in the world and only 12 hours direct flight from the west coast of North America, then New Zealand as a medical travel destination looks set to develop.

Philippines

The Philippines has been growing as a destination for medical tourism. The US Medical Tourism Association magazine reported that this services sub-sector grew 8.0% in 2007. The number can be expected to grow as American health-care costs rise, or if pending legislation results in an increase in patient wait times for surgical procedures (as has been seen in other countries where care has been nationalized), due to the traditional political, economic and cultural connections between the United States and the Philippines.

The Philippines is one of a few countries that sends qualified nurses, physicians and dentists to the US, the thousands serving in American medical facilities being a testament to its quality of medical education. According to year 2000 WHO rankings of the world's health systems, the Philippines takes its position on no.60.

Singapore

Singapore has a dozen hospitals and health centres with JCI accreditation. In 1997 (published 2000), the World Health Organization ranked Singapore's health care system sixth best in the world and the highest ranked system in Asia.

"Singapore Medicine" is a multi-agency government-industry partnership committed to strengthening Singapore's position as a medical hub and promoting Singapore as a destination for advanced patient care. Patients come from neighboring countries, such as Indonesia and Malaysia, and patient numbers from Indochina, South Asia, the Middle East and Greater China are growing. Patients from developed countries such as the United States and the UK are also beginning to choose Singapore as their medical travel destination for relatively affordable health care services in a clean cosmopolitan city.

Taiwan

The Taiwanese government has declared its determination for the country to become a medical tourism centre. In 2007, the Department of Health launched a campaign to promote inbound medical tourism, focusing on integrating the resources of the government and academia to build Taiwan's brand as a medical tourism destination. Costs for procedures remain comparatively low. Taiwan is known for liver transplants, joint replacement surgery, bone marrow transplants, and reconstructive and plastic surgery.

Thailand

Medical tourism has been a growing segment of Thailand's tourism and health-care sectors. In 2005, one Bangkok hospital took in 150,000 treatment seekers from abroad. In 2006, medical tourism was projected to earn the country 36.4 billion baht.

Treatments for medical tourists in Thailand range from cosmetic, organ transplants, cardiac, and orthopaedic treatments to dental and cardiac surgeries. Treatments also include spa, physical and mental therapies. One patient who had coronary artery bypass surgery at Bumrungrad International hospital in

Bangkok said the operation cost him US$12,000 (8,200 euros), as opposed to the $100,000 (68,000 euros) he estimated the operation would have cost him at home. Bumrungrad treated approximately 55,000 American patients in 2005 alone, a 30% increase from the previous year.

Hospitals in Thailand are a popular destination for other Asians. Bangkok Hospital, which caters to medical tourists, has a Japanese wing, and Phyathai Hospitals Group has interpreters for over 22 languages, besides the English-speaking medical staff. When Nepal Prime Minister Girija Prasad Koirala needed medical care in 2006, he went to Bangkok.

Many Thai physicians hold US or UK professional certification. Bumrungrad International hospital states that many of its doctors and staff are trained in the UK, Europe and the US. Bumrungrad International was accredited most recently in 2005 by the Joint Commission. Some of the country's major hospitals have also achieved certification by the International Organization for Standardization's ISO 9001:2000. However, ISO 2000 is not an accreditation scheme.

The World Health Organization's 2000 ranking put the Thai healthcare system at number 47, below the USA's ranking at 37 and the United Kingdom's ranking at 18.

Serious political problems during late 2008, including mass demonstrations and the complete closure of major airports, have made travel to Thailand less appealing than in the past, and the US State Department has issued a travel alert for the country.

Europe

Countries in Europe that have active medical tourism sectors include Turkey, Cyprus, Germany, Hungary, Lithuania, Malta, Poland, Portugal, Czech Republic, Slovakia, Spain, and Ukraine.

Czech Republic

Czech Republic has built its medical tourism on spas and medical care equalling the world standards.

Germany

Germany is a destination for patients seeking advanced medical technology, high standards, safety, and quick treatment. All German citizens have health coverage, resulting in a high hospital density, with twice as many hospitals per capita as the United States. The high hospital density results in shorter waitlists for treatment. Costs for medical treatment compete well with other developed European countries and are commonly 50% of those in the USA.

Germany is an attractive destination for patients from the Middle East since travelling to the USA has become more difficult for them since the September 11 attacks. US citizens sometimes travel to Germany to seek treatments such as artificial cervical disc replacement that are not US Food and Drug Administration (FDA) approved.

Poland

Since 2004, when Poland joined the European Union, it has become another locale for people seeking cheaper medical treatments. The quality of care in Poland must comply with EU standards.

Turkey

Turkey has since many years attracted medical tourists from Europe and the Balkans, the United States, Eurasia and the Middle East.

The Turkish private healthcare system is striving to become a strategic global health service provider manufacturing centre. The site contains information on prices and hospital statistics, information about the healthcare, pharmaceutical and insurance environments as well as an international patient guide.

Turkey has the highest number of JCI accredited healthcare institutions in the world except for the US. The German Hospital in Istanbul operates the country's first ISO-certified IVF centre, while Memorial Hospital was the first private hospital to receive American JCI accreditation. Since then, over 34 hospitals and medical institutions have achieved Joint Commission International accreditation.

Tourism Development in Kerala

Kerala, a state situated on the tropical Malabar Coast of southwestern India, is one of the most popular tourist destinations in the country. Named as one of the *ten paradises of the world* by the National Geographic Traveler, Kerala is famous especially for its ecotourism initiatives. Its unique culture and traditions, coupled with its varied demography, has made Kerala one of the most popular tourist destinations in the world. Growing at a rate of 13.31%, the tourism industry is a major contributor to the state's economy.

Until the early 1980s, Kerala was a hitherto unknown destination, with most tourism circuits concentrated around the north of the country. Aggressive marketing campaigns launched by the Kerala Tourism Development Corporation—the government agency that oversees tourism prospects of the state—laid the foundation for the growth of the tourism industry. In the decades that followed, Kerala Tourism was able to transform itself into one of the niche holiday destinations in India. The tag line *Kerala- God's Own Country* was adopted in its tourism promotions and became synonymous with the state. Today, Kerala Tourism is a global superbrand and regarded as one of the destinations with the highest brand recall. In 2006, Kerala attracted 8.5 million tourists–an increase of 23.68% in foreign tourist arrivals compared to the previous year, thus making it one of the fastest growing tourism destination in the world.

Popular attractions in the state include the beaches at Kovalam, Cherai and Varkala; the hill stations of Munnar, Nelliampathi, Ponmudi and Wayanad; and national parks and wildlife sanctuaries at Periyar and Eravikulam National Park. The "backwaters" region—an extensive network of interlocking rivers, lakes, and canals that centre on Alleppey, Kumarakom, and Punnamada—also see heavy tourist traffic. Heritage sites, such as the Padmanabhapuram Palace, Hill Palace, Mattancherry Palace are also visited. Cities such as Kochi and Thiruvananthapuram are popular centres for shopping and traditional theatrical performances.

The state's tourism agenda promotes ecologically sustained tourism, which focuses on the local culture, wilderness adventures, volunteering and personal growth of the local population. Efforts are taken to minimise the adverse effects of traditional tourism on the natural environment, and enhance the cultural integrity of local people.

Historical Context

Since its incorporation as a state, Kerala's economy largely operated under welfare-based democratic socialist principles. This mode of development, though resulted in a high Human

Development Index and standard of living among the people, lead to an economic stagnation in the 1980s (growth rate of 2.3% annually) This apparent paradox — high human development and low economic development — lead to a large number of educated unemployed seeking jobs overseas, especially in the Gulf countries. Due to the large number of expatriates, many travel operators and agencies set shop in the state to felicitate their travel needs. However, the trends soon reciprocated with the travel agencies noticing the undermined potential of the state as a tourist destination.

By 1986, tourism had gained an industry status. Kerala Tourism subsequently adopted the tagline *God's Own Country* in its advertisement campaigns. Aggressive promotion in print and electronic media were able to invite a sizable investment in the hospitality industry.

By the early 2000s, tourism had grown into a fully fledged, multi-billion dollar industry in the state. The state was able to carve a niche place for itself in the world tourism industry, thus becoming one of the places with the 'highest brand recall'. In 2003, Kerala, a hitherto unknown tourism destination, became the fastest growing tourism destination in the world.

Today, growing at a rate of 13.31%, Kerala is one of the most visited tourism destinations in India.

Major Attractions

Beaches

Flanked on the western coast by the Arabian Sea, Kerala has a long coastline of 580 km (360.39 miles); all of which is virtually dotted with sandy beaches.

Kovalam beach near Thiruvananthapuram was among the first beaches in Kerala to attract tourists. Rediscovered by back-packers and tan-seekers in the sixties and followed by hordes of hippies in the seventies, Kovalam is today the most visited tourist destination in the state.

Other popularly visited beaches in the state include those at Alappuzha Beach, Nattika beach[Thrissur], Vadanappilly beach[Thrissur], Cherai Beach, Kappad, Kovalam, Marari beach, Fort Kochi and Varkala. The Muzhappilangad Beach beach at Kannur is the only drive-in beach in India.

Backwaters

The backwaters in Kerala are a chain of brackish lagoons and lakes lying parallel to the Arabian Sea coast (known as the Malabar Coast). Kettuvallam (Kerala houseboats) in the backwaters are one of the prominent tourist attractions in Kerala. Alleppey, known as the "Venice of the East" has a large network of canals that meander through the town. The Vallam Kali (the Snake Boat Race) held every year in August is a major sporting attraction.

The backwater network includes five large lakes (including Ashtamudi Kayal and Vembanad Kayal) linked by 1500 km of canals, both manmade and natural, fed by 38 rivers, and extending virtually the entire length of Kerala state. The backwaters were formed by the action of waves and shore currents creating low barrier islands across the mouths of the many rivers flowing down from the Western Ghats range.

Hill Stations

Eastern Kerala consists of land encroached upon by the Western Ghats; the region thus includes high mountains, gorges, and deep-cut valleys. The wildest lands are covered with dense forests, while other regions lie under tea and coffee plantations (established mainly in the 19th and 20th centuries) or other forms of cultivation. The Western Ghats rises on average to 1500 m elevation above sea level. Certain peaks may reach to 2500 m. Popular hill stations in the region include Devikulam, Munnar, Nelliyampathi, Peermade, Ponmudi, Vagamon, Wayanad and Kottanchery Hills.

Wildlife

Most of Kerala, whose native habitat consists of wet evergreen rainforests at lower elevations and highland deciduous and semi-evergreen forests in the east, is subject to a humid tropical climate. however, significant variations in terrain and elevation have resulted in a land whose biodiversity registers as among the world's most significant. Most of Kerala's significantly biodiverse tracts of wilderness lie in the evergreen forests of its easternmost districts. Kerala also hosts two of the world's Ramsar Convention-listed wetlands: Lake Sasthamkotta and the Vembanad-Kol wetlands are noted as being wetlands of international importance. There are also numerous protected conservation areas, including 1455.4 km^2 of the vast Nilgiri Biosphere Reserve. In turn, the forests play host to such major fauna as Asian Elephant (*Elephas maximus*), Bengal

Tiger (*Panthera tigris tigris*), Leopard (*Panthera pardus*), and Nilgiri Tahr (*Nilgiritragus hylocrius*), and Grizzled Giant Squirrel (*Ratufa macroura*).

More remote preserves, including Silent Valley National Park in the Kundali Hills, harbor endangered species such as Lion-tailed Macaque (*Macaca silenus*), Indian Sloth Bear (*Melursus (Ursus) ursinus ursinus*), and Gaur (the so-called "Indian Bison" – *Bos gaurus*). More common species include Indian Porcupine (*Hystrix indica*), Chital (*Axis axis*), Sambar (*Cervus unicolor*), Gray Langur, Flying Squirrel, Swamp Lynx (*Felis chaus kutas*), Boar (*Sus scrofa*), a variety of catarrhine Old World monkey species, Gray Wolf (*Canis lupus*), Common Palm Civet (*Paradoxurus hermaphroditus*). Many reptiles, such as king cobra, viper, python, various turtles and crocodiles are to be found in Kerala – again, disproportionately in the east. Kerala's avifauna include endemics like the Sri Lanka Frogmouth (*Batrachostomus moniliger*), Oriental Bay Owl, large frugivores like the Great Hornbill (*Buceros bicornis*) and Indian Grey Hornbill, as well as the more widespread birds such as Peafowl, Indian Cormorant, Jungle and Hill Myna, Oriental Darter, Black-hooded Oriole, Greater Racket-tailed and Black Drongoes, bulbul (*Pycnonotidae*), species of Kingfisher and Woodpecker, Jungle Fowl, Alexandrine Parakeet, and assorted ducks and migratory birds. Additionally, freshwater fish such as *kadu* (stinging catfish – *Heteropneustes fossilis*) and brackishwater species such as *Choottachi* (orange chromide — *Etroplus maculatus*; valued as an aquarium specimen) also are native to Kerala's lakes and waterways.

Festivals

The major festival in Kerala is Onam. Kerala has a number of religious festivals. Thrissur Pooram and Chettikulangara Bharani are the major temple festivals in Kerala. The Thrissur Pooram is conducted at the Vadakumnathan temple, Thrissur. The Chettikulangara Bharani is another major attraction. The festival is conducted at the Chettikulangara temple near Mavelikkara. Parumala Perunnal, Manarkadu Perunnal are the major festivals of Christians. Muslims also have many important festivals.

Radiation Tourism

Karunagappally Taluk Karunagappalli#Places of Interest in Kollam District is the world's hottest spot of natural radiation. The radiation is caused by monazite sands which contain the radioactive element, thorium. The people in the area are exposed to radiation which is 10 times greater than the worldwide average. Tourist spots that offer the chance of the Radiation experience are very rare in the world.

Ayurveda

Medical tourism, promoted by traditional systems of medicine like Ayurveda and Siddha are widely popular in the state, and draws increasing numbers of tourists. A combination of many factors has led to the increase in popularity of medical tourism: high costs of healthcare in industrialised nations, ease and affordability of international travel, improving technology and standards of care.

However, rampant recent growth in this sector has made the government apprehensive. The government is now considering introduction of a grading system which would grade hospitals and clinics, thus helping tourists in selecting one for their treatments.

Culture

Kerala's culture is mainly Dravidian in origin, deriving from a greater Tamil-heritage region known as Tamilakam. Later, Kerala's culture was elaborated on through centuries of contact with overseas cultures. Native performing arts include *koodiyattom, kathakali* – from *katha* ("story") and *kali* ("play") – and its offshoot *Kerala natanam, koothu* (akin to stand-up comedy), *mohiniaattam* ("dance of the enchantress"), *thullal, padayani,* and *theyyam*. Other arts are more religion- and tribal-themed. These include *chavittu nadakom, oppana* (originally from Malabar), which combines dance, rhythmic hand clapping, and *ishal* vocalisations. However, many of these artforms largely play to tourists or at youth festivals, and are not as popular among most ordinary Keralites. These people look to more contemporary art and performance styles, including those employing mimicry and parody. Additionally, a substantial Malayalam film industry effectively competes against both Bollywood and Hollywood.

Several ancient ritualised arts are Keralite in origin; these include *kalaripayattu* (*kalari* ("place", "threshing floor", or "battlefield") and *payattu* ("exercise" or "practice")). Among the world's oldest martial arts, oral tradition attributes *kalaripayattu*'s emergence to Parasurama. Other ritual arts include *theyyam, poorakkali* and *Kuthiyottam*.

Kuthiyottam is a ritualistic symbolic representation of human bali (homicide). Folklore exponents see this art form, with enchanting well structured choreography and songs, as one among the rare Adi Dravida folklore traditions still preserved and practiced in Central Kerala in accordance to the true tradition and environment. Typical to the Adi Dravida folk dances and songs, the movements and formations of dancers (clad in white thorthu and banyan) choreographed in Kuthiyottam are quick, peaks at a particular point and ends abruptly. The traditional songs also start in a stylish slow pace, then gain momentum and ends abruptly.

Kuthiyotta Kalaris', run by Kuthiyotta Asans (Teachers or leaders), train the group to perform the dances and songs. Normally, the training starts about one to two months before the season. Young boys between 8 to 14 years are taught Kuthiyottam, a ritual dance in the house amidst a big social gathering before the portrait of the deity. Early in the morning on Bharani, after the feast and other rituals, the boys whose bodies are coiled with silver wires, one end of which is tied around his neck and an arecanut fixed on the tip of a knife held high over his head are taken in procession to the temple with the accompaniment of beating of drums, music, ornamental umbrellas, and other classical folk art forms, and richly caparisoned elephants.

Advertising Campaigns

Kerala Tourism is noted for its innovative and market-focused ad campaigns. These campaigns have won the tourism department numerous awards, including the *Das Golden Stadltor Award for Best Commercial, 2006, Pacific Asia Travel Association- Gold Award for Marketing, 2003* and the Government of India's *Best Promotion Literature, 2004, Best Publishing, 2004* and *Best Tourism Film, 2001*. Catchy slogans and innovative designs are considered a trademark of brand Kerala Tourism. Celebrity promotions are also used to attract more tourists to the state. The Kerala tourism website is widely visited, and has been the recipient of many awards. Recently, the tourism department has also engaged in advertising via mobiles, by setting up a WAP portal, and distributing wallpapers and ringtones related to Kerala through it.

5

Programmes and Policies of Tourism

National Tourism Policy of India

Tourism emerged as the largest global industry of the 20th century and is projected to grow even faster in the 21st century. India has immense possibilities of growth in the tourism sector with vast cultural and religious heritage, varied natural attractions, but a comparatively small role in the world tourism scene. A New Tourism Policy, which builds on the strength of the national Tourism Policy of 1982, but which envisages new initiatives towards making tourism the catalyst in employment generation, environmental re-generation, development of remote areas and development of women and other disadvantaged groups in the country, besides promoting social integration is, therefore, vital to our economy. It would lead to larger foreign exchange earnings and create conditions for more Foreign Direct Investment.

The Mission

To promote sustainable tourism as a means of economic growth and social integration and to promote the image of India abroad as a country with a glorious past, a vibrant present and a bright future. Policies to achieve this will be evolved around six broad areas such as Welcome (Swagat), Information (Suchana), Facilitation (Suvidha), Safety (Suraksha), Cooperation (Sahyog) and Infrastructure Development (Samrachana). Conservation of heritage, natural environments, etc. and development and promotion of tourist products would also be given importance.

Objectives

The objectives of tourism development are to foster understanding between people, to create employment opportunities and bring about socioeconomic benefits to the community, particularly in the interior and remote areas and to strive towards balanced and sustainable development and preserve, enrich and promote India's cultural heritage. One of the major objectives is the preservation and protection of natural resources and environment to achieve sustainable development.

Given the low cost of employment creation in the tourism sector and the low level of exploitation of India's tourism potential, the new tourism policy seeks to expand foreign tourist arrivals and facilitate domestic tourism in a manner that is sustainable by ensuring that possible adverse effects such as cultural pollution and degradation of environment are minimised.

The New Tourism Policy also aims at making the stay of foreign tourists in India, a memorable and pleasant one with reliable services at predictable costs, so that they are encouraged to undertake repeated visits to India, as friends. This would be in tune with India's traditional philosophy of giving the highest honour to a guest (Atithi debo bhava).

Tourism A Multi-Dimensional Activity

(a) The Government will aim to achieve necessary linkages and synergies in the policies and programs of all concerned Departments/agencies by establishing effective coordination mechanisms at Central, State and District levels. The focus of national policy, therefore, will also be to develop tourism as a common endeavour of all the agencies vitally concerned with it at the Central and State levels, public sector undertakings and the private sector.

(b) It will be the policy of government to encourage people's participation in tourism development including Panchayati Raj institutions, local bodies, Co-operatives, non-governmental organisations and enterprising local youth to create public awareness and to achieve a wider spread of tourist facilities. However, focused attention will be given for the integrated development of identified centres with well directed public participation.

(c) Public and Private Sector Partnership: A constructive and mutually beneficial partnership between the public and the private sectors through all feasible means is an absolute necessity for the sustained growth of tourism. It is, therefore, the policy of the Government to encourage emergence of such a partnership. This will be achieved by creating a Tourism Development Authority consisting of senior officials of the Government and tourism experts and professionals from the private sector.

(d) Role of the Government: Tourism is a multi-sectoral activity and the industry is affected by many other sectors of the national economy. The State has to, therefore, ensure intergovernmental linkages and coordination. It also has to play a pivotal role in tourism management and promotion. The specific role of the Government will be to :

i. Provide basic infrastructural facilities including local planning and zoning arrangements.

ii. Plan tourism development as a part of the over all area development strategy.

iii. Create nucleus infrastructure in the initial stages of development to demonstrate the potential of the area.

iv. Provide the required support facilities and incentives to both domestic and foreign investors to encourage private investment in the tourism sector.

v. Rationalise taxation and land policies in the tourism sector in all the States and Union Territories and in respect of land owned by Government agencies like Railways.

vi. Introduce regulatory measures to ensure social, cultural and environmental sustainability as well as safety and security of tourists.

vii. Ensure that the type and scale of tourism development is compatible with the environment and socio-cultural milieu of the area.

viii. Ensure that the local community is fully involved and the benefits of tourism accrue to them.

ix. Facilitate availability of trained manpower particularly from amongst the local population jointly with the industry.

x. Undertake research, prepare master plans, and facilitate formulation of marketing strategies.

xi. Organise overseas promotion and marketing jointly with the industry.

xii. Initiate specific measures to ensure safety and security of tourists and efficient facilitation services.

xiii. Facilitate the growth of a dynamic tourism sector.

(e) Role of Private Sector : Tourism has emerged as the largest export industry globally and all over the globe private sector has played the lead role in this growth. The private sector has to consider investment in tourism from a long term perspective and create the required facilities including accommodation, time share, restaurants, entertainment facilities, shopping complexes, etc. in areas identified for tourism development. Non-core activities in all airports, major stations and interstate bus terminus such as cleanliness and maintenance, luggage transportation, vehicles parking facilities, etc. should be opened up to private operators to increase efficiency and profitability.

The specific role of the Private Sector will be to :

i. Build and manage the required tourist facilities in all places of tourist interest.

ii. Assume collective responsibility for laying down industry standards, ethics and fair practices.

iii. Ensure preservation and protection of tourist attractions and give lead in green practices.

iv. Sponsor maintenance of monuments, museums and parks and provision of public conveniences and facilities.

v. Involve the local community in tourism projects and ensure that the benefits of tourism accrue to them in right measure.

vi. Undertake industry training and man-power development to achieve excellence in quality of services.

vii. Participate in the preparation of investment guidelines and marketing strategies and assist in database creation and research.

viii. Facilitate safety and security of tourists

ix. Endeavour to promote tourism on a sustained and long term perspective.

x. Collaborate with Govt. in the promotion and marketing of destinations.

Role of voluntary efforts: Voluntary agencies and volunteers have to contribute their expertise and understanding of local ethos to supplement the efforts of other sectors to provide the human touch to tourism and foster local initiatives. All such efforts shall be encouraged.

Tourism Development Fund and Resources for Development

It would be the policy of the Government to facilitate larger flow of funds to tourism infrastructure and to create a Tourism Development Fund to bridge critical infrastructural gaps.

Priority would be given for development of tourist infrastructure in selected areas of tourist importance and for those products which are considered to be in demand in the existing and future markets so that limited resources are put to the best use.

Foreign Investments and Incentives and Rationalization of Taxes

In order to off-set the specific constraints of tourism industry and to put in place the required infrastructure as quickly as possible, particularly in less developed areas, appropriate incentive schemes would be considered. It would also be the endeavour of the Government to persuade the State/UT Governments to rationalise taxes, to put a cap of 20% on all taxes taken together on the accommodation and hospitality units, to allocate suitable land for tourism purposes at reasonable prices, harmonize movement of tourist transport across State borders, etc.

Adoption of New Technologies

Efforts will be made to adopt the technological advances in the tourism sector to provide better facilities to tourists and to market the tourism product, to the benefit of all concerned.

Information technology shall be given the pride of place in the efforts to promote Indian tourism. Evey endeavour in this regard would increasingly rely on optimising the use of e-commerce/m-commerce, use of internet for disemination of tourism related information, increasing use of portals as gateway to accessibility to tourism information, development of Handy Audio Reach Kit

(HARK) Tourist Guidance System at important monuments and heritage sites, networking of States, setting of tourist information Kiosks, encouoragement to information technology and eco-friendly practices by the private industries and above all keeping abreast with the global technologies for promoting and facilitating tourism. It shall be ensured that Information Technology(IT) and Indian Tourism(IT) become synonymous.

The Central Government will set up a Paryatan Bhawan in New Delhi as a modern Tourist Interpretation Centre to cater to various needs of travellers, foreign as well as domestic and to offer facilities for air and train reservation, money changing counters and information about all tourist centres in the country. The Centre will be equipped with e-connectivity and networking facility to all state tourist offices. Efforts will be made to have similar state level Paryatan Bhawans in state Capitals.

The economic and social benefits of tourism and its importance as an instrument of economic growth have to be fully recognised by all sections of the society. It would, therefore, be the endeavour of the Government to bridge the information gap through proper statistical documentation of the impact of tourism and its wide publicity to create awareness so that the economic and social significance of tourism is well recognised and tourism is given due attention and national priority

Safety and Security

The safety and security of tourists are of primary importance both from the point of view of tourism development and the national pride. It will be, therefore, given high priority in the national strategy for tourism development. Central Government will take up with the State Government to enact suitable legislation on travel trade/ tourist police for protection and security of tourists and for providing institutional mechanism to deal with complaints received from tourists and the industry so as to create a better security perception amongst actual and potential visitors.

Facilitation Services

Tourists have to pass through several Government agencies so as to meet the requirements under various laws. These include obtaining visas, undergoing immigration checks, obtaining permits to visit certain areas, payment of fees for certain facilities, etc. The endeavour of the Government would be to improve efficiency in providing such facilitation services and make travel to and within India a pleasant experience. Introduction of issue of Visa on arrival at least for 15 days at all the airports, computerisation of the system of issue of Visa, streamlining of luggage handling system at airports improving tourist facilitation services at the airports by adopting technological solutions are some of the important facilitation services proposed in this regard.

Tourism Economic Zone, Tourist Circuits, Special Tourism Area and Areas of Special Interests

Tourism Economic Zones will be created with private participation based on the intrinsic attractions, potential for development and availability of resources in these zones. Air, road and rail connectivity to these areas will be established to facilitate direct and easy access to these zones from international and domestic destinations. Adequate backward and forward linkages will also be established to ensure flow of benefits to the local community. The development of such zones will be guided by well conceived Master Plans and executed by specific Tourism Development Authorities which will be created by the Government involving senior officers from the Department of Tourism, and other relevant Ministries/Departments of the Govt. of India, professionals from tourism industry and representatives of Industry & Trade Associations.

India with vast cultural and religious heritage and varied natural attractions has immensed potential of growth in the tourism sector. 25 travel circuits and destinations have already been identified for development through joint efforts of the Central Govt., the State Governments and the private sector. State Governments of Kerala, Tamil Nadu, Orissa and Maharashtra and Union Territory Administration of Daman & Diu have also declared Bekal Beach, Puri-Konark, Sindhudurg, Muttakadu-Mamallapuram and Diu as Special Tourism Area for integrated development. Steps will be taken to work towards the integrated development of all the tourist circuits of the country with the involvement of all the infrastructural departments, State Governments and the private sector.

Areas of Special Interest: Government would initiate and support special programmes and schemes for the development of tourism in North Eastern States, Himalayan region and island

States/U.Ts with a view to achieve overall economic development of the regions, and as part of the strategy for removing regional imbalances.

Sustainable Development and Perspective Plans

The principle of sustainable development stipulates that the level of development does not exceed the carrying capacity of the area. It will be governments' policy to ensure adherence to such limits through appropriate planning instruments, guidelines and enabling regulations and their enforcement. Efforts will be made to diversify the tourism products in such a way that it supplements the main stream of cultural tourism. Comprehensive perspective plans for developing sustainable tourism by assessing the existing tourism scenario in each State/Union Territory with respect to availability of natural resources, heritage and other socio-cultural assets, quantitative/demographic factors like population, employment, occupation, income levels etc., services and infrastructure will be developed by initiating immediate action in this direction.

Conservation and Development

Tourism development needs to be properly guided and regulated to avoid adverse impact on the natural environment and cultural heritage which constitute the tourist attraction. A judicious balance needs to be maintained between conservation and development. Government will continue its policy of trying to maintain balance through planning restrictions and by educating the people in appreciating their rich heritage and by eliciting their cooperation in preserving and protecting it.

Promotion and Marketing

Promotion and marketing is an important component of tourism development and needs to be undertaken along with product development in conformity with consumer profiles and product characteristics. The policy of the Government therefore will be to develop and implement cost effective marketing strategies based on market research and segmentation analysis in each of the tourist generating countries.

International Cooperation

Tourism is a global industry requiring inputs from various international agencies and collaborations with other countries.

The policy of the Government therefore will be to foster positive win – win partnership with all the international agencies and other countries.

Professional Excellence

Tourism being a service industry it is necessary to enhance its service efficiency. The new policy will strive towards excellence by introducing professionalism through training and re-training of human resources and providing memorable visitor experience to both domestic and international tourists.

Placing Tourism in the Concurrent List of the Constitution of India

Tourism as a separate subject does not find a place in the Seventh Schedule of the Constitution of India even though a number of its components are either in the Union List or in the State List or in the Concurrent List. Under the new Policy, Tourism will be placed in the Concurrent List as such a step will provide a Constitutional recognition to the tourism sector and help in channelising development of tourism in a systematic manner by enabling the Central Government to bring in legislation governing the activities of various service providers in the tourism sector.

Action Programme

The following is a list of action points emerging from the National Tourism Policy indicating the Ministries/Departments/ Agencies responsible for implementing these actions.

Action Points Relating to Suvidha (Facilities)

Paryatan Bhawan in Delhi and at State Capitals: Setting up of Paryatan Bhawan in Delhi as one stop tourist reception centre to cater to various needs of travellers, foreign as well as domestic and offer air and train reservations, money changing counters and information about all tourist centres with e-connectivity and networking facilities to all State tourist offices. Construction of similar State level Paryatan Bhawans at State Capitals.

Augmentation of International Air Seat Capacity:-

- Assessing sector wise and season wise air seat capacity, and load factors and augmentation of capacity in the critical sectors either by the National Airlines or by encouraging Foreign Airlines.

- Improvement of accessibility in States and regions of tourist interest. Special interest would be given to areas having important tourist centres which are not connected by trains/ buses. Promoting arrivals in destination of interest by creating hub and spoke operations. Giving impetus to Heli Tourism and Helicoper services to areas not serviceable by fixed wing Aircraft.

Construction of airports on Built-Operate-Transfer (BOT) through private sector participation.

Rail Services:-

- Increasing the number of tourist trains. Special funds need to be earmarked for this purpose.
- Improving hygienic conditions, environment and passenger facilities in and around Railway Stations serving important tourist centres.
- Construction of budget hotels at important railway nodes.

Road Network:-

- Providing wayside amenities along with filling stations or otherwise at a distance of about 100 kilometres on all the highways connecting important tourist centres.

Providing standard signages on all roads leading to tourist spots.

- Ensuring uninterrupted inter-state movement of tourist coaches and vehicles through rationalisation and single point collection of taxes.

Maintenance of Heritage Sites and Improvement of Tourist Facilities:-

- Ensuring proper maintenance and professional site management of important tourist attractions/monuments under the control of Archaeological Survey of India/State Archaeology Departments.
- Involving local authorities, trusts, etc. in the restoration/ preservation of tourist attractions and maintenance of the surroundings.
- Providing world class tourist facilities, amenities and land scaping of area around important monuments in a phased manner.
- Identification, documentation and video publishing of all the monuments which are great tourist attractions.

General Improvement of Tourist Facilities

- Computerisation of the system of issue of visas by the Embassies/High Commissions.
- Introduction of issue of visas on arrival atleast for 15 days at all the airports.
- Distribution of tourist information brochures through Indian Emabssies/High Commissions.
- Streamlining of luggage handling systems at the airports to ensure that the luggage is transported and cleared within about 30 minutes after the arrival of the flights.
- Improving tourist facilitation services at the airports by adopting technological solutions and imparting training to functionaries at the cutting edge level like customs and immigration officials, taxi drivers, guides, etc.
- Introduction of airconditioned taxis with electronic fare metres in all the international airports.
- Provision of special taxi and coach enclosures extending from arrival halls in all the international airports and controlled by security staff so that passengers can queue up easily and pick-up taxis and coaches without hassles.
- Mounting Video-Cameras in strategic places inside and outside arrival areas to prevent corruption.
- Providing direct access to airport hotels and railway platforms in all the international airports.
- Augmenting information services at the airports.
- Removal of RAP/PAP restrictions from most parts of the country.
- Provision of money changing facility in all the tourist centres.
- Providing international standard signages at tourist centres, airports, railway stations, bus stands, etc.

Action Points Relating to Soochana (Information)

- Setting-up a chain of exclusive souvenir shops stocking specially manufactured and beautifully packed information books and other souvenir items at all the nationally important tourist places in a professional manner.

- Introduction of audio-guides at the important tourist places on a commercial basis.
- There have been revolutionary changes in the computer and communication technologies and other relevant sectors, which are still changing. Such technologies have helped sharing of information globally to the advantage of all. Information Technology for improving visitor information and facilitation should be effectively used. Setting up of Touch Screen Information Kiosks , development of Tourism Portals with links to all tourism related web sites, production of CD-ROMs, creation and maintenance of websites, introduction of computer based information and reservation systems, use of virtual reality systems and video-conferencing for tourism promotion, etc. are the activities proposed in this regard.

Action Points Relating to Safety and Security (Suraksha)

- Launching of campaigns through local bodies, non-governmental organisations, youth centres, etc. to create awareness about the traditions of Indian hospitality and the importance of providing an assurance of safety and security to tourists so as to control touting, extortion and harrasment to tourists.
- Providing a legal framework for the protection of tourists and their belongings.
- Providing an institutional mechanism to deal with the complaints received from tourists and the industry so as to create a better security perception amongst actual and potential visitors.
- Introducing tourist police at important tourist centres through the respective State Governments.
- Strict prohibition of soliciting and enticing of tourists both within the airport premises and in its immediate neighbourhood by unethical operators and traders and keeping both the airports and its vicinity tout free.
- Central Government to take up with the State Governments to enact suitable legislations on travel trade/tourist police for protection and security of tourists. Model guidelines to be circulated to the State Governments.

Action Point relating to Infrastructure Development

- In order to off-set the specific constraints of tourism industry and to put in place the required infrastructure as quickly as possible, particularly in less developed areas, appropriate incentive schemes would be considered. It would also be the endeavour of the Government to persuade the State/UT Governments to rationalise taxes and to allocate suitable land for tourism purposes at reasonable prices, harmonize movement of tourist transport across State borders, etc.
- Efforts will be made to prepare Master Plan for land use in each tourist destination/urban centre for infrastructure purposes. Ministry of Tourism & Culture will also be the agency to effect any changes in the master plan relating to land use for tourism infrastructure.
- It will be the endeavour of the Govt to provide single window clearance facilities in the areas like allotment of lands, environment, electricity, water, sewerage, etc. in order to facilitate speedy implementation of tourism projects.
    - Tourism being an area where generally strategic issues are not involved, maximum impetus and incentives need to be given to FDI and involvement of NRIs, PIOs and OCBs to evolve appropriate means to facilitate FDIs such as Special Purpose Vehicles (SPVs). At present NRIs & PIOs are allowed 100 percent investment in tourism projects.
- Development of tourism to the extent desired would involve heavy investments in infrastructure. The resources for such investments have to come mostly from private investors, financial institutions and external borrowing. Financial viability and commercial returns are the guiding factors in such investments. Very often, it would depend on investments to bridge certain critical gaps in infrastructure which by itself may not be commercially remunerative. Special funds have to be therefore, created for such investments. The Institutions like Tourism Finance Corporation of India (TFCI) will be strengthened and a special fund namely Tourism Development Fund will be set up for development of Tourist Infrastructure.

Action Point Relating to Cooperation

- Encouraging Panchayati Raj Institutions, local bodies, religious trusts, co-operatives, and other community level institutions to take up tourism promotion activities through the general rural development and employment generation programmes and specific rural tourism development schemes.
- Encouragement of non-governmental organisations to create and manage tourist facilities.
- Involvement of non-governmental organisations to create environmental awareness on Eco-tourism, national parks, coastal tourism and urban/rural hygiene in tourist centres.
- Involvement of local community in the formulation and implementation of tourism development plans through District Tourism Promotion Councils, etc.

Action Point relating to Conservation

- Formulation and publication of appropriate policies and guidelines, creation of public awareness about such guidelines, etc. are the activities envisaged in this regard apart from providing the requisite legal frame work for ensuring social, cultural and environmental sustainability.
- Despoilation of natural environment, archaeological monuments, beaches, mountains and places of natural beauty; disruption in the eco-system of environmentally sensitive regions; destruction of traditions in the culturally sensitive areas; clandestine selling of antiques and vandalism are some of the possible adverse effects of unimaginative and unregulated development of tourism.

Action Point Relating to Product Development and Promotion

- Giving guidance and financial assistance to State/Union Territory Governments for preparing tourism Master Plans and perspective plans identifying tourism resources, prioritising development circuits and projects and specifying the most suitable forms of tourism.
- Implementing integrated/intensive development of tourist destinations after assessing the carrying capacity, local aspirations and the benefits likely to accrue to the community.

- Involving the town and country planning agencies of Central and State Governments and integration of spatio-economic development plans with tourism development.
- Focussing on the development of Eco-tourism.
- Developing the places of pilgrimage by providing the requisite infrastructural facilities with a view to promote domestic and international pilgrim tourism.
- Develop a clear identity/theme around some important existing attractions and package them to offer an attractive product e.g. Varanasi as the present living city with roots into deep ancient civilisation on similar lines as Jericho/ Rome/Bethlehem;
- Expand "Events Tourism" through organisation of international events such as sports, conferences etc.; also market existing cultural and religious festivals as tourist attractions.
- Expand "Shopping Tourism" through good value for money with the exquisite range of hand-crafted products made in the country.
- Expand "Cruise Tourism", in view of the huge coastlines and large number of ports.
- Developing heritage and village tourism as a package by identifying and developing villages around heritage properties, which have already been restored.
- Diversifying the tourism product to make India a unique multi-attraction tourism destination which can meet the needs of all forms of tourism particularly rural tourism, spiritual tourism, eco tourism, adventure tourism, incentive tourism, conference and convention tourism, etc.
- Developing natural health resorts of Yoga, Ayurveda, etc. as unique tourism products of India.
- Developing seamless inter-modal transfers by improving linkages.
- Involvement of NRIs and PIOs in product development.
- Amusement parks promote tourism by attracting both international and domestic tourists, generate demand in the transport, accommodation and service sectors and

create employment opportunities. The Government will prepare appropriate guidelines to encourage private sector to invest in development of amusement parks.

- Peoples Participation in Development of Tourism : - Tourism policy 1982 envisaged a selective approach based on travel circuit concept in the provision of tourism infrastructure to achieve intensive development of selected centres. The National Action Plan for Tourism 1992 also reiterated the need for such a policy to achieve significant impact on infrastructural development with the limited resources available. These policies, however, did not succeed in view of persistent demands for several small projects to meet the needs of domestic tourists in almost every place of tourist interest. Even the Government of India essentially followed a scheme approach instead of area approach in providing financial assistance for the development of tourism infrastructure. The approach for the future development of tourism has to, therefore, take into account both the needs for selective development and the demands of a wide cross section of domestic tourists. The activities in this regard would include:
- Creating public awareness about economic and social benefits of tourism amongst administrators, planners and the masses through seminars, workshops, presentations, etc.
- Launching entrepreneurship development and self employment programmes to involve the educated youth in providing various tourist facilities and services and thereby creating employment opportunities.
- Integrated development of special tourism areas and selected circuits.
- *Integrated Development of Tourist destinations: In*ternational tourist traffic to the country is largely confined to certain selected centres and destinations at present. There is also a fair level of seasonality in the international tourist arrivals. As a result there is a good deal of congestion and scarcity of facilities in some of these centres during peak seasons. The tourist traffic to some of the centres have even exceeded the carrying capacity with the attendant problems of

environmental degradation. It has, therefore, become necessary to go beyond the beaten tracks and to facilitate direct visit of tourists to new destinations. However, the choice of such new destinations for development will have to be based on their intrinsic attractions, potential for development and the carrying capacity as well as availability of resources. Such development will be guided by well conceived master plans, and executed by specific Tourism Development Authorities. Adequate backward and forward linkages will also be established to ensure adequate flow of benefits to the local community.

- Creation of Tourism Economic Zones
- Constitution of Tourism Development Authorities
- *Diversification of Tourism Products:* - The main strength of Indian tourism at present is its cultural attractions, particularly, the large number of monuments and archaeological remains scattered through out the country, its art and artefacts and colourful fairs and festivals. The country is also endowed with a number of other tourist attractions and options including beach tourism; forests, wild life and land scapes for eco-tourism; snow, river and mountain peaks for adventure tourism; technological parks and science museums for science tourism; centres of pilgrimage for spiritual tourism; heritage trains and hotels for heritage tourism; etc. The tradition of Indian system of medicine and its curative and preventive effect are well known the world over. Yoga, Ayurveda and other forms of natural health resorts have thus become unique tourist attractions of the country. There are also facilities for conference and convention tourism, cruise tourism and shopping tours. The development of natural health resorts of Yoga, Ayurveda etc. along with rural tourism, spiritual tourism and eco-tourism will be given adequate attention.
- *Sustainable Development of Tourism:* - Assessment of carrying capacity and Environment Impact Assessment studies would be insisted while developing tourism in ecologically fragile areas and all developmental activities will be guided by such studies. The other activities in this regard would include:

i. Providing a legal frame work through appropriate legislation for ensuring social, cultural and environmental sustainability of tourism development and protecting the tourists.

ii. Evolving specific policies and guidelines for the development of specific forms of tourism like ecotourism, adventure tourism, etc.

Action Points Relating to Promotion and Marketing

- Achieving effective coordination and synergy with other Departments, agencies and the private sector in tourism promotion and marketing.
- Fully utilising the Indian missions abroad for tourism promotion and related activities.
- Identifying potential tourism markets and segments and adopting focussed marketing strategies based on research to make promotional and marketing efforts cost effective.
- Enhancing the image of India as a fascinating multi-attraction and multi-activity destination with rich cultural heritage and a vibrant society.
- Observing 1999-2000 as Millennium/Explore India Year.
- Developing a Millennium Yatra Package and Youth packages.
- Organising Bauddha Mahotsav with international seminars and exhibitions at Sarnath/Bodhgaya.
- Organising photo exhibitions and creation of a photo library.
- Launching of a multi-media CD-ROM and creating an integrated website on Indian tourism.
- Developing a clear identity of Indian tourism product by promoting selected theme based tourist attractions.

Action Points Relating to International Cooperation

- Ensuring active participation in the activities of international agencies like United Nations Development Programme (UNDP), Economic and Social Commission for Asia and Pacific (ESCAP), World Tourism Organisation (WTO), Pacific Asia Travel Association(PATA), Indian Ocean Tourism Organisation (IOTO).

- Enhancing multilateral cooperation in tourism with different groups of countries like Association of South-East Asian Nations (ASEAN), Bangaldesh-India-Myanmar-Sri Lanka- Thailand-Economic Cooperation (BIMSTEC), South Asian Association for Regional Cooperation (SAARC), etc.
- Strengthening tourism promotion and investment through multilateral and bilateral agreements.

Action Points Relating to Areas of Special Interest

The seven States of the North East with beautiful landscapes, lush green forests, exotic wildlife, unique forms of art and culture and affable tribal societies have hitherto remained backward due to various reasons including poor infrastructure. These States alone offer enormous potential for the development of eco-tourism. At least ten percent of Plan funds of the Ministry will be used for the promotion of tourism in North East apart from taking up special projects and schemes for the development of the area. Other Special Tourism areas such as Himalayan areas, Islands and coastal areas which are identified will also be developed.

Action Points Relating to the Economic and Social Benefits

- Standardisation of statistical definitions and methods of data collection, tabulation and dissemination.
- Strengthening of statistical machinery and improvement of statistical systems on tourism both at the Central and State levels.
- Development of Tourism Satellite Accounts in association with the Department of Statistics to estimate the economic benefits of tourism precisely and regularly.
- Undertaking tourism impact assessment studies and case studies.
- Launching of tourism awareness campaigns at all levels of society.

The Action Points Relating to Professional Excellence

- Strengthening the institutional set-up for human resource development including the setting-up of an Advanced Institute of Hotel Management and a Culinary Institute.

- Qualitative improvement and modernisation of existing training institutions.
- Setting-up atleast one Food Craft Institute in each State, particularly in North Eastern States.
- Improving the standards of training in private institutes through accredition and quality control.
- Setting up a National Tourism Documentation Centre equipped with modern technology systems to function as a repository of research findings and publications on tourism.
- Involving the tourism industry in human resource development activities and encouraging them to set-up independent training facilities.
- Streamlining and strengthening of guide training and training of other grass root level workers.
- Introduction of optional courses in tourism related topics at Graduate and under Graduate levels in order to meet requirement of trained personnel in this sector.

6

Marketing of Modern Tourism

The marketing mix-the 4 Ps-target audience-segmentation-objectives-evaluation. These and other terms are all used in the process of "marketing." In tourism and tourism related industries, success means understanding this process.

This bulletin is designed for those in the tourism industry who may not be completely familiar with marketing or who may simply wish to refresh their basic marketing skills. Covered will be important concepts used in marketing, the relationship of marketing to tourism, and a process for developing a marketing plan for tourism/recreation businesses and/or communities. It will be impossible to cover in detail all the aspects of marketing within the scope of this bulletin. There are, however, other bulletins in this series that will provide more in-depth information on the different components of a marketing plan.

What is Marketing

People hold a variety of misconceptions about marketing. Most common is its confusion with selling and advertising. Selling and advertising are actually types of promotion which is only a component of marketing.

Marketing involves much more, including product/service development, place (location and distribution), and pricing. It requires information about people, especially those interested in what you have to offer (your "market"), such as what they like, where they buy and how much they spend. Its role is to match the right product or service with the right market or audience. Marketing, as you will see, is an art and a science. According to the American Marketing Association, marketing is "the process of planning and executing the conception, pricing, promotion, and distribution of ideas, goods, and services to create exchanges that satisfy individual and organizational objectives." Simply stated it is creating and promoting a product (ideas, goods or services) that satisfies a customer's need or desire and is available at a desirable price and place. Modern marketing is a way of doing business, heavily based on the "marketing concept" which holds that businesses and organizations should:

(1) design their products/services to meet customer needs and wants;

(2) focus on those people most likely to buy their product rather than the entire mass market; and

(3) develop marketing efforts that fit into their overall business objectives.

By adopting this concept you not only provide your customers with better products, you will avoid wasting valuable time and money developing and promoting a product or service nobody wants.

Recreation and Tourism Marketing

Earlier it was mentioned that a product can be "ideas, goods, or services." Since tourism is primarily a service based industry, the principal products provided by recreation/tourism (R/T) businesses are recreational experiences and hospitality. These are intangible products and more difficult to market than tangible products such as automobiles. The intangible nature of services makes quality control difficult but crucial. It also makes it more difficult for potential customers to evaluate and compare service offerings. In addition, instead of moving the product to the customer, the customer must travel to the product (area/community). Travel is a significant portion of the time and money spent in association with recreational and tourism experiences and is a major factor in people's decisions on whether or not to visit your business or community. As an industry, tourism has many components comprising the overall "travel experience." Along with transportation, it includes such things as accommodations, food and beverage services, shops, entertainment, aesthetics and special events. It is rare for one business to provide the variety of activities or facilities tourists need or desire. This adds to the difficulty of maintaining and controlling the quality of the experience. To overcome this hurdle, tourism related businesses, agencies, and organizations need to work together to package and promote tourism opportunities in their areas and align their efforts to assure consistency in product quality.

The Marketing Plan

One of the most important steps a business or community can take to improve the effectiveness and efficiency of their marketing efforts is to develop a written marketing plan. This plan will guide their marketing decisions and assist them in allocating marketing resources such as money and personnel time. The plan should include:

(1) the overall business objectives—what you want to accomplish;
(2) an assessment of the market environment—what factors may affect your marketing efforts;
(3) a business/community profile—what resources are available,
(4) market identification (segmentation)—the specific groups or clientele most interested in your product;
(5) the marketing objectives for each segment;
(6) the marketing strategies (or mixes) for different markets you target—the best combination of the 4 Ps (product, price, place, promotion) for each segment;
(7) an implementation plan—how to "make it work;"
(8) the marketing budget-how much you have to spend; and
(9) a method for evaluation and change.

A framework which can be used to develop a marketing plan. Each component will be briefly discussed in the remainder of the bulletin. For more information regarding different components of the plan be sure to consult other bulletins in this series.

Overall Business Objectives

Businesses, agencies, and communities should develop overall objectives and regularly monitor their progress. The objectives should provide guidance for all decisions including finances, personnel and marketing. They should be quantitative and measurable statements of what the business or community wants to accomplish over a specified period of time. Business objectives are often stated in terms of sales, profits, market shares and/or occupancy rates. Communities frequently establish objectives relating to such things as increasing the number of tourists, developing or changing their image, facility and activity development, cooperation among tourism related businesses and increasing length of stay and local expenditures. It is important that the objectives be reasonable given the market conditions and the firm's or organization's resources. Establish a few reasonable objectives instead of a long, unrealistic "wish list." This is especially true for new businesses or communities which do not have much experience in tourism development and/or marketing.

Market Environment Analysis

The next step in developing a marketing plan is to assess the impact of environmental factors (such as economic, social and political) on present and future markets. Changes in these factors can create marketing opportunities as well as problems.

Demographic and Lifestyle Trends

Changing demographics and lifestyles are having a major impact on R/T participation. An assessment of these trends is important to understand how they will likely affect your business or community. Some of the important trends that bear watching:

(1) population growth and movement;
(2) rural community growth compared to metropolitan areas;
(3) number of adult women employed outside the home;
(4) the number of households is growing, especially non family and single parent households, but family size is decreasing;
(5) the impact of two wage earner households on real family income;
(6) the number of retired persons with the financial ability to travel;
(7) better health to an older age; and
(8) continued aging of the population (we are becoming a middle aged society).

Economic Conditions

Overall economic conditions can have significant impacts on recreation and tourism markets. A marketing strategy that is effective during periods of low unemployment rates may have to be significantly adjusted if unemployment increases.

Businesses and communities should monitor and assess the likely impact of factors such as unemployment rates, real family income, rate of inflation, credit availability, terms and interest rates. Consideration should also be given to the prices of complementary products, such as lodging, gasoline and recreation equipment.

Laws and Government Actions

As a complex industry, tourism is significantly affected both positively and negatively by laws and by actions of governmental agencies. For instance, rulings on such things as liability issues or decisions regarding building and health codes may change or possibly prevent the construction of a proposed facility. If a public facility changes the prices of its services, this could affect the service offerings of associated private businesses. These actions may have both positive and negative effects on the marketing efforts of the business and community. To avoid wasting valuable resources it is important that R/T businesses, agencies, and communities continually monitor and evaluate governmental actions.

Technology

Technological developments are increasing rapidly. New recreation products, such as all-terrain vehicles and wind surfers, provide new ways for people to satisfy their recreational preferences. New production technologies and materials offer recreation and tourism businesses ways to reduce costs and improve the quality of their products/services. Advances in telecommunications have and will continue to create new promotional opportunities. Technological innovations, in relation to jobs and the home, have resulted in increased leisure time for many people.

Competition

Businesses and communities must identify and analyse existing and potential competitors. The objective of the analysis is to determine the strengths and weaknesses of the competition's marketing strategies. The analysis should include the competition's:

(1) product/service features and quality;

(2) location relative to different geographic markets;
(3) promotional themes and messages;
(4) prices; and
(5) type of customer they are attracting.

Business and Community Profiles

Too many communities attempt to market themselves as tourist destinations without accurate information about their resources (facilities, services, staff), image (projected vs. Actual), and how well their customers are satisfied. Without this information, it is difficult to make other decisions in the planning process. Included should be such things as recreational and entertainment facilities, cultural and historic sites, overnight accommodations, restaurants, shopping opportunities, special events and activities, staff size, and transportation. Each item of the "inventory" should also be assessed in terms of quality and availability.

Market Segmentation (Identification)

Recreation and tourism businesses and communities often make the mistake of attempting to be all things to all people.

It is difficult, and risky, to develop marketing strategies for the mass market. Strategies designed for the "average" customer often result in unappealing products, prices, and promotional messages. For example, it would be difficult to develop a campground that would be equally attractive to recreational vehicle campers and backpackers or promote a property to serve both snow mobilers and nature oriented cross country skiers.

Marketing is strongly based on market segmentation and target marketing. Market segmentation is the process of:

(1) taking existing and/or potential customers/visitors (market) and categorizing them into groups with similar preferences referred to as "market segments;"
(2) selecting the most promising segments as "target markets;" and
(3) designing "marketing mixes," or strategies (combination of the 4 Ps), which satisfy the special needs, desires and behaviour of the target markets.

There is no unique or best way to segment markets, but ways in which customers can be grouped are:

(1) location of residence—instate, out-of-state, local;
(2) demographics—age, income, family status, education;
(3) equipment ownership/use—RV's, sailboats, canoes, tents, snowmobiles;
(4) important product attributes—price, quality, quantity; and
(5) lifestyle attributes—activities, interests, opinions.

To be useful, the segment identification process should result in segments that suggest marketing efforts that will be effective in attracting them and at least one segment large enough to justify specialized marketing efforts.

After segments have been identified, the business or community must select the "target markets," those segments which offer them the greatest opportunity. When determining target markets, consideration should be given to:

(1) existing and future sales potential of each segment;
(2) the amount and strength of competition for each segment;
(3) the ability to offer a marketing mix which will be successful in attracting each segment;
(4) the cost of servicing each segment; and
(5) each segment's contribution to accomplishing overall business/community objectives. It is often wiser to target smaller segments that are presently not being served, or served inadequately, than to go after larger segments for which there is a great deal of competition.

Marketing Objectives for Each Segment

Marketing objectives which contribute to the accomplishment of the overall business objectives should be established for each target market. Objectives serve a number of functions including:

(1) guidance for developing marketing mixes for different target markets;
(2) information for allocating the marketing budget between target markets;
(3) a basis for objectively evaluating the effectiveness of the marketing mixes (setting standards); and
(4) a framework for integrating the different marketing mixes into the overall marketing plan.

The target market objectives should:

(1) be expressed in quantitative terms;
(2) be measurable;
(3) specify the target market; and
(4) indicate the time period in which the objective is to be accomplished.

For example, increase the number of overnight stays by people from the Chicago market over the next two years by five percent.

Remember, rank objectives by priority and carefully evaluate them to ensure that they are reasonable given the strength of the competition and resources available for marketing.

Marketing Strategy (Mix)

The marketing strategy, or mix, should be viewed as a package of offerings designed to attract and serve the customer or visitor. Recreation and tourism businesses and communities should develop both external and internal marketing mixes for different target markets.

External Mix

The external marketing mix includes product/service, price, place/location, and promotion.

Product

Earlier we said the principal products that recreation and tourism businesses provide are recreational experiences and hospitality. The factors that create a quality recreational experience often differ among people. A quality experience for one skier might include an uncrowded, steep slope. To another it might be a good restaurant and a chance to socialize. Decisions on what facilities, programs and services to provide should be based on the needs and desires of the target market(s). They should not be based on the preferences of the owner/manager or necessarily on what the competition is providing.

Recognize that a recreational/tourism experience includes five elements: trip planning and anticipation; travel to the site/area; the experience at the site; travel back home; and recollection. Businesses should look for ways to enhance the quality of the overall experience during all phases of the trip. This could be accomplished by providing trip planning packages which include maps, attractions en route and on site, and information regarding lodging, food and quality souvenirs and mementos. Recreation and tourism businesses should also view their service/product in generic terms. Thinking of products/services in this manner helps focus more attention on the experiences desired by customers and also the facilities, programs and services that will produce those experiences. For example, campgrounds are the business of providing recreational "lodging" not just campsites to park an RV or set up a tent. Marinas should provide recreational "boating" experiences, not just slippage.

Location and Accessibility—Place

Too many tourism businesses and communities fail to recognize their role in improving travel to and from their areas. They focus instead on servicing the customer once they arrive at the site/community. A bad experience getting to or leaving an R/T site can adversely affect a person's travel experience. Ways to help prevent this include:

(1) providing directions and maps;
(2) providing estimates of travel time and distances from different market areas;
(3) recommending direct and scenic travel routes;
(4) identifying attractions and support facilities along different travel routes; and
(5) informing potential customers of alternative travel methods to the area such as airlines and railroads.

Potential businesses should also carefully assess alternative locations for:

(1) distance and accessibility to target markets;
(2) location of competitors with respect to target markets;
(3) modes of travel serving the area; and
(4) other attractions and activities that might induce travel to the area.

Pricing Price is one of the most important and visible elements of the marketing mix. When setting prices it is important to take into consideration all of the following:

(1) business and target market objectives;
(2) the full cost of producing, delivering and promoting the product;

(3) the willingness of the target market to pay for the product or service you provide;

(4) prices charged by competitors offering a similar product/service to the same target market(s);

(5) the availability and prices of substitute products/services;

(6) the economic climate (local and national); and

(7) the possibility of stimulating high profit products/services (such as boats) by offering related services (such as maintenance) at or below cost.

When establishing prices, R/T businesses should give attention to pricing strategies which may encourage off season and non-peak period sales, longer stays, group business, and the sale of package plans (combination of room, meals, and recreational facilities). For additional information on pricing.

Promotion

Promotion provides target audiences with accurate and timely information to help them decide whether to visit your community or business. The information should be of importance and practical use to the potential or existing visitor and also accurate. Misrepresentation often leads to dissatisfied customers and poor recommendations.

Don't make claims you cannot live up to. Developing a promotional campaign is not a science with hard and fast rules. Making decisions regarding which type or combination of promotion types to use (personal selling, advertising, sales promotions, or publicity) is not always easy. If, however, you follow a logical process and do the necessary research, chances for success will be improved. It will be necessary to make decisions regarding:

(1) Target audience—the group you are aiming at;

(2) Image—that which your community or business wants to create or reinforce;

(3) Objectives—those of the promotional campaign;

(4) Budget—the amount of money available for your promotion;

(5) Timing—when and how often should your promotions appear;

(6) Media—which methods (television, radio, newspaper, magazine) will most effectively and efficiently communicate your message to the target audience; and

(7) Evaluation—how can the effectiveness of the promotional campaign be determined.

Internal Mix

As stated, marketing services such as recreation and tourism differ from marketing tangible products. Recreation and tourism businesses must direct as much attention at marketing to customers on site as they do to attracting them. In this respect, internal marketing is important because dissatisfied customers can effectively cancel out an otherwise effective marketing strategy.

The success of internal marketing is dependent on creating an atmosphere in which employees desire to give good service and sell the business/community to visitors. To create such an atmosphere requires the following four important elements:

(1) Hospitality and Guest Relations—An organization wide emphasis on hospitality and guest relations, including a customer oriented attitude on the part of the owners and managers as well as the employees. If the owner/manager is not customer sensitive, it is unlikely the lower paid employees will be.

(2) Quality Control—A program which focuses on improving both the technical quality (the standards associated with what the customer receives) and the functional quality (the standards associated with how the customer receives the service). All employees who come into contact with customers should receive hospitality training.

(3) Personal Selling—Training the staff in the selling aspects of the property (business) or community. This also includes rewarding them for their efforts. By being informed about the marketing objectives, and their role in accomplishing those objectives, they can help increase sales.

(4) Employee Morale—Programs and incentives aimed at maintaining employee morale. The incentives can be both monetary and nonmonetary.

A customer oriented atmosphere usually results in customers that are more satisfied, do less complaining and are more pleasant to serve. This helps build employee morale, their desire to provide good service and their efficiency.

Marketing Budget

Successful marketing requires that sufficient money and personnel time be made available to implement activities comprising the marketing strategy. A marketing budget is a financial plan which shows the total amount to be spent on marketing during different times of the year and how it is to be allocated among alternative activities. Separate marketing budgets should be developed for each marketing mix strategy. The separate budgets should then be aggregated to develop an overall marketing budget. If the total amount is too great it will be necessary to modify the overall objectives and the target market objectives, narrow down or drop target markets, or adjust marketing mixes. The final budget should be realistic given your objectives. When deciding on a marketing budget, consideration should be given to the job that needs to be done as defined by the objectives. Basing marketing budgets on some percent of sales or what the competition spends usually leads to over spending or under spending. Decisions should also be based on the costs, projected revenues, and desired profitability of different activities, not just costs alone. Successful marketing activities will generate additional revenues which can be projected based on the marketing objectives (such as increase off season stay by 5%).

Although budgets should be viewed as flexible plans, every effort should be made to adhere to them. Revisions in the budget should only be made after careful consideration of the likely impact of the change on the marketing mix and accomplishment of your objectives.

Implementation

Many well designed marketing plans fail because they are poorly executed. Businesses, agencies, and communities can increase the likelihood of successful implementation if they:

(1) Identify specific tasks which must be accomplished;

(2) Assign people or departments specific responsibility for different tasks;

(3) Provide employees with information on the marketing plan (rationale, objectives, strategies);

(4) Develop time lines and deadlines;
(5) Adhere as much as possible to the budget; and
(6) Regularly monitor and evaluate progress.

Evaluation

It is important that marketing efforts be continually evaluated. This will improve the effectiveness of marketing strategies by quickly identifying differences between actual results and expected performance and determining likely reasons for the success or failure to realize objectives.

A framework for evaluation would include:

(1) Determining which elements of the different marketing mixes are most important to evaluate.—-It is rarely possible or cost effective to evaluate all elements;
(2) Establishing performance standards to compare against actual results.—Marketing objectives, if properly formulated, should serve as performance standards;
(3) Development of formal and informal methods for collecting data on actual results.—There are many ways different elements of the marketing mix can be evaluated. For example, promotions can be evaluated with money off coupons. Special information request forms, telephone numbers to call or post office box numbers to write to can identify the area the request is coming from. Also, formal (written) and informal surveys can be used to determine the promotional material the customer used in planning the trip;
(4) Comparison of results with objectives;
(5) Determination of needed change(s).

Conclusion

Customer satisfaction in tourism is greatly influenced by the way in which the service (hospitality) is delivered and the physical appearance and personality of the business. It is critical that these elements be communicated in the best possible manner to convince people to come and experience what your business or community has to offer. Equally important is the ability to generate repeat business because of your efforts. Thus, marketing becomes the method to reach potential visitors. It is a vital part of tourism management and can be done effectively and well, with sophistication and tact, or it can be done poorly in a loud, crass and intrusive manner. Hopefully, this bulletin has given you the basics for the former rather than the latter. Remember that to do an effective job at marketing:

(1) Adopt a strong customer orientation which includes regular research and assessment of their needs, wants and attitudes;
(2) Allocate sufficient resources and time to marketing;
(3) Assign formal responsibility for marketing to one person or department; and
(4) Develop and regularly update a marketing plan.

Information Supply in Tourism Management

Operators in tourism management, compared to other management sectors, are confronted with a vast field of complex aims, requiring different plans of action. The special working requirements of the services sector are a result of its business peculiarities. Problems instrategic, and frequently operational planning, are characterized by their complexity, often being intermingled, non-transparent, individualistically dynamic and requiring the achievement of multiple goals. The vast amount of information or complex weighting of the different sectors can present an insurmountable problem for human resources. As are sult there are high expectations of decision-makers' trouble-shooting abilities.

In order to solve complex problems, decision-makers need to have a factual knowledge of the industry (declarative knowledge) and the methodology used (procedural knowledge). The wealth of knowledge is drawn from two pools; that obtained from the "storage" of already existing experiences, and by generating knowledge in the respective field. Com-bining these two pools creates an arena for problem solving.

Declarative Knowledge – Decision Basis in Tourism Planning

Currently, information gains more and more importance, leading legitimately to the development of a fourth economic sector – the information sector. Information also plays a vital role in tourism for entrepreneurs and managers who spend the whole day involved in information processing. In the tourism industry there is no lack of market research data, on the contrary, there is a rather uncontrolled growth of various data sources, each having different survey purposes and survey designs. Tourism surveys of national and international market research institutes are published in ever shorter intervals and the level of itemization of market data increases rapidly. Information collected by these means has indicated data which can be organized into the following groups:

1. Information on markets and environment,
2. Information on customer behaviour,
3. Information on competition in the industry, and
4. Internal information for executive boards.

The first three information groups are predominantly non-discretionary from a manager's point of view as the information can very rarely be directly influenced by an individual company. Information from these groups are similar in nature and scope for most sectors represented in the tourism industry (hotel trade, restaurant trade, tour operators, travel agents, common carriers, pressure groups, etc.). In the fourth group however, there is a larger scope for variety. Due to high costs for primary market research many tourism managers abandon market research in general. Even the larger businesses and tourism organizations lack market research departments and employees rarely work exclusively on market research items. This results again in an inconsistent development of marketing aims and strategies, as businesses as often as not grope in the dark for their direction.

In Europe the most frequent or highly recognized of the commissioned tourism studies are either publicly financed, directly by national or local authorities, or indirectly by government agencies. This method of procuring market research, is important and often a condition for its development, as the expensive primary studies cannot be financed by the numerous small or medium-scale businesses. The resulting obligation to pass on information, created by the above mentioned research financing, has lead to a wider search-inregional tourism organizations, and other bodies representing tourism-to find means of successfully sharing and communicating information.

Traditional data resources in tourism market research are reports, records and statistics which may be presented either in printed format or are electronically driven (CD-ROM). Computer-based information systems (databases) are currently a rarity, but usually can be found either in connection with the official statistical data of a country or a region or international institutions. The information available by this method is rarely used since it ignores the special information requirements of the end-user (managers), or is simply inaccessible due to high fees, complicated application procedures or is simply not user friendly.

The lack of practical relevance, of these information systems, can be explained by their bias toward representing the economic interest of the sponsors and data collectors and/or by the universal requirements the systems have to meet in the collection, storage and search of statistical data from other industries. Market research results are mainly available in print and they can be obtained either in bookshops, online or directly from the author. From the consumer's perspective this way of passing on secondary information has a number of disadvantages:

- Due to the complex design of market research reports the surveyed data is not up to date any more.
- Data from different sources cannot be easily compared especially if it has been surveyed for different purposes.
- Information contained in reports is often of limited relevance for the particular problem.
- Presentation of data is either not detailed enough, not significant enough, or supplementary information is missing which prevents a faultless interpretation of results.
- Often only very specific data from a more comprehensive study is required and thus the cost-benefit-ratio becomes unattractive.

There is usually an overabundance of available information leaving managers to cope with determining which is the best source. Often the entrepreneur has to rely on external consultants and market research specialists resulting in additional costs.

Procedural Knowledge – Decision Basis in Tourism Planning

"The big problem with management science models is that managers practically never used them." More than 20 years ago John Little described the discrepancy between the scientific development of planning instruments, models, level of itemization and the fact that, when available, the knowledge gathered is rarely put into practice. This is caused by the numerous, often poorly documented assumptions of model architects, which was denoted as model plutonism by Hans Albert. As a response to this problem Little suggested that the manager is included in the model. He postulated in his article on the Decision Calculus, aniline models with the following features: robustness, ease of control, simplicity, completeness of relevant detail and suitability for communication.

The communication problem is of vital importance in the every day life of managers' daily events. It is still common practice to employ various levels of change rather than continue-ally observe the changes in market share and volume. Many entrepreneurs do not even know terms such as market segmentation or market positioning and they do not regard them as essential. They keep on looking for measures to expand seasonal business but lack knowledge of methods that will measure their success. Corporate planning only takes place if external financing is required and supporting documents have to be submitted to the lender. Heuristic forecasting methods are hardly ever used, accordingly quantitative methods are never used. Models of strategic market plan-ningportfolio analyses and analyses of the lifestyle of a product-employed in other industries are hardly ever used in tourism management. The grounds for the poor employment of methodological processes in tourism management can be divided into two groups; technological development and insufficient training. Issues related to the technological development of existing information processing and transmission systems are:

- Data required for the application of tourism models is either not up-to-date or unsuitable.
- Standard software is not able to support the relatively complex tasks in tourism management.
- Specially developed software is too expensive for single tourism businesses. Issues related to the insufficient training of tourism managers are:
- Managers have little knowledge of existing methods or available data.
- Managers are confronted with various data sources and different results and they do not know how to cope with this situation.

- Managers do not know which data sources and models are suitable.

The Transmission of Market Research Data in the Internet

Due to the vital role of tourism in many countries and regions in Europe a number of programs concerning tourism promotion have been installed. Government and private tourism organizations have been established in order to strengthen a tourism destination. Usually the aim is to increase the added value of a region. The major tasks of these bodies are:

- To provide consumers with information about the destination,
- To coordinate and implement sales promotion measures,
- Tourism advertising,
- Support in sales and distribution, and
- To coordinate and implement market research projects.

For most of their tasks (except the coordination and implementation of market research projects) these tourism promoting bodies provide efficient methods. The actual effect of the last item mentioned has been lost in the past due to inefficient instruments relating to the transmission and utilization of declarative and procedural knowledge. Now with the development of cheaper hard-and software many tourism organizations are reconsidering their promotion policy.

In almost all industries systems are being developed in order to support investment and marketing planning. Also the tourism industry has developed decision support systems and the most important applications are: (1) systems supporting marketing decisions in national tourism organizations, (2) travel counselling systems for shipping clerks, (3) systems supporting regional planning regarding the optimal selection of locations in which to invest (4) systems providing tourism portfolio analyses, (5) simulation tools for forecasting travel behaviour in certain regions. In Austria in 1982 the Austrian Society of Applied Research in Tourism (ASART) started a project aiming at the development of a marketing information system for the national tourism organization in Austria (Austrian National Tourist Office). The first version of the tourism marketing information system (TourMIS) consisted of a database installed in a host system of the

Scientific Computer Centre Vienna and an optimization programme for the advertising budget of the Austrian National Tourist Office. Though the programmes were adapted in 1991 in favour of PC-software, and hence became accessible for a greater number of people (mainly employees of tourism organizations in the federal provinces), the area-wide information supply for top managers in the tourism industry did not begin until 1999 when the internet version was introduced.

Tourism Marketing Information System

The major aim of Tour MIS is an optimal information supply and decision support for the tourism industry. The first step is to provide aniline tourism survey data, as well as evaluation programmes to transform data into precious management information. Tour-MIS predominantly comprises:

1. A database containing tourism market research data (declarative knowledge),
2. Various program modules (method-base, procedural knowledge) converting acknowledged methods/models into simple surfaces, and
3. Various administrative programmes which assist the maintenance of the database and track and control the information search behaviour of users.

The internet supports the transport and presentation of animated and unanimated pictures, sound and video recordings and text and numerical data and is expandable. A high-performance SQL-database and a functionally designed user interface for Tour MIS based on hypertext and Perl permits the development of interactive applications. The programme modules contained in the method-base are developed according to the specific requirements of tourism managers. The internet offers a number of advantages against the old PC-solution. Since changes in the database have immediate worldwide effect the speed of information transmission can be reduced to the availability of the information source. For example, Tour MIS makes the monthly projections of Statistics Austria available within only a few seconds to all regional managers of the Austrian National Tourist Office regardless of whether they are located in New York, Sydney, Tokyo or Madrid. Anybody provided with access to the internet and entitled to use Tour MIS may access data and information, make calculations or simulations send or receive data – without tiresome postal procedures, danger of loss, delays and costs. All these advantages have led to a significant expansion in the number of users.

Conditions for the Use of the System

In the beginning Tour MIS was provided with strict access control and used to be only accessible to certain users. In this respect the application did differ from traditional internet offers. However, the present concept is also not an Intranet. Unlike the Intranet which supports internal information management systems Tour MIS is not owned by a certain organization but is open to all authorized tourism organizations, societies, tourism consultants, companies, tourism training centres, pressure groups, etc. in Austria and abroad. By covering the maintenance costs, a consortium of 12 of the most important initiators of market research projects in Austria (Austrian National Tourist Office, nine provincial tourism organizations, the two special interest associations for Hotel Trade and Restaurant

Trade of the Federal Chamber of Commerce, Federal Ministry for Economic Affairs and Labour Tourism and Recreational Commerce Section) guarantee the continuous updating of the comprehensive database. Since 2000 this initiative has provided the Austrian tourism industry with free access to overall data and functions (with some exceptions) of Tour MIS. The necessary hardware resources are situated at the Institute for Tourism and Leisure Studies at the University of Economics and Business Administration in Vienna where a major part of the necessary maintenance work is carried out.

The Tour MIS Database

In the beginning Tour MIS contained data that was strongly influenced by the internal interests of its commissioner, the Austrian National Tourist Office. In this respect international tourism statistical data, empirical tourism studies and economic indicators for the most important markets of origin for the Austrian tourism industry have been collected in Tour MIS. The PC-version, developed in the early nineties, contained more than 10,000 time series. The periodicity of information was generally based on annual data, however the most significant time series have also been recorded for periods of less than a year. Over the years the database has continually expanded. Due to the increasing importance of overseas markets further information has been required. Unequal needs of provincial tourism organizations led to additional statistics regarding the federal provinces and Vienna, being city and federal province at the same time, acquired an exceptional position. Furthermore data on the Austrian and international city tourism has been added. This information was collected at the branch offices of the Austrian National Tourist Office, transmitted by fax and data was entered manually into the marketing information system in order to be available to users. Later based on international cooperation (European Cities' Tourism, European Travel Commission) the first online maintenance agreements with local tourism organizations were initiated. The most important available data sources of Tour MIS are indicated in. Besides the basic information search functions the method-base has also been continually upgraded. In this respect the system more and more meets the requirements of an efficient decision support tool. In the next paragraphs the most important data sources and the facilities for analysis and reporting are discussed.

National Tourism Statistics Austria

One of the first data sources which was installed in Tour MIS was the official tourism statistics in Austria. Data generated from the registration with accommodation suppliers is one of the fundamental supports of the official inbound tourism statistics in Austria. Accommodation statistics are divided into two different kinds of survey: the accommodation for inbound travel and the accommodation capacity. The data on arrivals and over nights are surveyed for 50 generating countries related to 13 different accommodation types and 1,600 municipalities (= report communities) on a monthly basis.

Thus the official travel survey offers 25 million data points per annum which can be transformed into precious information for tourism managers. From the data material important information on tourism development, trends in markets of origin and accommodation types, evaluation of the competing situation can be derived. For example, for each of the 1,600 municipalities the database allows the user to regularly monitor the development of the average duration of stay, the seasonality, market shares, guest-mix structure, and, in connection with the capacity statistics, the occupancy rate.

Tour MIS presently offers official tourism statistics only at the provincial basis which nevertheless requires maintenance work of 11,700 data sets per month. The necessary data transfer from the host system of Statistic Austria (ISIS) to Tour MIS takes place automatically each time after the arrival of new data segments and in accordance with various maintenance routines.

The information supply of Tour MIS users takes place by means of predominate tables and reports created for the user in real time operations. The content and design of tables or reports plays an important role in the user's perception of the system's usefulness and usability. Only if the information supply meets the users' needs will the system achieve its aim of providing a high-performance usage of market data and improve the information supply in tourism management.

Source Feature Evaluation Period Update Data

Statistic Austria bed nights, arrivals, capacity (suppliers and beds) 50 countries of origin (markets), 13 types of accommodation – for Austria and her 9 provinces since 1960 monthly secondary data in time series format

Austrian Guest Survey 250 variables incl. intention to revisit, guest satisfaction, type of travel, means of transport, duration of stay, travel motive, expenses, selection of accommodation, activities, net income of the household, profession, education, etc. 16 countries of origin (markets) – for Austria and her 9 provinces since 1991 each third year primary data ETC (European Travel Commission) bed nights, arrivals, capacities (beds) 21 countries of origin (markets) – for 33 destinations (countries) in Europe since 1990 annually secondary data in time series format ECT (European Cities' Tourism) bed nights, arrivals, capacities (beds) 21 countries of origin (markets) – for 80 European cities since 1983 annually secondary data in time series format

Number of visitations in Austrian attractions (Austrian National Tourist Office) number of visits for 240 Austrian attractions federal provinces of Austria since 1998 annually secondary data in time series format Austrian Hotel and Restaurant Panel 60 variables incl. net product, fixed and working assets equity and debt capital,, cash flow, profitability-ures, etc. location, size, category and type of business. Since 1982 annually primary data.

- No particular database knowledge is required by the user,

- The data transformations and calculations implemented in the method-base of Tour MIS allow for adequate problem reporting, and
- The user interface refers to a familiar technical terminology.

Especially for the requirements of the managers in the provincial tourism organizations. The comparison with the developments in other (competitive) destinations permits an evaluation of the market share development in Carinthia.

The analysis in indicates for example that Carinthia could defend its position regarding the three most important markets (Germany, Netherlands, Italy), shown in the increase of market shares, despite the fact that Carinthia experienced a severe loss in bed-nights. On the other hand an apparent success regarding the increased demand of American guests (+ 7,7%) has to be put into perspective since the other federal provinces outperformed Carinthia in this segment. Due to the comparative analysis and a simple and informative presentation of the statistics (using sorting features and different colours to distinguish between market share gains (green) and losses (red)) the data material is upgraded. The analysis presented in may be used for historical or current data, for each Austrian province, based either on arrivals or bednights for each of the 13 different accommodation types.

Competitive Analysis for Austrian Regions

The opportunities for implementing tools which use official tourism statistics for bench-marking analyses, the implementation of early warning systems and forecasting tourism trends is obvious. Due to the refinancing interests of data collection authorities and the lack of financial resources in the tourism industry, however, the data analysis for smaller tourism regions or report communities has been prevented in the past.

This factor must be regretted since it can be assumed that the evaluation of key success factors in tourism marketing will significantly improve when they are measured in smaller regional units. Also tourism managers, especially those operating on a regional level, usually have only very little influence in the organization of nationwide surveys. Therefore, many of the statistical series are based on administrative regions that are not always congruent with actual regional use and by tourists and subsequent flows.

Number of Visitations in Austrian Attractions

The collection of statistical data on leisure-time activities and especially the measurement of visitor arrivals in attractions is a rather complex project. It is rarely executed internationally on a systematic or continuous basis. The major problems lie in the delimitation of the study object and the methods of measurement. Since the early 90's the Austrian National Tourist Office has collected and distributed information on the visitation numbers in Austrian attractions. In close collaboration with the nine provincial tourism organizations a list of 240 Austrian attractions is checked for completeness and updated on an annual basis.

Number of Visitations in Austrian Attractions

Since 2001 this maintenance procedure is carried out online in Tour MIS. Here the market research specialists at the respective provincial tourism organizations enter their information into the system. Due to the newness of the database the reporting facilities are still very limited. The present tables either provide simple time series for a single attraction or list all attractions for one or more federal province(s) arranged according to frequency of visits.

Austrian Guest Survey

Since 1988 alternating each third year a comprehensive visitor survey in Austria has been carried out. The Austrian Guest Survey is one of the most important sources of information in tourism market research. It provides vital information on guest profiles, customer satisfaction, information and booking behaviour, type of travel, destination, means of transport, accommodation, activities, visitor expenditures and other current topics. The Austrian Guest Survey is financed and coordinated by a consortium of authorities responsible for tourism promotion in Austria (Austrian National Tourist Office and nine provincial tourism organizations), the Chamber of Commerce and the Federal Ministry for Economic Affairs and Labour (Tourism and Recreational Commerce Section). Since the Austrian Guest Survey is a primary study it presents some features which complicate the information diffusion in Tour MIS compared to the above mentioned secondary data sources. The main reasons for these additional difficulties are:

(1) The much wider scope of the study,

(2) The required data analyses are more demanding, and

(3) Interpretation possibilities are limited by the sample size and characteristics.

The Austrian Guest Survey has more than 200 features which are partially modified for each survey. Considering the scope of the study and that only descriptive evaluation is possible the Austrian Guest Survey offers more than 1 million findings per survey. Traditional forms of report (market research report, press releases etc.) cover just a small part of the real investigation and evaluation potential. Thus important questions managers would raise remain unanswered although theoretically the answers exist. Data of primary analyses are available unprocessed (disaggregated data format). Regarding the Austrian Guest Survey there are 10,000 interviews per survey, all of the features being available in quantitative form. However, information processing requires the application of analytical methods ranging from calculating simple mean values to complicated data mining procedures.

The necessary methodological knowledge has to be obtained from statistics experts who create costs which, in most cases, cannot be covered by the tourism industry. Therefore, due to a lack of know-how or lacking financial support, many questions managers raise remain unanswered although data actually would be available. Contrary to a census, as found in official statistics, sample surveys do not integrate all elements of the whole picture into the study. The major aim in statistics is to draw reliable conclusions regarding to the totality from a limited number of elements. The previously mentioned evaluation procedures take more effort and interpretation depends on the features of the sample (sample size and sampling technique).

Automatic Selection of Analysing Methods

In addition the user may select only a certain part of the overall data set for evaluation (i.e. data of a certain province or market). In order to prevent interpretation errors due to unreliability of results, those values based on a small sample are only indicated after informing the user about the problem.

The analysis takes place in real time. Tour MIS provides the facilities to evaluate more than one survey, at the same time offering two alternatives: longitudinal and cross section analyses. The first application informs the tourism manager about changes in the guest behaviour over a specified period of time. Query support is provided by offering only variables surveyed unmodified over the overall selected period of time (i.e. the standard questionnaire programme). The latter application increases the sample size (for 4 surveys more than 45,000 interviews) which makes answers to detailed questions possible (assuming a particular time invariance, of course). This function permits for example reliable results about the share of side expenses of Italian guests in the federal province of Salzburg during a particular season.

Comparison of Hotel and Restaurant Groups

The database supports regional planners and tourism managers in their decisions as well as managers in the hospitality industry. The results of the past 10 years of a project which has been executed by the Austrian Society of Applied Research in Tourism and commissioned by the Austrian Hotel and Restaurant Association situated within the Austrian Federal Chamber of Commerce are presented in Tour MIS. In this project operating data and annual financial statements for hotels and restaurants in Austria are compared on an annual basis. Information collected directly from the businesses with a high level of itemization is supplemented with comprehensive, compressed data stored at cooperative industry related organizations such as the Wirts chafts for derungs institute der Austrian Federal Economic Chamberund Tourism us bank and Burges Forder ungsbank of the Austrian Federal Ministry of Economic Affair and Labour. In connection with the design and evaluation of continually repeated surveys a number of new approaches for the diagnosis and comparison of industry groups are developed. Tour MIS presently provides the following applications:

- Industry information for more than 1,300 hotels and restaurants per year since 1991.
- Various functions supporting key ratio analyses in the hotel and restaurant industry.
- The chance for hotel and restaurant managers to participate online in the most significant hotel and restaurant panel survey in Austria.

Information about more than 50 different key ratios is provided in the form of arithmetic mean and median values for 30 distinguished industry groups. Within the industry groups additional evaluations for businesses of excellent profitability (best practice enterprises) are available. For the hotel and restaurant panel database Tour MIS users are provided with the following query and analysing facilities:

- Evaluation of a key ratio for all industry groups referring to a certain year.
- Comparison of all key ratios for a particular industry group.
- Development of a key ratio uncovering the main industry developments.
- Benchmarking analysis for a particular hotel or restaurant (only provided when managers are actively participating in the study).

The quality of information based on the results of the survey is strongly influenced by the number of participating businesses. Due to the chance for interaction in the internet the first results may be obtained straight after entering business data. In this context the problem of how to prevent participants from entering incorrect data occurs. Tour MIS offers a number of plausibility controls during data entry and records data in a second, temporary database. At regular intervals experts determine which records are qualified to be stored in the general database.

Analysis of the User Behaviour of Tour MIS

How do we know that we have successfully implemented a system? Researchers have not really agreed on an indicator for successful implementation. One appealing approach is a cost-benefit study. In this evaluation, one totals the costs of developing a system and compares them with the benefits resulting form the system. In theory, this sounds like a good indicator of success, but in practice it is difficult to provide meaningful estimates. Obtaining the cost side of the ratio is not too much of a problem if adequate records are kept during the development of the system. However, an evaluation of the benefits of a computer-based information system is difficult. How can the value of improved information processing be measured? With transactions processing and some operational control systems, it is usually possible to show tangible savings. For example, many transactions systems have resulted in increased productivity in processing paperwork without a proportional increase in cost. Operational control systems, such as those used to control inventories in large hotels and restaurants, may reduce inventory balances, saving storage and investment costs while maintaining existing service levels. For systems that aid a decision maker, it is much more difficult to estimate the benefits.

For a marketing information system, like Tour MIS, use of the system is voluntary. A manager or other user receives a report but does not have to use the information on it or

1. Council of the European Union, Council Directive 95/97/EEC of 23 November 1995 on the collection of statistical information in the field of tourism, Official Journal. L291 of 6 December 1995.
2. Commission of the European Communities Report to the Council, the European Parliament, the Economic and Social Committee and the Committee of Regions on the Application of the Directive of the Council 95/97/EEC on the compilation of statistical data in the field of tourism, 17 January 2001, even read the report.

In particular systems that provide aniline retrieval of information from a database can be classified as voluntary since the use of such a system is frequently at the discretion of the user. For this type of system where use is voluntary, it is generally accepted that high levels of use is a sign of successful implementation.

In this case the economic or personal success of its users is indirectly measured by the frequency of usage. Several authors have shown that the frequency of usage is determined by the perceived usefulness (textual component) and the ease of use (technical component).

The acceptance of Tour MIS can be determined by means of constantly updated and aniline available access statistics. Contrary to other internet applications the accesses to websites is not counted but the number of virtually answered queries is. Results of the Tour MIS statistics are therefore not influenced by website characteristics (number of graphics or distortions due to the application of window techniques), but do represent the 'genuine user acceptance'. In addition, the comprehensive protocol system permits the analysis of queries broken down into various user groups, information sources and the type of query.

The community of Tour MIS users has continually developed. In 1998 there were only 50 registered users at the Austrian National Tourist Office and at the end of 2001 more than 1,000 registered Tour MIS users have been counted. The distribution of user groups indicates that Tour MIS is not only favoured by tourism managers (44.6%), but also by employees, students and pupils of education and research institutes (31.6% of all queries) and other non-tourism professionals or private persons (23.8%). The distribution of various user groups is present. The average number of queries per user in 2001 and therefore indicates the frequency of use for a specific Tour MIS user group. The employees of provincial tourism organizations use Tour-MIS most (92 queries per user) due to the comprehensive data material available on the federal provinces. The students, as the largest user group, show a relatively low number due to only temporal interest (for a seminar paper or a diploma thesis they need access to data material only once). The number of accommodation providers and F&B managers using the system is, considering the number of existing businesses, very low. A reason for this is probably that the most interesting information source for this user group (the Austrian hotel and restaurant panel database) is a relatively new data set that is simply not known by the managers. Overall, 34.538 queries have been processed in 2001, signifying an increase of 35.5% in comparison to the previous year (25,492 queries).

About half of all queries are made regarding the official tourism statistics in Austria. The industry appears to be very interested in the development of the major markets of origin and accommodation types in the federal provinces (on average approx. 50 queries per day). Regarding the official statistics for Austria most queries are made in connection with information concerning monthly statistics (20% of all queries). The international data sources ECT and ETC gained 18.7% respectively and they rank behind the official Austrian statistics. The significant increase of queries regarding these two international data sources as well as the tendency towards English queries, however, indicate a growing international interest in Tour MIS.

The assessment of demand of information certainly needs a more detailed investigation than simply monitoring the current use of market research resources. However, in Tour-MIS 'demand of information' not only refers to the principal (statistical) sources, but also to the sort of data transformations (analysis) and formats of automatically generated reports available to the users. The functional characteristics and the design of the system have always been developed in close collaboration with the affected managers. For instance, concerning the development of the decision support tools part of the international data sources in the system, the developers have met more than 20 times in form of working group meetings and seminars with representatives (CEOs and research directors) of European Cities Tourism and the European Travel Commission. The involvement of the managers in the design and operation of the information system resulted in favourable user attitudes and perceptions of the information system and led to higher levels of use. In the beginning only a few members were able and willing to actively contribute to this project by entering their data on a regular basis. Today, more than 100 managers working in different tourism destination marketing organizations, based in more than 30 different European countries, and speaking more than 15 different languages, are obviously convinced by the significance of the project and the value of the system as they regularly and voluntarily enter their data into the system.

Conclusions

Generally speaking tourism managers benefit from access to the internet in two ways: the internet provides the opportunity to communicate and serves as a platform for new distribution channels. The present article does not deal with new distribution channels and new booking systems in the tourism industry. This undoubtedly important topic has been discussed in an number of publications and symposia.

The present article introduced Tour MIS, an aniline accessible decision support tool for tourism and hospitality management which has been successfully used by more than 1,000 users for three years. According to Ritchie and Ritchie for the development of an industry supported destination marketing information system, information must be both generally accessible and widely advertised so that managers are aware of the benefits it offers. In lieu of a more preferable cost-benefit analysis, the success of Tour MIS was analysed by studying actual system use observed from various log files generated by the system. The merits of this form of evaluation lie in the objectivity of the findings, the cost-effective procedure, and the comparability of the estimates when the analysis are performed on a regular basis.

The major reason for the poor application of management science models and methodologies in tourism management is the insufficient education of practitioners and the inadequacy of problem solving features of standard software solutions. The development of simple, affordable (shareware) programs, downloadable for every tourism manager, is the first step into a new era of dialogue between research and practice. Within a short time, for internal diagnosis, forecasts and simulations on the net there will be high-performance computer languages available which are now being developed by major international software producers.

Technological progress will also offer benefits for the electronic transmission of tourism market research data. Interdisciplinary research projects will be challenged with tourism research, research in statistics and commercial information technology. For example there are still a number of problems to be solved in order to be able to jointly use ecoscopic and demoscopic tourism data within a marketing information system. These combination options require a constant standardization of information sources as well as new approaches towards the methodological processing of data gained from various studies. Another vital research initiative will be the development of information systems about themselves? Optimizing the knowledge presentation of 'service quality in information services' has been neglected in the past. By applying and accepting decision support systems the significance of this field of research will increase. Another important factor will be the role system imminent? Protocol presentations play, which are continually improved. Thus data on the user behaviour offers not only information on necessary improvements in the data processing of tourism market research results, but also on the future focus of tourism market research.

The sudden explosion of data and the growing need for information challenges basic research as far as data reduction and decision support methods are concerned. Therefore existing concepts for qualitative forecasts and market reaction models and their calibration options in a marketing information system have to be reconsidered. In this respect projects which aim at a systematic and regular compilation of experiences experts made with regard to various technical subjects (i.e. short-term development of singular markets of origin) are considered to be promising. It is their aim to provide an improved evaluation of future market developments and eventually to integrate the findings into the strategic planning of national and regional tourism organizations and businesses. Another necessary development regards already existing data collections and the processing of the European cities' statistics. In this respect this author has observed many shortcomings relating to the international comparability of the data. The improved communication possibilities provided by the new medium stimulates critical discussions and behavioural learning among all participants. Within European Cities Tourism, among other things, new initiatives to evaluate one city's major competitors have been released due to the managers' increased awareness of the importance of this problem.

The trend towards globalization in research, where the internet plays a vital role, refers also to tourism research. To those critics who refer to the internet as uncontrolled growing, complicated and in its applications too playful, supporters used to point out that one day smart and profitable applications would be found. That is where we stand now. The new areas of responsibility regional and national tourism managers are confronted with today, not only suggest shortcomings in education but also promise new opportunities for the next manager generations to acquire status.

7

Tourism as Employment Opportunity

Tourism is an economic tool which, when planted in a community expresses its positive presence through the jobs that spring from it. It then also contributes to the particular place's exposure to its external world drawing attention to it and with its visits that create the establishment of the logistics to address the needs of the visitors while they are there; food, drinks, transportation, communication, friendship, souvenirs.

Tourism is therefore a tool for poverty alleviation and social cohesion. The abject poverty in our rural areas could be reduced if tourism is developed. This is because most of our attraction sites are dotted in the rural areas where poverty is prevalent. Tourists spend on accommodation, food, souvenirs and so on at places visited. However, the fact that tourists embark on return visits and sleep in the urban areas after visiting the sites does not augur well for poverty reduction. The provision of social amenities in such areas will therefore go a long way to open up these areas to entice tourists to spend days at the attraction areas.

Tourism also orientates the community towards new introductions which may be positive or negative or both. Tourism never leaves a place without planting its footprints in there. It also makes a people conscious of their environmental cleanliness, and good conservation practices in a very sustainable way, because so long as the community area is acceptable to the visitors, they will continue to arrive and drop some benefits to the host community.

It addresses the social and cultural issues of the community in a very positive way. In Ghana, tourism as a tool for poverty alleviation is not in doubt. What is in doubt is the understanding of the industry because not much by way of education as to what it is and is not is brought home to the Ghanaian society. Tourism enjoys a lot of global attention due to its economic power to generate huge incomes to nations and its massive job creation base. The potential of tourism to transform developing economies and leapfrog them into middle income economies within record times has never been doubted both by economists and politicians.

The advanced countries commit so much budgetary allocations to the tourism industry and they receive the biggest chunk of business travellers who have all the money to spend. In recent times, developing countries especially those in Africa have taken to tourism as one of the possible panaceas for their economic challenges. Notable among nations that have given priority to tourism on their developmental agenda are Malaysia, Morocco, Mauritius, Kenya, Egypt and Singapore. These countries invested so much into developing tourism and are making gains.

We are told that Ghana's tourism makes almost $1.1bn USD in foreign exchange earnings, contributing four percent to the national Gross Domestic Product and creates about 220,000 direct formal employments across the country.

Tourism Development

Tourism has become a major global economic activity. In many countries it has overtake agriculture and manufacturing. The diversification of Ghana's economy in 1985 and the need to shift focus from the over-reliance of the economy on the traditional commodities brought the tourism sector into the front line as a major economic activity that has the potential of resuscitating the ailing economy. Ghana offers a wide range of unique and exciting natural, cultural and historical resources which are highly undeveloped but must be developed. As a traditional export, tourism has the potential to become a powerful tool in pro-poor development strategies. It has the ability to create jobs and wealth. This potential can be realized if sound economic and social development strength of tourism is effectively mobilized to create wealth and fight poverty in the communities in particular and the country at large. The positive impact of tourism can be assessed in terms of foreign exchange earnings, employment and income as well as a conservation of the biodiversity and also a catalytic tool for the growth of other businesses. Indeed, the tourism sector in Ghana is experiencing some significant growth since 1996 with tremendous positive impact from the year 2000. The growth experienced re-emphases the government's commitment to the development of the tourism sector. This statement has been re-echoed by President John Agyekum Kufuor in his 2005 sectional address to parliament when he said, "tourism is a gold mine that must be tapped." Tourism in Ghana is indeed the untapped gold mine of the economy.

Even though about 80 percent of the tourism potentials of the country remains untapped it is the fourth foreign exchange earner of the country after remittances from abroad, Cocoa and Gold. However, the Ministry of Tourism and Diasporan Relations is the least resourced. This has led to little publicity, poor marketing, sites are not properly developed, no promotional materials, and hence, tourism is relegated to the background. Looking at the fact that tourism is the fourth foreign exchange earner in Ghana's economy without any efforts, imagine what will happen if it is given little push with funding and support.

Though the country is blessed with pristine beaches stretching over 500 kilometres, these beaches are left undeveloped while portions have been turned into places of conveniences. Our habitual littering is also anathema to tourism development. How do we expect tourists to repeat their visits if we are misusing our tourism assets? We are renowned for our hospitality but when it comes to providing services we are not up and doing. Tourism is a very competitive business as people demand value for money if we wish to make the requisite gains then we should put our house in order.

Tourism Development and Poverty Aliviation

The Tourism Ministry in Ghana recently adopted a new approach to tourism development that maximizes the net benefit of tourism to the poor. This concept "Pro-poor Tourism" enhances the linkage between tourism businesses and poor-people so that tourism's contribution to poverty reduction is increased through the active participation of the local people in the development of the tourism product. The travel and tourism industry is itself human-resource intensive due to the service nature of the industry. Additional, one job in the core tourism business creates about two additional jobs (indirect) in the tourism-related economy. Available statistics indicate that in the area of employment, between year 2000-2003, total employment in the tourism sector in Ghana increased from 90,000 (direct-26,000; indirect-64,000) to 127,645 (direct – 37,283; indirect-90,362) representing 42 percent increase. Of those employed 56 percent were males and 44 percent females. It is projected that by the year 2009, tourism will employ about 300, 000 people. The gender dimension here is very important: according to the United Nations Development Programme empirical evidence which suggests developing countries with less gender inequality tend to have lower poverty rate. The implication for us is that gender equality through creating opportunities for women, as is typical of the tourism industry, has much stronger effect on poverty and the national economy.

Ghana is certainly endowed with a wide range of unique and exciting natural, cultural, historical and heritage resources, majority of which are located in the rural areas of where poverty is endemic. These resources are however, underdeveloped to harness the fullest potentials for the benefit of the communities within which they are located. City, district, municipal and traditional authorities who make efforts at developing the tourism resources within their localities are making gains from their investment.

This effort offers a wide range of service providers in the community economic and social benefits. It enriches members of the community, thereby enhancing their social life since they could afford the very basic necessities of life through descent work. Tourism is said to have a multiplier effect, once it is well developed and promoted. A case study is the Hohoe Municipal Assembly that declared its highest revenue coming from their investment in tourism. About 19 ecotourism sites around the country are not exceptions.

Tourism is also a catalytic tool that boosts growth in the other sectors of the economy which equally employs a good number of people. The agricultural sector employs about 60 percent of the country's total labour force. The tourism sector provides ready market for farmers at the restaurants and traditional/indigenous restaurants thereby helping to sustaining farmers in their trade. It is an undeniable fact that, tourism also sustains the industrial sector by patronizing their product likewise the manufacturing sector. Producers of local textiles, that is, tie-dye and batik fabrics have their products highly patronize by tourists as unique identification of "been to" a destination.

The vision of the Tourism Ministry to support and promote the achievement of the overall vision of the Government of Ghana aims at achieving a per capita income of USD$1,000 by 2015 through the realization of the sector's full potential in contributing to economic wealth creation, employment generation, poverty reduction, environment conservation, as well as national and international cohesion. To achieve this vision, the Ministry seeks to attract about a million tourists which imply a corresponding growth in the expansion of tourism plants across the country including restaurants, pubs, night clubs, tourist receptacles, and the like. With the current incentives available to attract investors L.I. 1817 when effectively implemented there is the likelihood to realize the continued and fast growth in the expansion of tourism plants that create more descent jobs for the citizens.

Challenges Facing the Tourism Industry

The tourism industry is beset with scores of challenges. These include; poor marketing of Ghana as a destination; lack of Ghana Tourism Brand; low awareness of the potential of tourism as a viable economic sector; poor infrastructure especially poor condition of access roads to tourist sites; inadequate funding from government for the sector; and inadequate skilled manpower as well as lack of professionalism to enhance service delivery. Paucity budgetary allocation, lack of logistics, poor human resource base, lack of domestic awareness and patronage, waste management, lack of corporate support, lack of favourable credit facilities, the perception of tourism as a high risk sector, quality products and services, lack of branding, marketing and a respectable attractive tourism image abroad, rampant road accidents among others are myriad of problems that the Ghanaian tourism sector has to contend with. Other challenges include poor institutional commitment, collaboration and support for tourism development at the District level; slow private sector investment in the sector; limited capacity and access to credit especially women entrepreneurs such as caterers and local fast food vendors; poor waste management and sanitation especially in the major cities; Ghana perceived as a high cost destination in the sub-region due to relatively high air fares and hotel tariffs; and low budget allocation

Justification for Government Support to the Tourism Sector

The vision of Government is aimed at achieving a per capita income of USD$1,000 by 2015. This implies that all sectors of economy must ensure growth to aggregated meet this target. The tourism sector has the magic to attain the overall vision of the country. A simple statistical calculation as follows proves this magic. Considering the fact that, the average spending of a tourist as at 2006 is US$1,985 and average length of stay is 10-days. Ghana attracted 497,129 tourists. Mathematically, revenue accrued in 2006 total US$986,801,065. This imply that tourism per capita in Ghana is US$41.12 with the assumption that the population at then stood as 22 million. However, the ratio of international tourists to domestic tourist generated is 1:7, meaning each international tourist arrival has a complimentary seven domestic tourists. Conventionally, both tourists have the same expenditure pattern, it signifies that total receipts from the tourism sector is approximately US$ 6,907,607,455.00 and holding constant the total population, it's very convenient to conclude that the per capital income of tourism is say US$ 314.

Given that the Ministry is adequately resourced and all other factors favouring growth of the sector are conducive and we attract a million tourists as targeted it is very comfortable to say that the tourism sector could drive the growth Ghana needs to become a middle level income country. Therefore, we need a tourism fund, and serious talk on this is very important factor for tourism development. Financing and management are the most critical factors for tourism development.

Everything including product development, training and human resource development as well as marketing and promotions are directly dependent on financing and management. The financing factor or lack of it has had the most debilitating effect on our tourism development: the terms of banks for long-term financing are quite prohibitive and tourism projects tend to have long gestation periods. The solution to this palpable situation is the National Tourism Fund, whether it takes the form of a special bank or a revolving fund for the private sector tourism service and plant operators.

Tourism marketing starts with the products that we are promoting. Financing will determine how well we add value to our tourism resources. Financing will also determine how accessible our tourist products become to both our domestic and international markets. We need money to develop our attractions where value-adding is necessary. The Metropolitan, Municipal and District Assemblies need to invest in tourism and support tourism investments. Financing is necessary for reaching the markets that we find lucrative to tap and exploit. Marketing and promotions has become a complex, competitive and highly technology-based activity, not aided at all by the facts that tourism is highly competitive and has a highly elastic demand. The industry needs soft financing to support facility development, to provide infrastructure at our tourism hot spots, to do good maintenance on existing facilities and amenities, and to start new projects in an expanding industry. We need to use the opportunity to as a matter of urgency review outdated and archaic legislation and regulation that regulate our tourism industry, since the sector is very robust and dynamic. Sadly the Ghanaian sector is being regulated by laws as old as thirty years and above. The Ghanaian sector deserves better attention, since each and every hamlet, village, town, city, district or region in Ghana has one unique tourism plant or facility that are scattered around the country, whose potential is crying for exploration and development, which has the potential to ensure an even development of the country to above all stop the rural-urban drift, in search of non-existing white collar jobs.

Tourism thrives on good roads, portable water. Electricity and effective telecommunications apart from the attraction itself. Unfortunately, most, if not all, of our attraction sites are in their raw state and the only way to exploit this gold is to develop them to meet international standards. If the Ministry of Tourism and Diasporan Relations target of attracting one million tourists annually is attained, tourism will rake in $1.5 billion with the corresponding 300,000 employees in the sector.

Indeed, Ghana is endowed with a lot of natural resources, and there is enough we can do to compete with the International Community in terms of development. What we have, no country has, as far as Tourism is concerned. The industry is the only area that brings in foreign exchange earning without export It is an indisputable fact that Ghana has today emerged as a special African tourist destination, drawing people and visitors to experience not only its fascinating cultural diversity, history and natural endowments, but all that there is to go with peace, stability, good governance and a hospitable people.

It plays a central and decisive role in promoting the development of responsible, ?sustainable and universally accessible tourism, paying particular attention to the ?interests of developing countries.? Ghana's opportunity to use tourism as a major pillar for its economic growth is realistic. Globally, Tourism today, is the second largest industry, which employs the most people and it is still growing. It is the major foreign exchange earner of more than 60 countries. It creates jobs at all levels. From shoe shine boys and porters, through receptionists, tour guides, accountants, managers, and the like, tourism also creates micro and small enterprises. Tourism will create jobs, jobs, jobs-attractive jobs; productive jobs and for that matter reduce poverty.

Customer-Driven 'Green' Tourism

In its efforts to diversify the nation's economy, the Government of Trinidad & Tobago has identified tourism as an area of potential growth. In this respect, we may consider ourselves fortunate that several of our Caribbean neighbours have many years experience in the Tourism Industry. Barbados and Jamaica, for example, have been established tourist destinations for many decades. Even in the relatively new ecotourism thrust, Belize and Dominica have more experience than we do. Thus, the opportunity presents itself for us to learn from the experience of our neighbours. In particular, we can identify problems which they have experienced, and study how they sought to solve those problems.

This paper discusses the issue of Customer-driven Green Tourism, which is increasingly becoming an issue in neighbouring Caribbean islands. There are those who would consider Green Tourism to be a benefit to our countries, but anecdotal evidence suggests that the demands of the Green Movement are posing significant problems to the owners and operators of tourist plant. Specifically, questions have been raised about:

* The criteria applied by the «Greens»,
* The sources of data used to evaluate individual facilities,
* The transparency of the process, and
* The lack of recourse by facility owners/operators.

Each of these issues will be addressed in this paper, but first there is a brief introduction of the concept of «Green Tourism».

Green Tourism

Customer Discretion

Of all industries, Tourism is the one in which the customer has absolute discretion. The tourist may choose one destination or another, or none at all; applying any criteria he sees fit. Destinations and individual facilities must therefore seek to provide a product which will satisfy the requirements of a suitably large number of customers, or they will face financial ruin. After all, in this industry the Customer is Always Right!

Environmental Concerns

There has been a growing trend of environmental consciousness among tourists, particularly those from Europe. This has led to two trends:

* Ecotourism, and
* Green Tourism.

The Eco-tourist is one who has a keen interest in nature, and seeks a vacation which will maximize the naturalist experience. Ecotourism is the fastest-growing segment of the tourist industry, and Eco-tourists tend to spend more at their destination (per person, per day) than other types of tourist (Final Report on the Feasibility Study for the Bloody Nature Project, Tobago, prepared by Eco-engineering-Eco-logistics, 1997). In addition, many facets of nature can be used as the basis for an Ecotourism industry: mainland rain forests, island rain forests, coral reefs, marine turtle nesting, etc. It is therefore not surprising that many Caribbean countries (Belize, Dominica, Guyana and Trinidad & Tobago, to name a few) have opted to develop a strong Ecotourism component to their overall tourism product.

Green Tourists, in contrast, may not have as strong an interest in nature as Eco-tourists. However, they consider it important that the facilities which they use are designed and operated in such a way that adverse impacts on the environment are eliminated (or, at least, minimized). This is clearly a laudable approach, so why does it create a problem? Hotel operators in the Organisation of Eastern Caribbean States (OECS) can attest to the fact that enquiries received from European travel agents and tour operators now frequently include the question: «Is your hotel classified as environmentally friendly?». Implicit in this question is the assumption that there are accepted criteria for such classification; whereas in our region such criteria are not readily available. In the absence of ratings within the region, it appears that many potential tourists rely on environmental groups in their own countries to determine which facilities are «green», and which are not.

Green Classification

Criteria

Criteria for rating the «environment-friendliness» of any facility usually relate to:

* Operational Practices at the Facility,
* Services and Products used at the Facility, and
* Waste Disposal.

Operational practices cover a wide range of environmental concerns. External lighting of the facility and the nature and timing of sound emissions can affect neighbouring residents or wildlife in adjacent areas. The frequency of washing linen affects the water demand at the facility, as well as the volume of waste water that is generated. Similarly, the nature of detergents used will influence the type of impact which is experienced in receiving water bodies. In like manner, composting of part of the solid waste would reduce the load being placed on landfills.

In all cases, the diversity of the Caribbean region makes it very difficult to define a universally-applicable «best approach». For example, some facilities may reduce demand on the public electricity supply by the use of solar water heaters or on-site generation via windmills or solar cells.

This may not be a practical approach in other locations. Likewise, the use of treated waste water for irrigation of lawns and plants is very effective in dry islands like Barbados or the Bahamas. However, in places like Dominica or Trinidad & Tobago, irrigation during the rainy season has proved unmanageable.

In preparing this paper, enquiries were made to determine what criteria were used by international environmental groups in rating the «green» status of tourist facilities in our region.

Unfortunately, no definitive answers were received. However, there was a clear suggestion that the criteria are applied uniformly across the region, without considering the diversity of the region.

Rating

Having decided on a set of criteria, the second question relates to the actual process of rating. Simply put, there are concerns about the information being used to rate facilities. These concerns relate to:

* the Accuracy of the Information, and
* the Currentness of the Information.

As with the criteria, we were unable to ascertain the sources of information being used to rate specific facilities. It is doubtful if this information comes from «Official Sources», because few (if any) of our governments collect and publish data on this type. We are also unaware of any International Environmental Groups which actually visit our region to collect such information. This leaves two sources: local environmental groups and surveys/ questionnaires sent directly to owners/operators of tourist facilities.

The first concern is that the information used in rating facilities should be accurate. Regardless of whether the source of the information is a local environmental group or a questionnaire/ survey, the information must be validated. It would be foolhardy to assume that neither of these sources of information would bias the information to serve some ulterior purpose. In like manner, it is important that the information be kept up-to-date. Tourist facilities seldom remain in a fixed form over a long period. In the quest to satisfy their customers, frequent changes are made. Some of these changes would affect the «green» rating of the facility.

Transparency of the Process

Several owners/operators have complained that the present system of «green» ratings lacks transparency. Owners/operators of tourist facilities wish to know how the ratings are being done, and by whom. It is a fact that tourists (and by extension, travel agents and tour operators) consider these ratings (among other criteria) in deciding which facilities to use. The owners/operators feel that they should have access to the rating criteria (to make changes which would improve their rating), as well as the information used in rating (to ensure that it is accurate and current).

The enquiries made in preparation of this paper suggest that such transparency is lacking.

Lack of Recourse

Because of the lack of transparency, owners/operators of tourist facilities feel that they have no meaningful recourse if they are disadvantaged by the present rating system. If they do not know how the ratings are being arrived at, they cannot correct errors. Even where they learn «through the grape vine» that they have been given an undeserved poor rating, they are unsure where their complaint should be directed.

Environmental Management Systems

Benefits of EMS

The implementation of Environmental Management Systems (EMS) represents one approach to addressing some of the problems indicated above. These tools permit the facility operator to devise an Environmental Policy which recognizes the uniqueness of his facility as well as his country. By their very nature, these systems also address local regulations and standards. Finally, the EMS relies on progressive improvement toward the goals, so that the operator is not faced with a «pass/fail» choice, but rather one of management by objectives.

Cost Implications

Anecdotal evidence suggests that the cost of implementing an EMS, per se, is not necessarily prohibitive. However, the cost of certification can be significant. In the circumstances, the following suggestions are made to bring the EMS within the reach of small and medium operators in the tourism sector:

(i) The OECS Region should invest in the preparation of a Handbook on EMS, specifically designed for the needs of the Tourism Industry. This is not intended to «re-invent the wheel», but rather should be tailored to exclude many details which are included in general texts but which are not directly relevant to the Tourism Industry.

(ii) The OECS Region should also provide broad-based training to operators in the Tourism Industry to ensure that the nature, objectives and procedures of EMSs are generally understood.

(iii) The OECS should support initiatives by regional organizations to become registered as EMS Certifiers. For example, the Trinidad & Tobago Bureau of Standards has indicated that they will shortly seek such registration with the International Standards Organization. Having such a registered organization within Caricom (in contrast to bringing certifiers in from the metropolitan countries) will certainly lower the cost of certification.

(iv) The OECS should explore whether economies can be gained by grouping facilities for the purpose of EMS certification. The concept of «grouping» is different from the «generic EMS» which has been discussed in some quarters, in that it would involve the selection of facilities which have features in common, and are similarly located.

Dialogue

In suggesting an approach to solving the problems high-lighted above, several factors were considered:

* Customer-driven Green Tourism can be harnessed to the benefit of our Region. Thus, our thrust should be to improve, not to eliminate.
* International environmental groups tend to be very receptive to meaningful dialogue with local groups. Unfortunately, they have been less cooperative with «official» agencies.

The suggestion, therefore, is that the tourism industry in the Caribbean Region should engage the international environmental groups in a meaningful dialogue on the subject of «green» rating of individual facilities. This dialogue should be aimed at ensuring that ratings are based on criteria which are acceptable in the Caribbean and on data which is accurate and current. It should also seek to build the necessary transparency into the system. It is our opinion that an industry grouping, such as the Caribbean Tourism Organization, would be more likely to succeed in this endeavour than a governmental organization.

Tourism in the Polar Regions: Facts, Trends and Impacts

This section describes how polar tourism grew to become a mature and highly diversified industry in both Polar Regions; the characteristics of its current operations; and prominent factors that will affect its future. This information is essential for understanding tourism's present and future impacts on the Polar Regions.

Evaluating tourism impacts, both beneficial and otherwise, requires knowledge of total numbers as well as where, when, and how tourists cause impacts. For example, the many thousand cruise-ship passengers who passively view the Arctic from offshore, and occasionally disembark to visit land based souvenir shops, affect the region in ways that differ from the smaller numbers actively engaged in Ecotourism or wilderness recreations activities such as river rafting, mountaineering, and sport fishing. By accurately identifying the full array of tourist activities and their behavioural patterns, then placing that information within the context of their natural and human resource settings, we can begin to understand key relationships.

Nearly Two Centuries of Arctic Tourism

The Arctic has attracted tourists since the early 1800's. The earliest Arctic tourists were individual anglers, hunters, mountaineers, and adventurers attracted to abundant fisheries, exotic wildlife species, and remote regions. Many articles describing their recreational pursuits appeared in the growing genre of recreation, mountaineering, hunting, and fishing periodicals that emerged in the mid-1800's. During the same era, several pioneering travellers to the Arctic published journals that became popular guide books for future Arctic tourists.

Mass tourism in the Arctic has thrived since the mid-1800's when steamships and railroads aggressively expanded their transportation networks providing access to numerous destinations throughout the Arctic. Tourism entrepreneurs, such as Thomas Cook, formed partnerships with railroad and steamship companies and thereby pioneered the popular tourism industry. By the 1880's, the "Land of the Midnight Sun" in the Scandinavia Arctic, Alaska, and the popular excitement of the Klondike Gold Rushes firmly established the Arctic's mass tourism market.

During the past two centuries numerous advances in transport technologies have contributed to the steady growth of Arctic tourism. At the present time, advanced ship technologies together with improved marine charts and navigational aids have allowed cruise ship travel to increase exponentially. Diesel locomotives, four wheel drive and tracked vehicles further opened access to vast regions of the Arctic. And, most importantly, air transport in all of its forms, provides immediate travel to the Arctic. Collectively, these improved transport technologies not only added numbers of tourists, but also expanded the seasonal and geographical reach of Arctic tourism.

Antarctic Tourism

Antarctic tourism began in 1957-59 with four visits by Argentinean and Chilean naval transports, which accommodated tourists whose fares helped to pay costs of servicing the national expeditions. Antarctica received extensive international publicity from the explorations led by Richard Byrd, Vivian Fuchs and Edmund Hillary.

Entrepreneurial tour operators recognized the commercial value of feasible access and positive international publicity. In 1966 Lars Eric Lindblad began expedition cruising to the Antarctic and initiated the use of zodiacs to land passengers at diverse sites. As a result of the success of the Lindblad model, government affiliated voyages were quickly superseded by dedicated cruises in small 'expedition' ships carrying 50-120 passengers. For many years this type of travel dominated the trade. Increasing numbers of expedition ships are transporting larger numbers of passengers, and making more landings at several hundred sites. The first larger cruise ship to enter the field, Ocean Princess in 1990-93, had a capacity of 480 passengers, but carried only 250-400 on its annual Antarctic voyages. The most recent development has been the advent from 2000 of liners carrying between 800 and 3,700 passengers, including crew members.

Over the last decades, tourism activities have expanded tremendously with the number of ship-borne tourists increasing by 430 % in 14 years and land-based tourists by 757 % in 10 years (IAATO 2007). The tremendous increase of ship-borne tourism and its impacts on the Antarctic environment resulted in the members of the Antarctic Treaty adopting a resolution (May 2007) which recommends the Parties of the Treaty to:

1. Discourage or decline to authorize tour operators that use vessels carrying more than 500 passengers from making any landings in Antarctica; and
2. Encourage or require tour operators to:

a. Coordinate with each other such that not more than one tourist vessel is at a landing site at any one time;
b. Restrict the number of passengers on shore at any one time to 100 or fewer, unless otherwise specified in applicable ATCM Measures or Resolutions; and
c. Maintain a minimum 1:20 guide-to-passenger ratio while ashore, unless otherwise specified in applicable ATCM Measures or Resolutions.

Commercial air transport of tourists to the Antarctic includes both small groups travelling to the continent and larger numbers viewing from over flights. Adventure Network International (ANI) has been providing flight services to Patriot Hills in the Heritage Range since 1985 and other charter air companies have provided tourist transport between South Africa and Dronning Maud Land, and between Punta Arenas, Chile and King George Island.

Polar Tourism Today – Diverse and Growing

Polar tourism is now a mature industry providing diverse experiences in both Polar Regions. The polar tourism industry is enticing an increasing clientele with expanding numbers of attractions, recreational activities, international destinations, and visitor accommodations. And now that regularly scheduled excursion travel is provided to both the Arctic and Antarctic, year-round polar tourism has become a reality. Polar Tourism's Diverse Markets

Polar tourism is not a single, monolithic industry, but rather a collection of diverse specialty markets that appeal to an equally diverse clientele. Each of these distinct markets is growing and expanding for an obvious reason – they appeal to tourists who are willing to pay for the unique experiences they offer. The five highly specialized market segments currently dominating the polar tourism economy are best defined in terms of their primary attractions and the ways in which those attractions are experienced. This approach to classifying tourist markets explicitly acknowledges tourist expectations, the service delivery methods used to realize those expectations, and the distinct impacts resulting from those activities. The five markets are:

1. The mass market, comprised of tourists primarily attracted to sightseeing within the pleasurable surroundings of comfortable transport and accommodations.

2. The sport fishing and hunting market, with participants who pursue unique fish and game species within a wilderness setting.
3. The Ecotourism market, consisting of tourists who seek to observe wildlife species in their natural habitats, and experience the beauty and solitude of natural areas. These tourists are also concerned with conserving the environment and improving the wellbeing of local people.
4. The adventure tourism market, providing a sense of personal achievement and exhilaration from meeting challenges and potential perils of outdoor sport activities.
5. The culture and heritage tourism market, a very distinct market comprised of tourists who either want to experience personal interaction with the lives and traditions of native people, learn more about a historical topic that interests them, or personally experience historic places and artifacts.

Each market has distinct visitor experiences and economic dimensions, involving different tourists' motivations, expectations, on-site behaviour, and resource uses. Market segmentation provides a useful framework for understanding polar tourism in terms of the use of natural and cultural resources, economic activity, and visitor behaviour. But obviously, tourists themselves are not constrained by this classification: they participate freely in many types of activities.

The enormous geographic scope of the five markets deserves emphasis. All eight Arctic nations, and their seas and oceans host all five markets, while Antarctica hosts most of them with the exception of the sport fishing and hunting and the culture and heritage markets. Most of that geography consists of land masses that are true wilderness and oceans with the world's most severe maritime conditions. The challenge of managing tourism across those vast lands and seas is well known to the Arctic nations and to those concerned about Antarctic tourism.

Environmental, Economic, Social and Cultural Impacts of Polar Tourism

Environmental Impacts

There are serious concerns that tourism is promoting environmental degradation in the Polar Regions by putting extra pressures on land, wildlife, water and other basic necessities, and on transportation facilities (GEO 2002 and GEO 2006). According to the Arctic Council Working Group on the Conservation of Arctic Flora and Fauna (CAFF), the main environmental impacts of tourism in the Arctic are the following:

* The transport of tourists to the Arctic, in itself, increases the volume of ship and aeroplane traffic. In addition to the impacts on climate by long distance air and water traffic, increased ship traffic in these waters could lead to increased risks of groundings and other accidents, the results of which can include oil spills and other environmental consequences.
* Many visitors want to see areas of great beauty or richness, such as bird colonies, marine mammal haul-outs, and caribou aggregations. Because there are relatively few places where such sights are accessible and reliable, tourist traffic is often concentrated. Arctic vegetation is typically unable to withstand repeated trampling, and paths of bare ground have appeared in some heavily visited spots.
* Helicopters, used sometimes for recreational purposes, are noisy and produce a variety of sounds that are disturbing to seabirds. Helicopters cause panic flights and can lead to egg loss particularly in birds.
* In the forest-tundra areas of the Arctic, tourism, including sport hunting and fishing, attracts moderate though increasing numbers of visitors. This places additional pressure on the region's resources, sometimes leading to conflicts between local and visiting hunters. The forest-tundra in general has a low tolerance for trampling. Even the temporary presence of humans often leaves a lasting impact.
* Visits to Arctic seabird colonies by tourists are rapidly growing. Currently cruise ships visit or sail by colonies in the low and high Arctic of Canada, west Greenland, Iceland, Norwegian coast and Svalbard, eastern Russia, and the US (Alaska). Colonies chosen for visitation tend to be large and spectacular and usually are home to species such as murres, puffins, kittiwakes, and fulmars. During a colony visit, passengers typically board smaller boats

from the larger ships, and cruise by colonies observing the seabirds and taking pictures. Occasionally passengers make landings at suitable colonies and view the seabirds from above or below the cliffs.

* Recreational activities, such as boating and fishing, cause local disturbance at bird colonies in several Arctic countries. In the Russian far-east, coastal and lowland species such as ducks, gulls, terns and Spectacled Guillemots are frequently disturbed by visitors.
* Garbage, waste, and pollution are significant problems for many tourism operations, especially as decomposition is slow and waste remains visible atop the permafrost in many Arctic areas.

In the Antarctic the most important impact of tourism concerns the disturbance of cetaceans. Certain studies have lent increasing strength to concerns that human activities may be influencing the fitness of these animals. Tourism activities in Antarctica present also a risk to the marine environment (pollution resulting from operations or maritime accident (e.g. grounding)) as well as to terrestrial ecosystems as over 80 % of the tourists land one or more times during their journey (introduction of alien species; disturbance of birds colonies; damage to the vegetative cover (e.g. lichen). In addition, high-risk unsupported (adventure) tourism can potentially impact on national research programmes in terms of search and rescue operations. The main positive impact of polar tourism, if well done, is its educational value. Arctic and Antarctic visitors are fascinated by the sheer beauty, wilderness and natural phenomena of the polar environment. This can be used to make them not only to ambassadors for the protection of the visited regions, but also supporters of conservation activities and organizations worldwide.

Economic Impacts

Growing public and private resource commitments to promote and further develop tourism demonstrate strong intentions to strengthen tourism's economic role in the Arctic. Given these circumstances, economic impacts, both positive and negative, include the following:

* Many Arctic people seeking economic security perceive tourism as a positive means for improving economic

stability. From their perspective, reliance on predictably arriving tourists offers a more stable economic outlook than exhausting finite natural resources to meet the boom and bust needs of world markets.

* Arctic communities generally appreciate the economic benefits resulting specifically from the angling, hunting, and nature tourism market because most tourist expenditures remain in the community. Tourists employ local guides, pilots, charter boat captains and crews, outfitters, and suppliers. They use local transport, stay in local accommodations, and eat in local establishments.
* Culture and heritage tourism provides critical support for language preservation, the practice of traditional ceremonies, and the perpetuation of ancient customs and art forms. The presence of appropriate and effective interpretation and education methodologies will dramatically impact effectiveness. Additionally, this form of tourism creates a market for art and other native manufactures and services.
* The cost of building, operating, and maintaining tourism infrastructure is a huge economic burden for Arctic communities and governments. Support facilities and services of all types are built and maintained to serve relatively large numbers of persons that exceed the resident population. Transport facilities, law enforcement, medical services, other emergency services, water and waste water utilities, and waste collection and disposal incur capital and operating costs, require advanced work force skills, spare parts, and need specialized supplies in order to sustain there functions. Tourism normally occurs for a few months of the year, but the infrastructure must be maintained under adverse conditions for the entire year.
* The economic and human costs of providing emergency services deserve special attention. Highly trained personnel, many of whom are volunteers, risk their lives in search and rescue operations. Expensive transport and medical equipment and supplies are required to evacuate victims and treat their injuries. Law enforcement resources must respond to large populations visiting their

communities and need specialized equipment to patrol back country regions. Fire suppression service faces similar challenges.

* The cost of responding to environmental hazards is included in the budgets of all Arctic nations, but may not be sufficient. Oil spill containment and recovery, hazardous materials handling and storage, and hazardous waste disposal all represent substantial costs. Adequate funds and the availability of specialized equipment, trained personnel, and essential supplies may or may not be sufficient to respond to events.
* Finally, the question of who benefits economically from large-scale Arctic tourism is a very sensitive issue. Many of the transport, tour and hotel corporations conducting tourism in the Arctic are head quartered outside the region. Consequently, much of the money paid by polar tourists to those nonresident corporations escapes the Arctic people.

The continent of Antarctica derives absolutely no economic benefits from tourism, but can suffer environmental and heritage resource costs. Unlike most parts of the world, there are no indigenous people to benefit from tourism in Antarctica and thus tourism is not an alternative to local unsustainable economics activities. This blunt fact is a serious consideration for anyone motivated to propose tourism management practices on the southern continent. There is no continuous stream of money devoted to tourism management, environmental monitoring, emergency services, waste collection and disposal, the design and implementation of risk minimization or mitigation programmes, or any other "best practices" normally associated with reasonably managed tourism. Specifically:

* Aside from the fees collected by the Antarctic Historic Places Trust to maintain heroic era huts in the Ross Sea region, no revenues or fees of any sort are collected from either tour operators or the tourists themselves for the management of Antarctica's environmental resources. Some scientific stations and heritage sites generate revenues from the sale of souvenirs, but these are neither

dedicated to resource management nor sufficient to support tourism management programmes.

* As with all who travel to Antarctica, costs are incurred by tour operators for the preparation of environmental impact assessments required by the Protocol on Environmental Protection to the Antarctic Treaty. Scientific stations incur costs for the assistance they provide in emergency situations such as search and rescue or medical support. The true costs of emergency response include not only direct expenses for personnel and equipment, but the risk to additional lives and distraction from scientific missions.
* To the credit of many tourists who learn about Antarctica's economic dilemma, generous personal donations have been given in support of environmental research and heritage preservation projects in Antarctica and the sub-polar islands.

Social Impacts

There are serious concerns regarding the negative impacts of a growing tourism industry to the people in the Arctic world. Social norms, values and unique ways of life are all subjected to impacts from polar tourism. Tourism impacts affecting polar communities and their people are presented below.

* The most obvious social impacts result from the number of visitors that temporarily overwhelm the social norms of some Arctic communities during tourist season. Community institutions such as educational, religious, and civic organizations often experience altered roles and functions when the tourists are in town. Based on the attitude of the community, this may or may not be a major disruption, but large numbers of tourists relative to local populations always exerts a dominant presence.
* Social impacts of Arctic tourism can be mitigated by the terms and conditions of collaborative agreements between the tour operators and the local community. In some instances, tax revenues and special fees can offset local costs. When tourist seasons are expanded there are greater economies of scale and efficiencies result from the extended use of infrastructure and longer duration of employment and income benefits.

Cultural Impacts

The Arctic environment is not merely a setting in which a rich diversity of Native People live, but rather it encompasses the essential resources upon which the lives and culture depend. Consequently, any events that endanger those resources place Native People at grave risk. By their own declarations the most severe threat facing Native People is climate change. The loss of Arctic sea ice with its attendant effects on wildlife habitat, numbers, and migratory behaviour; the transport routes needed to subsist; the duration of seasons; and the condition of fisheries are of critical importance to the cultural and economic wellbeing of Arctic people. According to a statement by Sheila Watt-Cloutier, former International Chair, Inuit Circumpolar Conference:

"What is at stake here is not just the extinction of animals but the extinction of Inuit as a hunting culture. Climate change in the Arctic is a human issue, a family issue, a community issue, and an issue of cultural survival."

The cultural impacts described below must be evaluated from that perspective.

* Large numbers of tourists can produce significant cultural resource impacts. They further stress increasingly scarce natural resources and that results in a variety of pressures on indigenous subsistence practices and value systems.
* Ironically, as traditional indigenous lifestyles succumb to change resulting from climate change, there will be fewer opportunities for tourists to support authentic cultural traditions. This will affect Arctic culture and economies.
* In addition to their numbers, the introduction of technologies and tourist service amenities can impact Native People's desires to maintain traditional lifestyles.
* Intrusive, inappropriate visitor behaviour violates traditional customs. Tours that do not include educational practices can generate conflicts that damage both Native People's quality of life and the tourist experience. When that happens, both parties lose.
* In summary, the ways in which Arctic communities allow their natural and cultural resources to be used affects the character of those communities. As Arctic communities continue to achieve self determination, they will

increasingly decide how their natural and cultural resources will be utilized and this will ultimately determine how those resources are managed. Arctic communities and Native People must determine how tourism will, or will not, occur and how natural and cultural resources should be used and safeguarded. They can be aided by good management practices that are relevant to their objectives. But the final decisions regarding natural and cultural resource uses must be made locally. Any other solution would be yet another example of intrusion from the "outside".

The Outlook for Polar Tourism: Reduced "Barriers to Entry"

Polar tourism expands because of a continuous reduction of what economists call "barriers to entry". The concept suggests that the extent to which these barriers are increased, reduced, altered, or eliminated directly controls the amount, geographic distribution, seasonal duration, and types of tourism likely to occur. Since its inception, the most difficult barriers confronting polar travel include difficulty of access, environmental conditions (both real and perceived), cost of travel, time to travel, and jurisdictional restraints. Both human-induced and natural events are making the Polar Regions increasingly accessible. Vastly improved geographic and hydrographic knowledge; advancements in transport and navigational technologies; more comfortable clothing; more durable recreational equipment; significant reductions in the amount, extent and duration of sea ice; and a relatively more tolerable climate are all contributing to growing access to the Polar Regions. The cumulative impacts of these events are larger numbers of polar tourists spending more time in more locations.

Conclusion

Polar tourism was slow to start, but is now a popular and rapidly-growing industry that is expanding in terms of tourists, tour operators, diverse recreational pursuits, geographic scope, and seasons of use. Arctic economies have seen it evolve from an incidental activity to a vital sector upon which they increasingly rely. This has been particularly true for newly enfranchised indigenous people of the Arctic seeking self-sufficiency, and for gateway cities in the southern hemisphere eager to realize the economic benefits of Antarctic tourism.

Sustainable Tourism in the Polar Regions: Setting an Agenda

The conservation and sustainable management of polar environments and cultures including by means of good tourism practices will require both mutually accepted goals and a solid commitment to implement appropriate management techniques. Fortunately, the first of those tasks has been carefully deliberated by the international community. As previously stated, the United Nations Environment Programme and the United Nations World Tourism Organization engaged diverse stakeholders from around the world to establish 12 sustainability principles that are fully listed below. When summarized, those principles identify goals essential for achieving sustainable tourism. Again, those goals are:

* Conserving environmental quality.
* Preserving cultural and social values by means of participatory decision-making.
* Creating sustainable economies.
* Ensuring positive visitor behaviour, safety, and enjoyment.

Though relatively new, polar tourism is old enough to have established recognizable patterns of procedure, and mature enough-even in its newest venue Antarctica-to have accumulated extensive management experiences. Well documented knowledge of tourism management techniques, resource conservation programmes, industry practices, jurisdictional responses, economic strategies, and community opinions and expectations currently exist to provide the basis for sustainable polar tourism policies and practices.

Simultaneously, while tourism's presence is growing numerically and spatially, the polar environment itself is experiencing significant change. This section describes tourism management conditions, issues and techniques that are relevant to sustaining the environmental and cultural integrity of the Polar Regions. This information is further reinforced by examples of good polar management practices presented in the final section of this publication.

Management Conditions: Wilderness

Polar tourism most frequently occurs in immense wilderness regions, either de-facto or officially designated, and these vast areas are exceedingly difficult to manage. The Polar Regions contain the world's largest expanses of wilderness-places where human presence and development are virtually absent or not readily apparent. The continent of Antarctica is entirely a wilderness land mass. North America's and Eurasia's largest wilderness regions are located in the Arctic. Fully reliable sets of marine charts and hydrographic information for the Southern and Arctic oceans are not yet available.

These enormous wilderness areas and relatively unknown marine regions provide permanent habitat for highly adapted indigenous wildlife and seasonal habitat for immense populations of migratory wildlife. Arctic wilderness is the homeland of diverse Native Peoples who have practiced cultural traditions for millennia. The Antarctic contains important artifacts of the history of exploration and scientific discovery. Wilderness regions also possess highly esteemed scientific, inspirational and conservation values. For most of their existence these polar resources and values were protected by their remoteness and climatic conditions. Again, wilderness regions present unique management challenges. Comprehensive inventories of their natural and cultural resources are time-consuming and expensive to obtain. A competent knowledge of their dynamic ecological systems requires long-term investigations that are equally complicated and costly to accomplish. Establishing mutually acceptable methods to facilitate stakeholder participation in wilderness planning and management are difficult to implement, and frequently contentious.

Management Issues

Scarce Management Resources

The absence of development may be essential for sustaining the integrity of wilderness values, but it is also a huge obstacle in the performance of environmental and tourism management. The Arctic's scarce infrastructure in terms of transportation systems, number of trained personnel, and service facilities are severe constraints on managing the impacts of tourism. Operational functions essential for meeting the demands of large numbers of tourists, such as resource conservation, resource monitoring, scientific research, security patrolling, visitor safety, waste collection and disposal, and emergency response capabilities are all affected by the scarcity of infrastructure.

In the Antarctic the situation is even worse. Unlike the Arctic, there are no resources located on the continent specifically dedicated to supporting tourism's expanding presence and growing access. International policy strongly advocates environmental conservation of the entire continent, but the fact remains that because the Antarctic Treaty System cannot tax, there is no money to support on site management. Consequently, there are neither land nor marine Antarctic-based resources dedicated to the management of tourism activities. The Protocol on Environmental Protection to the Antarctic Treaty requires environmental impact assessments of tour operations. Although the inspection regime established under article 14 of the Madrid Protocol could also apply to tourism activities, there are no adequate international monitors to ensure compliance with assessment requirements or that proposed mitigation measures are implemented.

Both Arctic resource managers and Antarctic tour operators are keenly aware of these constraints and have adapted to them. Specialized wilderness management techniques affecting the number and distribution of tourists; educational programmes to promote appropriate behaviour; and self-reliant practices extending from waste collection to the provision of emergency services have been implemented. Valuable information regarding their effectiveness may be found in the wilderness recreation management studies published during the past 40 years.

Environmental Management Issues – Who did what?

Polar tourism must be conducted in a responsible manner and tourism management techniques are often suggested for conserving the polar environment. One of the supreme difficulties for accomplishing this objective is to accurately determine the environmental cause and effect and then manage tourism accordingly. In other words, when an environmental condition changes, the question becomes whether it was caused by a natural event, by tourism activity, or by some combination of both? The capacity to accurately monitor tourism, revise tourism management plans, alter visitor activities and behaviour, and implement appropriate environmental conservation measures depends on the answers to those questions. Realistically, the ability to assess and manage tourism impacts in the Polar Regions is vitally dependent on a competent understanding of those relationships.

Environmental cause and effect relationships affecting the Polar Regions also result from events occurring well beyond the high latitudes. Wildlife populations that seasonally migrate to the Polar Regions from other regions of the world are impacted by changing oceanographic conditions, environmental pollution, hunting and fishing pressures, and habitat transformations that are well beyond the jurisdictional boundaries of polar resource agencies. The cumulative impacts of these complex environmental changes are a colossal challenge to comprehend, much less competently manage. When polar tourism is mixed with this collection of dynamic, naturally occurring events, reliable understanding of those interdependency is further complicated.

Cultural Management Issues

Numerous cultural traditions pervade the Arctic, many of them derived from centuries of habitation by indigenous people. Others are the culmination of settlement patterns, resource uses, economic systems, and social customs evolved from empire building and the desires of sovereign nations. These very complex heritage and cultural traditions of Arctic societies are simultaneously tourist attractions and sensitive management issues. In Antarctica defining the 'allowable and acceptable' visitor uses of heritage sites and resources is a particularly difficult task. Internationally significant heritage resources associated with polar discovery, scientific inquiry, historical economic development, and human settlement are located throughout the southern polar region.

The abandonment of those sites, the absence of a permanent population to perform conservation, and severe weather has resulted in deterioration. Resource management issues at these sites include environmental remediation, heritage conservation, visitor safety, and the creation of interpretive services that simultaneously preserve the story of these places and enlist the respect of their visitors. These are daunting tasks given the absence of resources dedicated to these purposes.

The sub-polar islands in the southern hemisphere possess sovereignty status and the authority to implement heritage conservation programmes. Many resource conservation activities have taken place, but the scarcity of financial resources and the remoteness of the sites are ever-present impediments to this effort (UNEP-WCMC, 2006,a,b,c).

Managing Tourist Behaviour and Numbers

The history of tourism proves that increased access inevitably leads to increased numbers. This is a serious management concern. In fact, improved access causes various numbers to increase, e.g., number of sites visited, extended use of seasons, greater duration of stay, types of recreational activities pursued, additional support staff required, and more services needed. The results are an increased exposure of environmental resources to additional risks, the economic dependencies of local communities on tourism, threats to privacy, more cultural contacts, and growing demands on infrastructure.

An enduring criticism of tourism is tourist behaviour. Since its inception, tourists have been universally criticized for "inappropriate" behaviour and cultural insensitivities. When tourist behaviour results in resource damage, then condemnations and tough responses are well deserved. On other occasions, criticisms of visitor behaviour more accurately reflect opinion rather than proof of harm. In all instances, efforts are required to hold both the tourist and the tourism industry accountable.

From the tourist's viewpoint, the issue of numbers equates to perceptions of congestion, and this directly affects the quality of their tourism experience. The tourist's perception of congestion in the Polar Regions is an especially critical issue because these locations are strongly promoted as wilderness.

International Policy Issues

Polar climate and associated ecological changes are fueling international discussions concerning foreign policy. For tourism management, the resolution of those issues will be critical. Decisions regarding sovereign powers and jurisdictional boundaries determine the terms and conditions for allowable uses of Arctic resources. Alteration of wildlife, fishery and marine mammal treaty obligations, management practices and jurisdictional boundaries will directly impact tourism activities such as wildlife viewing, nature tours, angling, and hunting.

Arctic Governance Issues

The wilderness management dilemma faced by Arctic governments is to determine when, where, and how people should be allowed to use areas without destroying the natural character. In other words, what human activity should be permitted in an area universally defined as having no human presence? Governments throughout the world have responded to this challenge in a variety of ways. Management techniques range from strict restrictions of public access to participatory approaches that combine resource inventories, environmental assessments, and public involvement to define allowable uses. The most severe restrictions seek to achieve preservation by preventing human entry. The goal of the more collaborative approaches is to identify allowable uses based on science and citizen input and then test the effectiveness of those decisions by means of careful resource monitoring.

Enormous expanses of the Arctic are governed by the customs and traditional laws established and enforced by Native Communities. The Inuit in Canada, Greenland, and Eastern Russia, the Saami in Scandinavia, and diverse Native Peoples in both Russia and Alaska exercise combinations of traditions and sovereignty to determine the allowable recreational use of their land and water. These customs and the terms and conditions expressed in their management approaches offer valuable experiences that can be replicated in other parts of the Polar Regions.

Finally, it is acknowledged that politics and the competition for budgets are perpetual management issues affecting the governance of Arctic tourism. Officials responsible for wilderness recreation management realize that success in the political and budget arenas depends on providing quality tourism experiences to the public and economic benefits to local communities. They must demonstrate that the fees they collect from recreation activities and associated economic benefits to local communities justify their budgetary requests. Recreation managers have navigated this difficult course for a long time, and make considerable efforts to demonstrate that recreation participation is strong and growing.

Human activities in Antarctica are primarily regulated by the complex of multilateral agreements of the Antarctic Treaty System, in particular the Antarctic Treaty itself and its Madrid Protocol on Environmental Protection. The Antarctic Treaty was adopted on 1 December 1959. Its primary purpose is to ensure, in the interest of all mankind, that Antarctica shall continue forever to be used exclusively for peaceful purposes and shall not become the scene or object of international discord. The Treaty provides for freedom of scientific investigation and promotes international cooperation in scientific research. It also prohibits any nuclear explosions and the disposal of radioactive waste material in Antarctica. In order to further the protection of the Antarctic environment, a Protocol to the Antarctic Treaty on Environmental Protection was adopted in 1991.

The main purpose of the Protocol is to provide for the comprehensive protection of the Antarctic environment and dependent and associated ecosystems. The Protocol designates Antarctica as a natural reserve, devoted to peace and science; prohibits mineral resource activities other than scientific research; and sets principles and measures for the planning and conduct of all activities in the Antarctic Treaty area. Guidelines have been developed under this protocol to provide a framework for regulation of the potential negative impacts of tourism in the Antarctic. As tourist activities on the continent continue to grow the ATS is intensifying its focus on these issues.

Management Techniques

The UNEP and UNWTO have established 12 principles essential for accomplishing sustainable tourism. These principles represent guidelines for establishing and evaluating effective tourism management techniques. "The twelve aims for an agenda for sustainable tourism" are presented below and comprehensively discussed in the UNEP/UNWTO publication entitled Making Tourism More Sustainable A Guide for Policy Makers.

1. *Economic Viability:* To ensure the viability and competitiveness of tourism destinations and enterprises, so that they are able to continue to prosper and deliver benefits in the long term.
2. *Local Prosperity:* To maximize the contribution of tourism to the economic prosperity of the host destination, including the proportion of visitor spending that is retained locally.

3. *Employment Quality:* To strengthen the number and quality of local jobs created and supported by tourism, including the level of pay, conditions of service and availability to all without discrimination by gender, race, disability or in other ways.
4. *Social Equity:* To seek a widespread and fair distribution of economic and social benefits from tourism throughout the recipient community, including improving opportunities, income and services available to the poor.
5. *Visitor Fulfilment:* To provide a safe, satisfying and fulfilling experience for visitors, available to all without discrimination by gender, race, disability or in other ways.
6. *Local Control:* To engage and empower local communities in planning and decision making about the management and future development of tourism in their area, in consultation with other stakeholders.
7. *Community Wellbeing:* To maintain and strengthen the quality of life in local communities, including social structures and access to resources, amenities and life support systems, avoiding any form of social degradation or exploitation.
8. *Cultural Richness:* To respect and enhance the historic heritage, authentic culture, traditions and distinctiveness of host communities.
9. *Physical Integrity:* To maintain and enhance the quality of landscapes, both urban and rural, and avoid the physical and visual degradation of the environment.
10. *Biological Diversity:* To support the conservation of natural areas, habitats and wildlife, and minimize damage to them.
11. *Resource Efficiency:* To minimize the use of scarce and non-renewable resources in the development and operation of tourism facilities and services.
12. *Environmental Purity:* To minimize the pollution of air, water and land and the generation of waste by tourism enterprises and visitors.

As stated in the UNEP/UNWTO publication: "The order in which these twelve aims are listed does not imply any order of priority. Each one is equally important." While all of these principles cannot be applied in the Antarctic and some Arctic regions (because of the absence of indigenous population and the non existence of local economies), they provide a solid basis of management objectives and evaluative criteria for creating, implementing and evaluating sustainable polar tourism. Each principle also contains key words and phrases that identify factors that can be monitored to evaluate the effectiveness, equity and efficiency of those plans, strategies and techniques. Notably, the principles include factors that address both the quantity and quality aspects of the host region and the tourism experience. Given the diverse conditions found throughout the Polar Regions, the principles must be adapted to fit special circumstances.

The remainder of this section outlines tourism management techniques that have been effectively used in the Polar Regions. They are relevant to polar conditions and to the several distinct tourism markets operating in those regions.

Recreation Management in the Arctic Wilderness

As outlined in Section 3, the polar tourism market is now a highly diversified industry that attracts people to many wilderness recreation activities. Nature tourism, wildlife viewing, sport fishing, hunting, and wilderness adventures of all types are actively pursued throughout all regions of the Arctic. In response to these recreation demands, Arctic resource managers have established numerous, specialized techniques to safeguard both the environment and the tourist. These techniques have an extensive history of addressing the Arctic's environmental conservation issues and the opportunity exists to expand their use in the Arctic.

Wilderness recreation approaches used in the Arctic are normally an integral part of comprehensive wilderness resource plans. Responsible stewardship, defined as the conservation of its natural and cultural resources, requires the selection of objectives that define the appropriate and allowable uses of those resources and the establishment of management techniques that protect those resources from loss or damage. In the Arctic, as elsewhere, the primary wilderness management objective associated with tourism is to protect both polar resources and tourists from harm. This approach to wilderness management is employed by all Arctic nations.

Wilderness management plans and the recreation management techniques they endorse are the result of substantial stakeholder involvement. Government agencies responsible for resource management of protected areas seek advice from a variety of stakeholders. Participatory processes and competing interests vary among jurisdictions, but the issue of allowable tourism is always part of these lively discussions. Significantly, polar tourism is only one of many competing resource uses confronting Arctic wilderness managers as they attempt to reconcile economic development interests with the protection of wilderness values. A wealth of tourism management experience can be obtained from the public records that document those decision making processes.

The techniques described below are utilized by wilderness agencies to manage both the independent back country traveller and small groups pursuing recreation activities. The techniques are designed to optimize scarce management resources and, to a considerable extent, hold tourists personally responsible for their own safety. They also respond to the need to manage both general, short term use of wilderness resources and recreation activities requiring special expertise and the use of specific locations. They are especially applicable to three distinct polar tourism market groups: (1) the nature and Ecotourism market; (2) the sport fishing and hunting market; and (3) the adventure market.

Controlling and Monitoring Back country Use

Arctic wilderness managers implement land and water resource management plans that designate specific recreation entry points. These gateways to diverse wilderness experiences may be trail heads, information kiosks, interpretive centres, ranger stations, boat ramps, hunting zones, fishing sites, or kayak put-in sites. The primary purpose of these widely publicized locations is to intercept the tourist before they venture into the wilderness. When this "capture technique" is successful, managers can dispense vital information while simultaneously learning when, where, and how people are travelling through wilderness lands and waters.

This technique requires agencies to designate allowable recreation uses in specific locations and relies on tourists to let them know exactly how and when those resources are being used. Managers then monitor recreation activity locations to determine if current recreational use should be continued, modified or prohibited. Elements of this approach include:

* Before departure the tourists are advised to read all pertinent regulations, obtain maps, essential supplies and equipment, and relevant guide books.
* Given a scarcity of agency personnel or lack of funds for visitor centres, wilderness recreation information is often provided at entry kiosks, or by means of signage. Obviously, selecting the foreign languages to be used will directly impact the effectiveness of this information.
* Back country travellers are requested to identify their route and mode of travel. This is generally done by means of registrations at trailheads and boat launch sites. Identification of their intermediate camp sites and destinations is accomplished by back country permit registrations. Known hazards are identified and they are advised that their personal safety, including clothing and equipment, is their personal responsibility.
* In locations where search and rescue services are available, emergency instructions, such as communication frequencies and weather radio broadcasts, are provided with the assumption that the tourist has compatible communication equipment. Persons travelling by boat or kayak are required to possess proper vessel licenses and to have marine charts, tide tables, and adequate safety and navigational equipment on board. But there are rarely coast guard vessels to conduct inspections.
* Management objectives are enforced by periodic patrolling by authorized resource agency personnel. Patrolling is accomplished from strategically located fixed or seasonal bases. Patrols may be conducted by boat, aircraft and various modes of land travel. The availability and frequency of these enforcement resources is affected by financial and personnel resources, the ruggedness of the terrain, and weather conditions.
* Search and rescue and emergency response capabilities vary widely in the Arctic's wilderness areas. Their availability is generally dependent on agency resources, proximity to communities, terrain conditions, and the severity of the weather. For all remote Arctic settlements, the commitment by volunteers to perform these functions is vital.

* Resource monitoring is conducted by resource agency personnel or designated persons with special skills. The frequency and rigor of these monitoring and evaluation endeavors are dependent on the budgetary and personnel resources of the lead agency and support received from NGO's dedicated to support the agency's resource conservation mission. Arctic NGO's play a vital role in this regard. Their commitment of volunteer personnel, fund raising, public awareness, and political advocacy provide invaluable contributions to the conservation of Arctic resources. Therefore, it is well justified to ask polar tourists to become active supporters of such organizations.

These management techniques have been used by Arctic resource agencies in national parks for more than a century. National governance of Arctic wildlife refuges, forest reserves, and UNESCO World Heritage and Biosphere sites rounds out a list of prominent environmental settings offering important sustainability experiences. Site management practices, participatory decision making processes, partnerships with stakeholders, and commitment to international resource conservation agreements are all embodied in the roles and responsibilities of these resource agencies.

Licensed Guides and Special Use Permits

One of the most successful management techniques for conserving Arctic resources and directly influencing lawful visitor behaviour is guide licensing. Wildlife managers realized long ago that an effective way to insure regulatory compliance was to require anglers and hunters to employ licensed guides. Guide licensing programmes have been established by wildlife management agencies in all Arctic nations. The programmes instruct specialized knowledge of environmental conditions, resource laws and regulations, survival skills, and emergency response skills. Guide licenses are issued based on demonstrated competency of that knowledge and skills. In most jurisdictions refresher courses are required to sustain both educational knowledge and practical skills.

Guide licensing in the Arctic has expanded well beyond angling and hunting. The pursuit of Arctic recreation activities such as mountaineering, rafting, kayaking, and wildlife photography frequently require licensed guides with the special skills required to safely conduct those activities. Licensing requirements vary considerably among Arctic jurisdictions and responsible resource agencies, but fundamental requirements required by all include: proven knowledge of specific locations, technical skills, safe and efficient recreation delivery systems, waste removal, emergency response systems, and detailed reporting of activities and observations. This skill and knowledge takes time to acquire, thus Arctic jurisdictions established a process that evolves from apprenticeship to master status.

States exercising jurisdiction in the Arctic hold guides directly responsible for both resource protection and visitor safety. Critical management issues concerning liability for resource damage and human harm are explicitly addressed by a combination of license requirements that include adequate insurance coverage, bonding, and indemnification. Based on the huge risks they are legally required to accept, guides very diligently monitor the behaviour of their clients. Guides accept the professional and financial risks of their profession for the privilege of pursuing a unique way of life.

They generally spend a considerable amount of time teaching their clients appropriate behaviour, and respond quickly to instances when clients willfully disregard this information. Guide licensing regulations not only have beneficial affects on tourist behaviour, but on tourist numbers also. Legal prescriptions effectively limit tourist access by requiring they be accompanied by a licensed guide. Numbers are controlled by means of guide to visitor ratios, length of season, and sometimes duration of stay at a particular location. All of these methods strictly control the maximum number of people that may be on site. These requirements may be further specified in special use permits used to govern recreation activities. By example, the terms and conditions of river rafting, mountaineering, and wildlife viewing expeditions can be defined by special use permits.

Arctic guide licensing and the issuance of special use permits have proven to be effective polar tourism management techniques. They are an integral part of resource conservation programmes, such as wildlife management; they directly affect appropriate visitor behaviour and numbers; and the reports filed by guides provide vital resource monitoring information that would otherwise be unavailable. This approach to sustainable tourism has also established mutually beneficial partnerships between local communities and resource agencies. Native People and local residents who depend on polar resources for their cultural and economic wellbeing often serve as guides or possess special use permits to conduct recreation activities.

They are the strongest advocates of sustainable management of polar resources, and as guides, they provide a direct method for accomplishing wise stewardship. The application of a guide licensing programme to Antarctica deserves serious consideration. To date, Antarctic tourism has been conducted by knowledgeable persons who often have distinguished records of scientific service in Antarctica, but no formal training in the skills and techniques of guiding. As the number of Antarctic tourists increase there will be a corresponding need to supply more qualified guides. Proficiency in variety of skills including subject expertise, knowledge of the landing sites, emergency response and communication skills, and tourist management should constitute the basic requirements of the Antarctic guide.

These skills would help protect Antarctic resources; enhance the safety of the tourism experience; and advance the development of universal operational and communication protocols needed to respond to emergencies. For ship-based tourism, in particular, an education programme in polar tourism for guides should be considered. Cruise companies interested in high quality educational skills of their guides may support such an initiative and could request a certificate for their guides. Cooperation with environmental organizations in this field could lead to increasing benefits for conservation through advanced education.

The Special Case of Adventure Tourism the Arctic

Significant management challenges confront those responsible for accommodating the adventure tourism market. Principally, it is nearly impossible for Arctic recreation resource managers and licensed guides to competently know if the skill levels, health and psychological preparation of the participant are sufficient to meet the rigors of their sports.

Inspection of equipment should be conducted, but managers, guides and operators rarely have that opportunity, and usually do not have spare parts and repair facilities to correct deficiencies.

Maps, marine charts, tide tables can be supplied and it is hoped that adventurers will responsibly seek these essential aids to navigation. Emergency communication instructions in the form of emergency radio frequencies, protocols, directional beacons, and Standard Operating Procedures for search and rescue (if available) can also be provided. Again, it is essential for the adventurer to avail themselves of these in order to safely pursue their activities.

The Antarctic

For several decades Antarctica has attracted increasing numbers of adventure tourists. These activities range from relatively traditional outdoor sports to extreme events. More traditional pursuits have included mountaineering expeditions and numerous cross country skiing challenges. The more extreme sports include sky diving at the South Pole and scuba diving. A comprehensive discussion of this market and its management implications are found in Lamers, Stel, Amelung 2007.

Cultural Resource Management

The Arctic

A fundamental Arctic tourism management goal is to achieve balance between the public, commercial display of cultural features and the preservation of cultural integrity. Each culture has its own tolerance level for visitation and sharing its resources. Individual Arctic societies define acceptable visitor behaviour in terms of the types, magnitude, geographic location, and seasons of resource use. Consequently, cultural tourism management in the Arctic is subject to a set of 'host conditions' in which cultural preservation, economic necessity, and scarce natural resources are continuously debated. The conservation of ancestral homelands, scarce resources, and vulnerability to irreversible change are all significant tourism management issues facing Arctic indigenous societies.

From approximately the mid-1970s to the present, Native People have implemented a variety of policies, programmes, and techniques designed to uniquely reflect their approach to cultural tourism. In many instances these approaches are an affirmation of self-rule. When Alaskan Native Corporations and Villages were established they were empowered and capitalized to create economic development programmes. Several organizations pursued very conventional tourism development, such as hotels and similar commercial attractions, others instituted heritage tour programmes that represented their cultures. In the Canadian Arctic, the Inuit attained governance of Nunavut, a territory spanning one fifth of Canada's entire land mass. Nunavut has pursued various forms of tourism development during the past 25 years in response to this opportunity.

Attainment of Homeland Rule by the Inuit of Greenland in 1979 resulted in the initiation of a very aggressive tourism development programme that includes ambitious commercial activity in Nuuk and diverse venues in rural areas. The Saami throughout Norway, Sweden and Finland are especially active in designing, funding, and operating numerous types of tourism venues that reflect the diversity of their cultures. And the most recent entrant to the Arctic cultural tourism market is Russia's Association of Indigenous People of the North (RAIPON), established in 1990 to accomplish many goals, one of which is tourism development.

As with other forms of tourism management, there is a substantial history of cultural tourism experience in the Arctic. The lessons learned, both good and bad, provide valuable guidance for those seeking to either establish or modify cultural tourism programmes. But the foremost lesson is that Native People and their governments must be vitally involved in decisions regarding how their culture and resources are shared with others.

The Antarctic

Antarctic heritage sites are popular attractions because of their historical significance and because of family and cultural ties to the pioneering settlers who once worked there. Management responses to these demands for visitation have ranged from prohibited entry to cordial invitations. For example, despite the popularity of Sir Ernest Shackleton's exploits, tourist access is denied to Stromness, South Georgia because of environmental protection concerns, while visitor access to Grytviken, where 'the Boss' is traditionally toasted at his graveside, is encouraged. Antarctic heritage sites in the Ross Sea are permitted with strict, but hospitable controls, and the refurbished 1940s research station at Port Lockroy, in the Antarctic Peninsula Region, actively promotes tourism to share its colorful heritage and to commercially support its postal concession.

Managing the Mass Market

The Arctic

The Arctic's tourism management opportunities and constraints are obviously well known to its people, governments, conservation organizations, and the tour companies that operate there. In response to a strong desire to influence the growth and development of polar tourism, a meeting of affected stakeholders was facilitated in 1995 by the World Wildlife Fund Arctic International Programme (WWF Arctic, 1996). The result of that collaborative effort was the publication in 1996 of Linking Tourism and Conservation in the Arctic which contains ten principles for Arctic tourism and associated codes of conduct for both tour operators and tourists.

The participatory process and its product, as described by WWF Arctic, involved: "Representatives from local communities, governments, different sectors of the tourism industry, conservation organizations and scientific institutions used their experience to create these guidelines for arctic tourism. The principles were also adopted into Codes of Conduct for tourism business and tourists which contain more specific information on what to consider when doing business or travelling in the Arctic."

The Arctic's consensus-based Principles and Codes of Conduct offer a responsible approach to polar tourism management. The ten principles contain an appropriate collection of resource conservation goals, the essential starting point for resource management. Environmental conservation, cultural integrity, economic benefits, visitor safety, and respect for polar resources are comprehensively included in the Principles for Arctic Tourism. The principles are to be realized by two ten point Codes of Conduct for Tour Operators and Tourists in the Arctic, respectively. The direct relationships between the conservation goals and tourism practices by both operators and tourists are clearly described and represent the strength of this approach. The Principles and Codes are implemented by means of a comprehensive advocacy programme. Stakeholders collectively promote the Principles and Codes through information dissemination, consumer education, and personnel training. To date, they have been diligent in their efforts. The Principles and Codes are described in further detail in the Good Practices section of this publication.

The Antarctic

The first tourism-specific regulations were adopted by the Antarctic Treaty as early as 1966 with the emergence of commercial tourism activities. These regulations were setting rules for visits by tourist groups to Antarctic stations maintained by the Parties. In 1975 a Statement of Accepted Practices was adopted. This was modified and expanded several times and resulted in the Tourism Guidelines adopted in 1994 by the Parties to the Antarctic Treaty. Aside from establishing guidelines for tourist expeditions, the Parties to the Antarctic Treaty also require tourist expeditions to submit reports on their visits.

On August 2005 the UN Secretary General reported on the UN General Assembly on the "question of the Antarctica". The report recognizes that "Antarctic tourism activities are increasing, as is their diversity (camping, climbing, kayaking and scuba-diving), presenting new management challenges". As a first step towards a more rigorous control of tourism activities, the Antarctic Treaty Consultative Meetings (ATCMs) adopted two resolutions to enhance information exchange and consultation and to further the development and implementation of site-specific guidelines.

However, according to the Secretary General report, "no consensus has yet been reached on critical issues, such as land-based and high-risk (adventure) tourism, leaving tourism to be regulated to a large extent by the industry itself". The annual Antarctic Treaty Consultative Meetings (ATCMs) have been discussing tourism and tourism regulation in details since 2001. The Antarctic Treaty parties have adopted guidelines for visitors to the Antarctic. These guidelines are intended to ensure that wildlife and vegetation are not disturbed, protected areas and research programmes are respected, and activities are conducted with a high regard for safety. Guidelines for operators request that they provide advance notification of their activities, confirm visits to scientific stations, ensure that their passengers are properly supervised and report on their expeditions.

The requirements of the Madrid Protocol and other components of the Antarctic Treaty System are implemented by each Treaty party in its own laws, according to its legal system. Visitors to the Antarctic should ensure that they are familiar with the legal requirements that apply to them-for example, the applicable laws may be those of the country where the expedition is being planned, or the country from which the expedition departs. The most important legal requirements relate to prior environmental assessment of the proposed activities, prohibition on taking or harming flora and fauna, waste disposal, contingency planning and the need for permits if visits to protected areas are contemplated.

Complimentary to the regulatory framework created by the Antarctic Treaty System, one on-site management technique currently available for conserving the resources of the entire continent is self regulation of tourist operations and behaviour. The International Association of Antarctic Tour Operators was founded by seven private tour operators in 1991 and, as of 2007, had grown to include 80 members from 14 countries. The majority of tourist ships to Antarctica are members of the Association and some yacht operators are joining them. The members of IAATO endeavored to comply with Recommendation XVIII-I: Guidance for Visitors to the Antarctic by creating visitor guidelines that addressed the environmental protection of landing sites, the safety of the guests, and the establishment of operational protocols to provide emergency assistance. Both guests and all tour operator personnel receive these instructions.

As the UN Secretary-General's Report to the GA in 2005 on the Question of Antarctica states, "since the Twenty-fifth Antarctic Treaty Consultative Meeting, the IAATO has continued to focus its activities on increasing cooperation and field coordination among its members; promoting effective environmental impact assessments; preventing the introduction of alien organisms; promoting self-sufficiency and proper conduct among visitors; developing emergency response and contingency plans; and promoting specific guidelines for sites where the growing bulk of tourism occurs".

The self-regulated approach to tourism management in Antarctica, developed in accordance with the existing regulatory framework, currently depends on the following premises: (1) the tourist industry instructs their clients about appropriate behaviour and does not alienate them; (2) voluntary coordination among cruise and tour directors is the only means of managing site visits; and (3) responses to emergency situations are completely dependent on voluntary efforts and the skills of those who, fortuitously, are willing to respond. To date this approach has been effective, but the inherent environmental conditions of Antarctica, its remoteness, and, most importantly, the growing number of tourists will test the sustainability of this approach. As passenger numbers increase, there is a need for increased vigilance at some of the sites. Towards this end, the indicators proposed by UNWTO for the assessment of the sustainability of tourism in Antarctica provide a good base for a monitoring programme.

Conclusion

Key elements of an agenda for sustainable tourism development in Polar Regions have been developed through the efforts of a combination of governments, intergovernmental bodies, NGOs, business initiatives. They are:

* The 12 principles for sustainable tourism development that have been endorsed by UNEP/UNWTO. While all of these principles cannot be applied in the Antarctic and some Arctic regions (because of the absence of indigenous population and the non existence of local economies), they provide a solid basis of management objectives and evaluative criteria for creating, implementing and evaluating sustainable polar tourism.
* In response to unique circumstances, Arctic governments, Arctic natural resource agencies, NGOs, the tour industry operating in both hemispheres, and Native People have created innovative management techniques that are now applied in both Polar Regions. Some of the most important of these techniques include the Antarctic Treaty tourism Guidelines, and the WWF 10 Arctic Principles.
* Recognizing the need to simultaneously protect many resources from adverse impacts, existing tourism management techniques employ a comprehensive approach to influence appropriate tourist behaviour and resource conservation practices.
* An immense amount of information pertaining to the laws, participatory decision-making process, native customs, and numerous techniques employed to manage polar tourism and polar resources has been produced.
* A multitude of good tourism management practices exist throughout both the Arctic and Antarctic that should be

evaluated for either expansion to new regions or modified for current tourist activity zones.

* Improved knowledge of the many natural events affecting the environmental conditions of the Polar Regions is growing rapidly. This knowledge is an essential ingredient in the design of tourism management policies and programmes, which must also be adjusted and as necessary reinforced in the face of growing tourist numbers.

What is now needed to advance sustainable polar tourism policies and programmes is the assembly of existing information and open access to that information. Since virtually all polar tourism management documents are in the public record and the Arctic is supremely well connected in this digital age, this is a very feasible agenda that can produce immediate positive results.

Remote Arctic communities seeking to manage tourism in a timely manner need immediate access to this type of information. Stakeholders concerned about Antarctic tourism should have access to the full spectrum of available resource conservation and tourism management techniques. The collection and dissemination of appropriate tourism management and resource conservation laws, customs, treaties, codes of conduct, techniques, and customs will provide significant benefits to both Polar Regions. This free flow of information will allow the benefits derived from tourism in Antarctica by a limited number of persons or commercial entities to be weighed against the global values at risk. Antarctica offers unique opportunities for scientific monitoring of, and research on processes of global and regional importance and was declared a natural reserve devoted to science and peace. A regime for its protection was also developed in the interest of mankind as a whole. As stated in the SG report, "the tourism industry has increased tremendously over the last decade. Efforts should be continued to ensure that commercial activities will not impact on the successes of the Antarctic Treaty system, in particular in securing Antarctica as a natural reserve, devoted to peace and science".

Defining 'Nature Tourism'

Nature in Tourism

In its broadest sense, nature in tourism involves experiencing natural places, typically through outdoor activities that are sustainable in terms of their impact on the environment. These can range from active to passive and include everything from bush walking and adventure tourism experiences to sightseeing, scenic driving, beach experiences and wildlife viewing. In many instances a visitor may combine several of these in the one trip. For keen outdoor enthusiasts, and there are many, the great majority of adventure activities directly depend on nature and natural environments for their successful conduct. Fundamentally, the role of nature can vary from 'crucial to the visitor experience' to 'enhances the visitor experience'-particularly in relation to such variables as active or passive measures of the activity involved.

For passive and active visitors alike, nature is also playing an increasingly important role in giving something back to people (relaxing, enriching the spirit, getting back to basics). By doing so, it is able to enhance their broader experience of a destination. And for mainstream domestic visitors, these benefits tap more accurately into nature's deeper meaning-see resource paper No 3, The deeper significance and role of 'nature' in tourism. Nature-based experiences are intimately linked to all other aspects of the visitor's total experience of a destination, such as food, culture, relaxation, health, escape, family needs, accommodation, transport, etc. All serve to complement each other and together form the basis of a visitor's overall satisfaction with their holiday.

Ecotourism

Eco tourists, with their strong focus on learning about the natural environment, minimising negative impacts and contributing to its care, lie at one specialist end of the nature in tourism spectrum, albeit an important one. They are in effect ambassadors (or early adopters) for a set of personal values towards which it now appears many other market segments, potentially comprising much larger visitor numbers, are moving. Conserved and protected areas (including Marine and National Parks), the Earth's biodiversity, and respect for local culture and those who have been traditional guardians of our natural environments, can be central to their interests. Eco tourists are also characterised by knowing what they want and being strongly self-active in accessing it. They will often plan and book their experiences and travel needs themselves, leaving tourism operators with more time and the broader opportunity to pursue tourists with more mainstream nature-based interests, and those seeking adventure activity.

Soft and Hard Adventure Tourism

Soft and hard adventure tourism activities also comprise a subset of activities strongly associated with the natural environment and nature-based tourism. Related market segments include 'adventure sports' such as mountain biking. Anecdotal evidence from Australian tourism operators suggests that demand for both soft and hard adventure tourism is growing. Research suggests that spending by nature-based tourists (particularly those with an interest in adventure activities and visiting significant nature destinations including national parks) is often substantially above average, per visitor and per night.

It is important to recognise that international source markets can culturally differ over which activities they will describe as 'soft' and which as 'hard' (e.g. snorkelling, surfing, ballooning and orienteering may be viewed as soft by one market and hard by another). Similarly, differences in outlook can arise between younger and older visitors from the same source market.

For many major international markets (e.g. Asian and American), soft activities rather than hard are more frequently preferred by those interested in adventure-based experiences in natural areas. Soft adventure activities commonly require a moderate level of physical involvement by participants and are less physically challenging than hard activities. They can include– hiking/bush walking, mountain biking/bicycling, camping, horseback riding, orienteering, walking tours, wildlife spotting, whale watching, river and lake canoeing and fishing. The numbers undertaking such activities can be substantial – e.g. the NSW Fisheries estimates that recreational fishing is enjoyed by over 1 million New South Wales residents each year, as well as around 300,000 visiting anglers.

There is evidence from leading natural destinations that bush walking activity rates are also significantly increasing, particularly when support facilities are good, with highest participation rates in the 'under 2 hours' and '2 hours to a full day' categories. Wildlife viewing also achieves high levels of participation. Hard adventure activities commonly involve a higher level of physical or rugged involvement or a potentially greater personal challenge for participants. The risk factor can also increase. Hard adventure activities with a nature basis or need include– caving, scuba diving, trekking, white water rafting, kayaking, rock and mountain climbing, cross-country skiing, safaris, surfing, windsurfing, ballooning and ocean sailing. By contrast, bungy jumping does not depend on a nature setting. At the more challenging end of the hard adventure scale, support equipment can be involved or be absolutely necessary-e.g. climbing gear, oxygen tanks, ocean-going kayaks.

Special Interest Tourism

Nature-based tourism and its various subsets can also encompass some particularly challenging, but potentially high spending, special interest market segments. These often comprise socially and environmentally aware, highly educated and potentially demanding visitors who travel both to learn and to achieve personal and social goals.

Most of these visitors are serviced and targeted by specialist tourism operators and suppliers who often provide highly expert guides as part of the service. Examples include the 'not for profit' travel sector in the United States whose interests can range widely, encompassing anything from wildlife expeditions to scientific and cultural tours.

The major non-profit institutions of North America, such as natural history museums, zoos, universities and botanical societies, commonly promote their own worldwide travel programs to membership, alumni and donor bases that can run into the millions. Accessing and converting their small groups travel market can be difficult. It takes time, effort and a great commitment to high quality standards and delivery. An equally dedicated nature-based special interest visitor segment exists with bird-watching. Enthusiasts will travel long distances (and often at short notice) to sometimes remote and hard-to-access destinations, in order to sight new and rare species. In addition, readily identifiable communication channels (such as the ornithologists' special interest newsletters) can exist for accessing such market segments.

Wildlife Tourism

Wildlife tourism involves travel to observe wildlife in natural environments and preferably their native habitat. It is a further subset of nature tourism and one in which significantly high levels of domestic and international interest exist. Wildlife tourism involves wild and non domesticated animals and can encompass free-ranging and captive circumstances. Given the unique character and special appeal of most of Australia's wildlife, this suggests it may represent a tourism opportunity area for some destinations. The Blue Mountains, Barrington Tops, North and South Coast areas and Outback New South Wales possess great potential in this regard given their species diversity and relative convenience as destinations from major source markets and ports of entry. Wildlife tourism encompasses the chance to encounter fauna (and flora) in terrestrial, aquatic/marine and aerial settings and to gain some further understanding of a wide variety of species (including viewing kangaroos, koalas, whales, dolphins, seals, fish and birds). Undertaking this activity in a manner that is environmentally responsible is important to ensure less disturbance to wildlife and habitats. In terms of major visitor trends, 'appreciative tourism' involving observation, photography and interaction with wild animals is large scale, prominent and growing. Consumptive tourism involving such activities as hunting and (non-catch and release) fishing is also large scale, but declining. Ideally, wildlife tourism should include some element of education and an increased appreciation of nature and conservation issues.

Potential new models for wildlife tourism in Australia are being developed. These involve wildlife sanctuaries with feral free habitats attempting to use tourism and other enterprise based revenue sources as a means to help protect endangered native species and develop recovery plans for the species. Activities directly related to wildlife viewing, such as scuba diving and whale watching, are experiencing rapid worldwide growth in popularity and it is clear that the concept of wildlife viewing itself is gaining global currency with visitors. It has been estimated to generate $30 billion worldwide in revenues each year. Alaska has experienced strong tourism growth in recent years, particularly in wildlife tourism, with more than 46% of its visitors engaging in this activity.

Nationally in the USA, wildlife viewing is the third highest purpose for trips each year (671 million) after sightseeing (1037 million) and family gatherings (778 million). It is expected that wildlife activities will increase 61% nationally over the next 52 years to Year 2050 (Outdoor Recreation in American Life: A National Assessment of Demand and Supply Trends, 1999 – quoted in

Nature: The leading edge for regional Australia). 43% of Canadians are involved in outdoor recreation each year and 18.6% have a wildlife component to their trip. 74.5% watch wildlife on the media and this is a major influence on driving wildlife tourism. The worldwide value of whale watching is estimated at over $2 billion. In Australia it has been estimated to generate $100 million with almost one million people watching each year. In New South Wales alone, more than 200,000 people annually pay for whale watching tours– double the number of 10 years ago.

Wildlife tourism should also seek to maximise the benefits to local communities, while avoiding problems such as disturbance to wildlife and pollution. Types and magnitudes of environmental impacts associated with wildlife tourism vary with the type of tourist activity pursued – some impacts are obvious and easily identifiable while others are indirect and difficult to quantify. The impacts on particular animals should not be considered in isolation from the broader environmental settings and wider animal population. The conservation benefits of wildlife tourism can include – its financial contribution; practical (in kind) contribution; socioeconomic incentive for conservation; and education.

Sustainable Tourism

Sustainable tourism is envisaged by the World Tourism Organisation (WTO) as "leading to management of all resources in such a way that economic, social and aesthetic needs can be fulfilled while maintaining cultural integrity, essential ecological processes, biological diversity and life support systems". Sustainable tourism might also be defined as "tourism which is economically viable but does not destroy the resources on which the future of tourism will depend, notably the physical environment and the social fabric of the host community". Furthermore, "A clear distinction should be made between the concepts of Ecotourism and sustainable tourism: the term Ecotourism itself refers to a segment within the tourism sector, while the sustainability principles should apply to all types of tourism activities, operations, establishments and projects, including conventional and alternative forms". The goal of 'ecologically sustainable development' is to improve the total quality of life, both now and in the future, in a way that maintains the ecological processes on which life depends. Supplementary definitions with significant relevance to nature in tourism.

Geotourism

Geotourism is concerned with sustaining or enhancing a destination's geographic character – the entire combination of natural and human attributes that make one place distinct from another. Geotourism encompasses both cultural and environmental concerns regarding travel, as well as the local impact tourism has upon communities and their individual economies and lifestyles. Aesthetics, heritage and the wellbeing of residents are included as some of its concerns. Geotourism has also been summarised as restorative and reconstructive forms of tourism that enhance a destination's natural and cultural distinctiveness, as well as provide a high-quality visitor experience. Geotourism is obviously closely related to sustainable tourism, even though it has its own refined concerns and focus.

Ecologically Sustainable Development

"Using, conserving and enhancing the community's resources so that ecological processes, on which life depends, are maintained and the total quality of life, now and in the future, can be increased."

Conservation

"The management of human use of the biosphere so that it may yield the greatest sustainable benefit to present generations while maintaining its potential to meet the needs and aspirations of future generations." (National Conservation Strategy for Australia.) "The protection, presentation, maintenance, management, sustainable use and restoration of the natural environment (and its ecosystems)."

The issue of management is vital in relation to tourism. The environmental impacts of tourism as a service industry must be recognised and never dismissed, but they also need to be placed in perspective. Ecological sustainability will never be achieved through a focus on environment and biodiversity alone. Social and economic values and needs must become integral concerns of nature conservation management. Likewise the tourism industry must address the concerns of natural area managers and recognise them as important partners in delivering sustainable experiences to visitors. Managed protected areas and other conservation sites now provide accessible means by which all visitors can experience at first hand nature in its wider diversity (and come to appreciate its values). Effectively planned and managed, this can foster conservation benefits – the basic challenge is to deliver good management, planning, education and resourcing. Interpretation (directed at visitors)

1. "A special process of stimulating and encouraging an appreciation of the natural and cultural heritage of a region, as well as a means of communicating nature conservation ideals and practices."
2. "A means of communicating ideas and feelings which helps people enrich their understanding and appreciation of their world, and their role within it." The first definition sees interpretation from a visitor's perspective as a means of value-adding to their experience because of the added interest it creates when more is known about an attraction or experience. The second definition places the responsibility back with the visitor to arrive at their own understanding based on their collective experiences.
3. "An educational activity which aims to reveal meanings and relationships through the use of original objects, first hand experience and illustrative media, rather than simply by communicating factual information."

Principles for Successful Interpretation

Successful interpretation typically reflects a number of key principles: People learn better when they are actively involved in the learning process. People learn better when they are using as many senses as appropriate. It is generally recognised that people retain approximately 10% of what they hear, 30% of what they read, 50% of what they see and 90% of what they do. Insights that people discover for themselves are the most memorable as they stimulate a sense of excitement and growth. Learning requires activity on the part of the learner. Being aware of the usefulness of the knowledge being acquired makes the learning process more effective. Enhancing the quality of interpretation at visitor centres, attractions, on tours, along trails/drives and 'in the field' or on site, is a major opportunity area for 'nature in tourism' in New South Wales.

As far as possible, interpretation needs to capture a visitor's imagination, intellect or emotions (even momentarily) and in so doing grab their interest. Differences such as age, and cultural background are also obvious considerations. When pursuing excellence in interpretation, there are as many paths of possibility open to visitor managers as there are creative ideas in the world. To fail to explore these is to risk having an audience label the interpretive approach adopted as too dull, tired, serious, patronising, over-complicated, overwhelming, superficial, cautious, etc. Great creative ideas resulting in exciting interpretation outcomes are often achieved more successfully if more innovative creative development processes (e.g. those developed by Edward De Bono) are applied, and the creative net cast more widely.

Building wider creative alliances by involving other people with different 'skill sets' (e.g. who are known for their innovative & 'wildcard' thinking capacities as well as essential sense of humour & fun) can often prove of value-particularly if they are properly rewarded for the business significance of their personal contribution to the results. A capacity for simple but effective delivery coupled with good commonsense and empathy also helps. Summarising its benefits, interpretation is an effective way of adding value to the experience, employing more locals, creating a cultural connection for visitors, building understanding and differentiating an operator's product in the market.

Tourism Feels the Heat of Global Warming

The promoters of 'adventure-' or 'Ecotourism' have popularized slogans such as: "Go visit the last paradises... before they'll be destroyed by tourist hordes." In a similar fashion, the British daily The Observer recently suggested that world travellers need to hurry up if they want to see the '10 wonders of a vanishing world'. According to the related article, the most wondrous natural tourist attractions we can no longer take for granted due to global warming include:

Africa's highest mountain-the spectacular Kilimanjaro in Tanzania will never look the same as snows are disappearing at an alarming rate.

The Caribbean coral reefs – particularly the Meso-American reef, the world's second biggest, stretching from the coast of southern Mexico down past Belize and into Honduras, is threatened by a threefold environmental disaster: Warmer water disrupts coral growth; acidic water affects coral's abilities to secrete new skeletons; and increasingly intense hurricanes break it up. As a result thousands of marine species are on the brink of extinction. The Maldives in the Indian Ocean-many tropical islands forming the Indian Ocean archipelago are likely to become submerged in the next two decades as a result of rising sea levels and increasing numbers of heavy storms.

Traditional ski resorts in the Alps such as Kitzbuhel in Austria for example will disappear from the tourist map within 20 years because of the lack of snow. Furthermore, the future of many unique animal species that have attracted wildlife tourism is in jeopardy as habitats, breeding grounds and migration routes are changing. If global warming gets worse, entire populations of polar bears in the Arctic region, Wildebeests in East Africa, Mountain Gorillas in Uganda and Rwanda or Monarch Butterflies in Mexico may be destroyed.

Tourism World Wakes up to the Climate Crisis

Climate is an essential resource for tourism, and especially for beach. nature and winter sport tourism, and the phenomenon of global warming already gravely affects the industry and an increasing number of destinations. In 2003, the Madrid-based UN World Tourism Organization (UNWTO) convened the 1st International Conference on Climate Change and Tourism in Djerba, Tunisia, to help the travel and tourism industry to respond to these issues. The UNWTO, that only a few years ago became a special UN agency, is traditionally driven by a strong Business Council that aggressively advances the interests of the world's most powerful tourism-related corporations.

That the UNWTO declared climate change a priority issue shows the growing awareness among industry leaders and policy-makers that the impacts of global warming pose a serious threat to tourism-one of the world's largest and fastest growing industries, generating over 10.4 percent of world GDP, according to the World Travel and Tourism Council (WTTC). Notably, the Djerba conference recognized that the relationship between climate change and tourism is twofold: Not only is tourism affected by a changing climate, at the same time it contributes to climate change by the consumption of fossil fuels and resulting greenhouse gas emissions.

It was concluded that there was an "urgent need for the tourism industry, national governments and international organizations to develop and implement strategies to face the changing climate conditions and to take preventive actions for future effects, as well as to mitigate tourism's environmental impacts contributing to climate change.". Also the burgeoning international Ecotourism industry feels challenged.

At the recent Global Ecotourism Conference 2007 (GEC07) that was jointly organized by The Ecotourism Society (TIES), Ecotourism Norway and the UNEP in Oslo, Norway, it was agreed that "Climate change has increasingly become a major threat affecting the very resources on which Ecotourism depends – natural areas and local and Indigenous communities around the world....Stronger leadership and strategies are needed in order to substantially decrease Ecotourism's carbon footprint generated from multiple sources including facility operations and transport-related greenhouse gas emissions."

This article will offer some explanations as to why travel and tourism leaders are now feverishly working at the climate change front. Firstly, the economic costs of climate change for the industry will rise inexorably if it takes a business-as-usual attitude. Secondly, tourism relies more than other industries on a good image, but its reputation as a beneficial and environmentally acceptable activity has rapidly faded during recent debates on the causes of global warming.

Aviation, Cruise Ship Industry Major Climate Change Culprits

The aviation industry in particular is now facing enormous pressure since the Intergovernmental Panel on Climate Change (IPCC) and environmental campaign groups have singled out the responsibility of air travel in accounting for a considerable portion of global greenhouse gas emissions. Globally, the world's 16,000 commercial jet planes generate more than 600 million tones of CO2 per year, almost as much as from all human activities in Africa each year, according to Friends of the Earth. The huge increase in aircraft pollution is largely due to the rapid growth of tourism and related air traffic. A WWF briefing paper on 'Tourism & Climate Change' (2001) states that the actual tonnage of CO2 emitted will increase by over 75 percent by 2015; concomitantly, from almost 700 million international travellers in 2000, numbers are expected to jump over one billion by 2010 and 1.6 billion by 2020. "As a consequence, the role of air travel within the tourism industry is likely to expand, cause considerable environmental damage, and to have knock-on effects on the tourism industry itself," concludes WWF. Given the recent negative publicity, tourists in Western countries are changing their behaviour and tend to fly less. There are now even voices in Europe that go so far to suggest that flying away on holiday is immoral and should be stopped altogether. "Warming stops global roaming", wrote the Australian newspaper Daily Telegraph recently. A survey in Australia done by a holiday website found nearly 20 percent of respondents considered giving up air travel as it causes irreparable harm to the environment, while only 16 percent said they do not care about climate change and it would not affect their travel choices at all.

Similarly, a study prepared for Greenpeace in the UK showed a clear shift in consumers' perception: 61 percent of the respondents were of the opinion that "We should limit our air travel voluntarily", 33 percent agreed that "Air travel is now too cheap", 52 percent agreed that "There should be a tax on fuel for air travel", and 61 percent of the respondents supported the idea that "There should be a pollution warning on air tickets".

Apart from aviation, the worldwide booming cruise ship industry has also come under fire. Cruise ships that can carry up to 5,000 tourists are not only notorious for creating tremendous amounts of waste and sewage but also belong to the biggest contributors to greenhouse gas emissions within the travel and tourism industry. The US-Bluewater Network that campaigns against the pollution of the world's oceans by ships has found that in one port visit, a single cruise ship can generate the emissions of more than 12,400 cars. The ship smokestacks release toxic emissions that lead to acid rain, global climate change, and damaging health effects to communities situated near ports. Despite the fact that ocean cruise liners are more energy efficient than other forms of commercial transportation, marine engines operate on extremely dirty fuels, known as 'bunker oil'. To compound the problem, engines on these ocean-going ships are currently not required to meet the same strict air pollution controls as cars and trucks are required to do.

Global travel and tourism could only grow by leaps and bounds because the transport networks that enable the movement of people and goods around the world are heavily subsidized. Tourists can enjoy to travel the world at incredibly low prices. As the New

Economic Foundation study 'Up in Smoke?' explains "...much international trade lives in a bubble. International aviation and marine fuels are immune from any kind of taxation that would indicate and internalize the real environmental cost of freight and shipping. Greenhouse gas emissions from international freight are also exempt from the emissions targets set for rich countries to meet under the Kyoto Protocol of the UN Climate Change Convention."

Growing consumer awareness on these issues and a burgeoning citizens movement calling for fuel taxes and stricter regulation of the transport industry can severely curb future tourism growth targets and, thus, cut deep into the profits of plane-makers, airlines, travel agencies, cruise ship-operators and other tourism-related businesses. No wonder then that companies are now scrambling to talk about hard-earned environmental advances and new initiatives to protect the environment.

At the Paris Air Show in June, for example, Airbus' top salesman John Leah, told a press conference that Airbus is "saving the planet, one A380 at a time". The company's promotional brochures featured a silhouette of the new two-deck super-jumbo-dubbed the "gentle green giant"-set against images of dolphins, rain forests and fishing boats on a misty pond. Boeing representatives were also keen to display ecological bona fides and claimed the industry has reduced fuel consumption by 70 percent since the jet age began, reported Dow Jones Newswires. While the global travel and tourism lobby has adopted the rhetoric of corporate social and environmental responsibility, reality checks on the ground show that tourism's environmental performance has remained very poor. Neither the UN-initiated International Year of Ecotourism 2002 or multilateral environment agreements such as the Tourism Guidelines under the Convention of Biological Diversity (CBD), have achieved anything to stop tourism from pervading pristine coastal areas, islands, forests and mountainous areas.

On the contrary, more fragile ecosystems and biodiversity are destroyed, local communities displaced and traditional livelihoods destroyed-all for the establishment of huge exclusive resorts, golf courses and marinas. These massive tourism complexes are also notorious for high per capita consumption of energy and water. But however damaging and wasteful these projects may be, with the right PR efforts, they can still pass as 'Ecotourism' developments and even raise their profile thanks to eco-accreditation schemes, or environmental Best Practices awards. As long as no proper legally binding frameworks are in place to check and redress excessive and damaging tourism activities, 'green-washing' continues and climate change culprits are likely to get away scot-free. Ecotourism promoters' intention to help minimize tourism's carbon footprint is laudable. The GEC07 Oslo Statement, for example, outlines an action plan that aims at "encouraging adapted travel patterns (e.g. increase length of stay per trip); promoting more energy-efficient, alternative or non-motorized transport options; utilizing reduced and zero-emission operation technologies; and increasing participation in reliable high-quality carbon offsetting schemes."

But many of the new initiatives that promote 'zero-carbon' or 'carbon-neutral' tourism businesses need critical examination because they may just be marketing gimmicks. For instance, The Guardian (UK) announced in January that Per Aquum, the brand behind some of the world's most luxurious resorts, was the owner of the first 'zero-carbon' five-star beach resort designed by architects in London. The developers of the resort, due to open in 2008, claim the project will have no negative environmental impact and will be totally self-sufficient, using only energy from the sun and wind and producing little waste or carbon emissions. "The only drawback, environmentally speaking, is its location-thousands of fuel-guzzling miles away in Nungwi, Zanzibar," cautioned The Guardian.

Six Senses Resorts and Spas, a Bangkok-based luxury hotel chain with properties in Thailand, Vietnam and the Maldives is now specialized in 'carbon-cutting getaways' for millionaires who do not want their "vacation dampened by global warming guilt". Apart from introducing energy-saving innovations at the luxurious island resorts, all visitors are required to pay a tax for their flight, which goes into a carbon offset fund. The project owners say the fund will be spent on renewable energy projects for villages in Sri Lanka and India, thus, offsetting among the poor the carbon emissions caused by jets transporting the rich to their holiday destination. Yet, can Six Senses really be called an environmentally friendly company considering that it consumes exorbitant amounts of water to run their spa facilities, for example?

Index

□□□